The War Against America's Public Schools

Privatizing Schools, Commercializing Education

Gerald W. Bracey

Allyn and Bacon

Boston • London • Toronto • Sydney • Tokyo • Singapore

Series editor: *Arnis E. Burvikovs*
Series editorial assistant: *Matthew Forster*
Manufacturing buyer: *Julie McNeill*
Senior marketing manager: *Kathleen Morgan*
Cover designer: *Suzanne Harbison*
Production coordinator: *Pat Torelli Publishing Services*
Editorial-production service: *Stratford Publishing Services, Inc.*
Electronic composition: *Stratford Publishing Services, Inc.*

Copyright © 2002 by Allyn & Bacon
A Pearson Education Company
75 Arlington Street
Boston, MA 02116

Internet: www.ablongman.com

Library of Congress Cataloging-in-Publication Data

Bracey, Gerald W. (Gerald Watkins)
    The war against America's public schools : privatizing schools, commercializing
education / Gerald W. Bracey.
        p. cm.
    Includes bibliographical references and index.
    ISBN 0-321-08073-4
    1. Privatization in education—United States. 2. Public schools—United States.
I. Title.

LB2806.36 .B73 2002
371.01'0973—dc21

                                                                2001022870

Printed in the United States of America

10   9   8   7   6   5   4   3   2   05   04   03   02

The War Against
America's Public Schools

Related Titles

The Leadership Assignment: Creating Change
Raymond Calabrese
ISBN 0-205-32183-6

Implementing Change: Patterns, Principles, and Potholes
Gene E. Hall and Shirley M. Hord
ISBN 0-205-16222-3

Testing! Testing!: What Every Parent Should Know About School Tests
W. James Popham
ISBN 0-205-30595-4

For further information on these and other related titles, contact:
College Division
Allyn and Bacon
75 Arlington Street
Boston, MA 02116
www.ablongman.com

Contents

Tables

Preface

The blue book of propaganda known as *A Nation at Risk* decried the state of the nation's public schools. Its message was "more": more hours in the school day, more days in the school year, more courses, more rigorous courses, more credits for both students and teachers, and so on. Soon after *A Nation at Risk* appeared, however, calls came for not more but "different." First, people said we had to "restructure" schools. But soon, people were saying we had to abandon the public schools for other structures altogether. Former assistant secretary of education Chester E. Finn, Jr. put it this way:

> The public school system as we know it has proved that it cannot reform itself. It is an ossified government monopoly that functions largely for the benefit of its employees and interest groups rather than that of children and taxpayers. American education needs a radical overhaul. For starters, control over education must be shifted into the hands of parents and true reformers—people who will insist on something altogether different than murmuring excuses for the catastrophe that surrounds us. (Finn, 1998)

I don't know if Finn has ever been in a public school. Nothing he has written indicates that he has. Like many reformers, Finn appears to peer at schools from afar. But he is symbolic of a certain class of reformers who feel that if we could just get those dumb, recalcitrant educators out of the schools things would be fine. Education reform has a long and ignoble history of searching for magic bullets. Those who hold beliefs similar to Finn's have engaged in experimentation with education that is unprecedented since the Common School was established: charter schools; vouchers; Educational Management Organizations; tuition tax credits. These and a high-standards movement run amuck are all part of the education landscape these days.

Some reformers are mere opportunists who look at the $700 million that the United States spends in all sectors of education and want some of those dollars. Others truly believe that a market-driven system would lead to a better education for all. Still others would like to teach religion in publicly supported schools without having to worry about the niceties of the First Amendment. And others, especially those starting charter schools, have a "vision" of what education should look like.

No one has summarized in one place these various types of experiments, and that is the purpose of this book. It is largely descriptive, even where describing experiments that I do not believe will help. There are some arenas, though, such as that of vouchers, where my negative conclusions are obvious. The opening sections of the book should also make it clear that none of the various experiments can be justified using the argument that the entire public school system is in crisis.

The first sections of the book establish a context for today's educational debates, examining the various philosophies that underlie different approaches to schools. They examine historically how we arrived at a place where parents are nervous about schools and then they look at the data that bear on that anxiety to see if it is justified.

Following these chapters, the book then describes the different kinds of experiments transpiring in education. It does not pretend to be exhaustive in naming all of the players, but provides information about those that are typical and those that are dominant in their particular arenas.

Acknowledgments

I would like to thank Bonnie Fisher of the College of St. Catherine, Anthony A. Koyzis of the University of Wisconsin–Oshkosh, Claire Sibold of Biola University, Sandra M. Stokes of the University of Wisconsin, and Angela Spaulding of West Texas A&M University for reviewing this manuscript and offering many helpful suggestions.

—Gerald W. Bracey

The War on America's Public Schools

Prologue

A war is being waged on America's public schools. They are under siege. Sometimes the war doesn't look like a war because it is a war waged mostly in the polite language of academic debates. Sometimes it is waged in the polite terms of new "partnerships," but it is a war nonetheless. Indeed, the polite language of the war is so important that when some of us have called it for what it is, we have been shunned. For instance, in 1993, Michael Usdan of the Institute for Educational Leadership and Lowell Rose, then the executive director of Phi Delta Kappa International, proposed a conference to be called "Common Ground" that would bring school critics and school defenders together to find out what they had in common. I learned that some from the Right (Dennis Doyle and Chester E. Finn, Jr., among them) had told Usdan and Rose that if I was invited, they wouldn't come.

I shamed Usdan and Rose into an invitation by pointing out that little common ground would be found if one side was allowed to set the rules. Still, it was offered only on condition that I not be a speaker. The conference was a bust—a very polite bust. The various antagonists danced around the issues for two days, and nothing came of it.

Jonathan Swift's "A Modest Proposal" is a polite essay. It induces horror only when one realizes what Swift's satire proposes. So it is with many of the polite proposals for modifying or replacing public schools. And it is not that the public schools don't *need* modifying. Frederick Wiseman's 1967 documentary *High School* sends the viewer to sleep with the trivial and stultifying atmosphere of what was supposed to be a good school.

Too many schools still bore too many kids. Indeed, they are likely to be even more boring today in spite of being much more exciting than in the past: Kids today are so much more sophisticated and knowledgeable about the world. The advent of niche magazines, targeted television, computers, CDs, and the

3

Internet have made it possible for students to amass vast amounts of specialized knowledge at very early ages. A lone teacher cannot keep up with all of the different directions that students can go. The Columbine killers, Eric Harris and Dylan Klebold, were said to be "high-ability" kids. In our need to view the Columbine tragedy as just that, no one to my knowledge has also observed that Harris and Klebold were also amazingly knowledgeable, resourceful, planful, and thorough. Other students demonstrate these qualities in more socially benign ways, but the Columbine killers demonstrated them nonetheless, posing powerful challenges to teachers.

Enemies of the Public Schools

Conservative Foundations: Follow the Money

The war is being waged by multiple enemies. Some of them can be spotted by observing the research they fund. "Follow the money" is one of the principles of data interpretation described in *Bail Me Out!* (Bracey, 2000a; advice given to *Washington Post* reporters Bob Woodward and Carl Bernstein by their Watergate investigation informant, "Deep Throat"). It's good advice. For instance, in August 2000, a report appeared finding that African American students using vouchers apparently scored higher than a matched sample remaining in public schools (Howell, Wolf, Peterson, and Campbell, 2000). The authors credit a virtual who's who of conservative foundations for funding the study: the Achelis Foundation, Bodman Foundation, Lynde and Harry Bradley Foundation, William Donner Foundation, David and Lucille Packard Foundation, Smith–Richardson Foundation, Spencer Foundation, and Walton Family Foundation.

As the National Committee for Responsive Philanthropy observed, these are not neutral, idea-oriented organizations (1997). While the mainstream foundations such as Carnegie, Rockefeller, Ford, and MacArthur followed a pragmatic, issue-oriented program of funding, the conservative foundations poured money into a single idea: the reduction of "liberal big-governmentism." Conservatives often refer to public schools as "government schools." Getting the government out of schools is part of the conservative agenda. The Milwaukee-based Bradley Foundation has actively promoted vouchers in that city. Members of the Walton family spoke at a voucher-privatization conference in Washington, D.C. Milton and Rose Friedman created their foundation precisely and solely to promote vouchers, an idea Milton Friedman put forward in 1955 and elaborated in his 1962 book, *Freedom and Capitalism*. On their website, the Friedmans have this to say:

> Since then [1955] we have been involved in many attempts to introduce educational vouchers—the term that has come to designate the arrangement we proposed. There is a distressing similarity to attempts made over three decades and from coast to coast. In each case, a dedicated group of citizens makes a well-thought through proposal.

It initially garners widespread public support. The educational establishment—administrators and teachers' unions—then launches an attack that is notable for its mendacity but is backed by much larger financial resources than the proponents can command and succeeds in killing the proposals. (Friedman and Friedman, 2000)

Interestingly, in the November 2000 elections, voucher proposals in California and Michigan went down in flames, with 70 percent of voters in both states saying no. In these instances, the proponents of the vouchers had outspent the "educational establishment" opponents by two to one. When I asked Friedman how he interpreted this debacle, he said that the "defeats are highly relevant to the question of political tactics," and he retained his faith in the efficacy of vouchers (Friedman, 2001).

The person whose name appears on most evaluations of voucher programs is that of Paul Peterson at Harvard University. In 1990 Peterson described himself and fellow voucher advocates as, "A small band of Jedi attackers, using their intellectual powers to fight the unified might of Death Star Forces led by Darth Vader whose intellectual capacity has been corrupted by the urge for complete hegemony" (Peterson, 1990, p. 73). This is not the perspective of a disinterested, objective researcher. According to Howard Nelson, senior researcher at the American Federation of Teachers, Peterson has also worked with the Institute for Justice, the principal legal organization behind the voucher movement. For example, it was lawyers from the Institute who argued before the Wisconsin Supreme Court that religious schools should be permitted access to publicly funded vouchers. Peterson's partisanship led researchers at Mathematica, Inc., to disavow his description of the results of a study they and Peterson had jointly conducted (Zernike, 2000). Had they not offered such a disavowal, their own credibility as disinterested researchers would have been called into question.

New enemies are appearing. On October 3, 2000, the day of the first debate between presidential candidates Al Gore and George W. Bush, a full-page ad appeared in the *Washington Post* decrying the low state of American students compared to those in other nations and declaring the system a failure: "Every year we pump more money into our public education system, and every year the system gets worse. . . . Only when schools are forced to compete for students will they be motivated to improve. Only then will the system open up, new options emerge and education look like the rest of America. Meanwhile, nearly 90% of American children are stuck in a failing system."

The ad was sponsored by the Campaign for America's Children, headed up by billionaire industrialist Theodore J. Forstmann and former secretary of education William J. Bennett. The slanted, spun, and distorted statistics that this group operates with can be found at http://www.putparentsincharge.org. Part of this book will show that the system is not only not failing, it is improving. It will also raise questions about whether or not education *should* look like "the rest of America" (whatever *that* means).

Higher Education: Biting the Hand That Feeds

Some enemies of the schools do not even perceive themselves as such. Large research universities often abet the more open enemies of public schools. To extract money from foundations and governments, they emphasize the negative. Susan Fuhrman, at the time a professor at Rutgers, now dean of the school of education at the University of Pennsylvania, once declared, "If you want money, ya gotta say the schools are lousy. So what else is new?" She said it in a room full of academics and the startle factor of her comment was such that she might as well have said, "The sky is blue."

Virtually all of the papers delivered to the group that produced *A Nation at Risk* were commissioned from professors at large research universities; a few went to think tanks, which are universities without students. The only paper written by a public school employee was an unsolicited critique of one of the commission's symposia. Although "the Commission was impressed during the course of its activities by the diversity of opinion it received regarding the condition of American education," no such diversity showed through in the papers or in the final report. Given this loading of the critical dice, the schools never had a chance.

The antischool position of university professors is hardly new. University of Illinois historian Arthur Bestor's 1953 book, *Educational Wastelands: The Retreat from Education in America's Public Schools*, laid waste to the schools and, especially, to the schools of education that prepared teachers to teach in them. For some reason, professors at colleges of arts and sciences have been unable to comprehend Harold Hodgkinson's observation that it's *All One System* and to assist rather than attack schools and schools of education (Hodgkinson, 1985). After all, the schools of education prepare the teachers who will teach the children who will attend the colleges of arts and sciences. The teachers groom the future students of the professors. The high schools also groom future professors. The Swedish sociologist Gunnar Myrdal, best known for his study of America's ethnic segregation, in another work expressed bafflement at the lack of support American universities showed for schools (Myrdal, 1969).

Business and Industry: A Workforce at Risk?

Business and industry have not always been antischool, although they have often taken this position in recent years. For many years, however, they have attempted to control the curriculum of the schools. As discussed in Chapter 4 (The Historical Context), for over a century, business and industry have prodded schools to turn out "products" that would more readily suit the businessmen's need for a docile yet energetic workforce.

Some who wish to eliminate the public school system simply want to do so for profit. The investment firm Lehman Brothers reportedly sent brochures to their clients saying, essentially, "We've taken over the health system; we've taken over the prison system; our next big target is the education system. We will privatize it and make a lot of money" (Chomsky, 2000). A number of articles have reported that investors are bullish on such efforts.

These various efforts have been coupled with deliberate attempts to mislead Americans about the nature of the future job market. The National Commission on Excellence in Education, Bill Clinton, Al Gore, and a host of others have produced bogus arguments and "facts" in this effort. "We have to prepare people for the jobs of the future," goes the refrain. Even as the low-skill service sector explodes, reformers are screaming that all jobs in the future will be infinitely more complicated and difficult than currently. The goal is simple: If you can make people anxious about their future, you can control them. People who are anxious about the future are less able to see their neighbors as fellow citizens and more likely to perceive them as competitors.

The National Commission on Excellence in Education accomplished this by putting forth an absurd theory about what makes a country economically healthy and competitive in a global marketplace. In its propaganda-laden 1983 publication *A Nation at Risk*, the commissioners had this to say: "If only to keep and improve on the slim competitive edge we still retain in world markets, we must dedicate ourselves to the reform of our educational system" (p. 7). The commission thus tightly yoked the economic health of the nation to the standardized test performance of children aged five to eighteen.

Wise observers saw this as the nonsense it was and responded with words similar to those of the education historian Lawrence Cremin:

> American economic competitiveness with Japan and other nations is to a considerable degree a function of monetary, trade, and industrial policy, and of decisions made by the President and Congress, the Federal Reserve Board, and the Federal Departments of the Treasury, Commerce, and Labor. Therefore, to conclude that problems of international competitiveness can be solved by educational reform, especially educational reform defined solely as school reform, is not merely utopian and millennialist, it is at best a foolish and at worst a crass effort to direct attention away from those truly responsible for doing something about competitiveness and to lay the burden instead on the schools. It is a device that has been used repeatedly in the history of American education. (1989, pp. 102–103)

Alas, only a few educators, not the general public, read Cremin's remarks and his sensible comments never caught the eye of the media. As the nation slipped into a recession in the late 1980s, the commission's theory gained widespread popularity. Variations on "Lousy schools are producing a lousy workforce and that is killing us in the global marketplace" could be heard in many quarters. By late 1993, however, the economy had come roaring back. "America's Economy, Back on Top" headlined the *New York Times* in early 1994. Many other publications ran similar banners. The *Times* author presented not only a positive picture of the present but also a glowing portrait of the future:

> A three percent economic growth rate, a gain of two million jobs in the past year, and an inflation rate reminiscent of the 1960s make America the envy of the industrialized

world. The amount the average American worker can produce, already the highest in the world, is growing faster than in other wealthy countries, including Japan. The United States has become the world's low-cost provider of many sophisticated products and services, from plastics to software to financial services.

For the most part, these advantages will continue even after countries like Japan and Germany snap out of their recessions. It is the United States, not Japan, that is the master of the next generation of commercially important computer and communications technologies and also of leading-edge services from medicine to movie making. (Nasar, 1994)

She was right, of course. The seven years since those words were written saw economic prosperity at heights previously thought unattainable. Unemployment dipped to a level considered theoretically impossible—until it happened. America's workers have become even more productive. And the increase in productivity has translated into gains in growth without any significant inflation. Although the Federal Reserve Board during one period raised interest rates six times in eighteen months to head off inflation, the economy raced ahead. In the first half of 2000, the economy expanded by a heady 5.5 percent.

The economy then began to cool. What followed was more a crisis of confidence—recessions are usually more about psychology than about the economy. While economists reaffirmed the basic health of the economy, President Bush, Vice President Dick Cheney, and Secretary of the Treasury Paul O'Neill seemed determined to bring on a recession by talking as if it had already happened.

Whether or not a recession actually occurs—and in the spring of 2001, it seems unlikely—the economic slowdown has been singular in one respect: No one has yet blamed the schools. The operative word might turn out to be "yet," but so far others have taken the hit, most notably Alan Greenspan, chairman of the Federal Reserve Board, whom critics contend did not lower interest rates fast enough or far enough.

The blame for the bearish market has been spread around, however, among venture capitalists who hyped the dotcoms, analysts who were "quoted incessantly as oracles for five years" but now are seen as corrupt and worthless, Wall Street in general, which consisted of an "unholy combination of venture capitalists and investment bankers" who "teamed up to fob off phantom companies" on the public, and the news media, who weren't skeptical enough (Barbash, 2001).

Meanwhile, Japanese students continued to score well on tests even as the Japanese economy continued to sink. William Safire (and many others) blamed the government's protection of bad loans and its unwillingness to let inefficient companies go out of business (Safire, 2001). George Will agreed with Safire that Japan's government exercised too much control over the economy and the economy therefore "has entered a second ghastly decade" (Will, 2001). All commentators observed that the Japanese government either didn't know what to do about their economic problem or knew what to do and simply lacked the political will to do it.

American educators should take no comfort in the disconnection between Japanese test scores and Japanese economic health except to point out that the disconnection is there. Despite its decline, the Japanese economy is the world's second largest and if that nation collapses, the rest of the world will suffer, the United States especially since Japan has invested so heavily in this country, investments that might have to be withdrawn in horrific economic conditions.

One might think that, at the very least, school bashing would be considered bad form in such good times. Yet, three months after the *New York Times* article quoted above appeared, IBM CEO Louis V. Gerstner, Jr., in the midst of firing 90,000 employees, took to the op-ed page of the *Times* to declare "Our Schools Are Failing." They are broken, said Gerstner, because they do not prepare students who can compete with their international peers.

Even after the "Asian tiger" economies had tanked, even after Japan had wallowed in recession for a *whole decade*, Gerstner continued his refrain. Remember, this is the man who organized three "education summits" and cajoled the nation's governors attending those summits to do his bidding. At the 1998 event, Gerstner convened the group with a speech outlining "the good, the bad, and the ugly of American education." It began with these words:

> The good: Our kids have the potential to be the best in the world. In science and math, our fourth-graders are right up there with the very best.
>   The bad: By 8th grade, we rank 28th, behind, among others, Russia, Thailand and Bulgaria.
>   The ugly: By 12th grade we trail every developed nation in the world. In fact, we're doing better than only Cyprus and South Africa. (Gerstner, 1999)

Gerstner's talk illustrates how school bashers often omit inconvenient statistics. Gerstner conveniently excludes science at eighth grade. The ranking of twenty-eighth is for math only. American eighth-graders ranked thirteenth in science among the forty-one nations taking part. Critics like Gerstner also accept uncritically statistics that make American schools look bad: The twelfth-grade data that Gerstner cites do not hold up under scrutiny as will be seen in Chapter 5.

For their part, Bill Clinton and Al Gore contributed to the distortion with a letter to the editor of *USA Today*. In it, they declared that "By the year 2000 60% of all jobs will require advanced technological skills" (Clinton and Gore, 1995). I wrote Messrs. Clinton and Gore, asking for a citation for their 60 percent figure and asking as well for a definition of "advanced technological skills." To increase the likelihood of a response, I sent copies to Richard Riley and Robert Reich, then secretaries of education and labor, respectively. My four epistles produced one response: Someone in Riley's office wrote to say that she was certain that someone in Reich's office could answer my queries.

Education and the Future of Work.   I should note in passing that many speakers, when referring to the jobs of the future, imply that advancing technology will make jobs more complex, sophisticated, and difficult. In fact, advancing technology often makes things easier. Who, reading this book, would trade their current

word-processing program for one from fifteen years ago? The development of
single-lens reflex (SLR) cameras with built-in light meters greatly simplified pho-
tography. Yet those same SLRs themselves seem cumbersome, unwieldy, and difficult to use compared to today's digital and point-and-shoot cameras.

The Jobs of the Future.   The Bureau of Labor Statistics provides a different
answer about what jobs of the future will look like. The most recent projections
are given in Table 1.1.

Occupations in the computer and health fields dominate the list—the latter, no doubt, in part because of the graying of the nation. The leading edge of
the baby boom generation is only a decade away from the benchmark retirement
age of sixty-five. Yet only five of these fast-growing jobs require "advanced technological skills," if one assumes that means something beyond simply sitting in
front of a personal computer (PC) and using a software package such as
Microsoft Office or Lotus SmartSuite.

However, as I have indicated elsewhere (Bracey, 2000a), statistical pictures
painted with rates often differ markedly from pictures painted in terms of numbers. When we look at "fastest growing" we are looking at a rate. Table 1.2 shows
the projections for the ten occupations with the largest increase in *numbers*.

Only three occupations are found on both lists. Of these, two require
sophisticated use of information technology (systems analysts and computer support specialists), and one does not (personal and home care aides). Note that
most of the jobs in this second list are occupations that have traditionally provided large numbers of jobs. Retail sales, for example, provides only 570,000
fewer jobs than the top ten fastest growing jobs *combined*, 4,620,000 versus

TABLE 1.1:   *The 10 Fastest Growing Occupations, 1998–2008 (In Thousands)*

		Employment		Change	
		1998	2008	Number	Percentage
1.	Computer engineers	299	622	323	108
2.	Computer support	429	869	439	102
3.	Systems analysts	617	1194	577	94
4.	Database administrators	87	155	67	77
5.	Desktop-publishing specialists	22	44	19	73
6.	Paralegals and assistants	136	220	84	62
7.	Personal care and home health aides	746	1179	433	58
8.	Medical assistants	252	398	146	58
9.	Social service assistants	268	410	141	53
10.	Physicians' assistants	66	98	32	48

Source: Bureau of Labor Statistics, *Occupational Outlook Handbook* (Washington, DC: Bureau of Labor Statistics, 2000).

TABLE 1.2: *The 10 Occupations with the Largest Job Growth, 1998–2008 (In Thousands)*

		Employment		Change	
		1998	2008	Number	Percentage
1.	Systems analysts	617	1194	577	94
2.	Retail salespersons	4056	4620	563	14
3.	Cashiers	3198	3754	556	17
4.	Managers and executives	3362	3913	551	16
5.	Truck drivers	2970	3463	493	17
6.	Office clerks	3021	3484	463	15
7.	Registered nurses	2079	2530	451	22
8.	Computer support specialists	429	869	439	102
9.	Personal and home care aides	746	1179	433	58
10.	Teacher assistants	1192	1567	375	31

Source: Bureau of Labor Statistics, Occupational Outlook Handbook (Washington, DC: Bureau of Labor Statistics, 2000).

5,189,000. High-tech jobs might be growing fast, but they are swamped by the growth in the low-tech, low-pay service sector.

For the most part the war on America's schools is *not* a conspiracy. It is too open for that. Ever since he proposed school vouchers in 1962, Milton Friedman has been arguing that we should replace "government" schools with vouchers and a privatized system of education. Ronald Reagan, a devotee of Friedman, made vouchers and tuition tax credits centerpieces of his education agenda.

Christian Conservatives

Attacks also come from Christian conservatives, who promote vouchers and tax credits in the hope of funding schools that can use tax dollars to teach religion without worrying about the First Amendment (others, however, as discussed in Chapter 8, oppose vouchers on the grounds that taking public money will inevitably result in government regulation and loss of independence). Catholic school officials have for the most part discreetly refrained from public comment on the war, but it is hardly a secret that many would like to see vouchers provide money to their financially ailing schools. One article on the exodus of teachers from Catholic schools because of low pay indicated that some Catholics "point to the growing national voucher movement, which would allow parochial and private schools to receive taxpayer funding in the form of student vouchers—perhaps freeing additional money for teacher salaries" (Massey, 2000).

Vouchers also would offer Catholic schools an opportunity to spread the faith, one of the functions of Catholic education. One study comparing public and private schools described a conflict between a Catholic school principal and the local priest. When the principal asked about academic achievement, the priest responded, in effect, "What profit it a man to gain Harvard if he lose his Catholicism?" (Rothstein, Carnoy, and Benveniste, 1999).

Although the various camps wage their war in polite terms, those who attack the schools do not fight honestly. Critics of public schools often present distorted, selected, or spun statistics to make their case. We have already seen such spinning in Gerstner's speech at his education summit. Similarly, in a speech celebrating the twenty-fifth anniversary of the Heritage Foundation, former secretary of education William J. Bennett declared flatly, "In America today, the longer you stay in school, the dumber you get relative to kids from other industrialized nations." To make this statement, Bennett had to accept uncritically results from one of the worst studies, methodologically speaking, ever conducted: the Third International Mathematics and Science Study's (TIMSS) Final Year Study. I have discussed the many problems with this study elsewhere (Bracey, 2000b). Bennett accepts unquestioningly the authors' interpretation of their data because this interpretation supports his own view of the problem.

The spectacle of a former secretary of education spouting lies about public schools is appalling, but there is apparently no limit to the depths to which Bennett can sink. For instance, in a September 4, 2000, op-ed essay in the *Washington Post*, Bennett wrote that "About half of high school graduates have not mastered seventh-grade arithmetic." This is a peculiar statement, on several counts. First, we don't test "high school graduates," so how could he know? Second, Bennett offered no definition of "mastery." Third, he offered no definition of "seventh-grade arithmetic," a phrase that has no currency among educators.

I called Bennett's office and was told that the figure came from *The Book of Knowledge*—not the familiar childhood encyclopedia but a book on how to invest in the "education industry," written by Michael Moe, director of Global Growth Research at Merrill Lynch (Moe and Bailey, 1999).

When I called Moe's office, I was told that the statistic was "an interpretation of 1996 NAEP [National Assessment of Educational Progress] mathematics test results." Rest assured, readers, that there is no possible way to go from the NAEP data to the "interpretation" that Moe gave them—the interpretation that Bennett uncritically accepted as correct.

Bennett is hardly alone. Consider the Hudson Institute's report "On Shaky Ground," an assemblage of statistics designed to make the Indiana public schools look bad and to grease the skids for vouchers and for conservative political candidates. At one point, the report gnashes its teeth over the fact that students in Connecticut who carry an A+ high school grade point average score 71 points higher (total score) on the Scholastic Aptitude Test (SAT) than Indiana students with A+ averages. A close look at the statistics, however, indicates that only 2 percent of Connecticut seniors report A+ averages, compared with 4% of Indiana students. When compared to other states with similar percentages, Indiana does not lag behind in SAT scores. One can wonder which states' teachers have the most accurate grading system, but when Indiana is compared like-against-like, it does not suffer in the comparison.

The report further states that "Being an A student in an Indiana public school still makes it difficult to compete with A students from other states, but being a B or C student makes it difficult to compete with just about anyone." This statement has no foundation. Indiana's B students scored 484 on both sections of the SATs. Ignoring New Hampshire and Connecticut for a moment, the range of verbal scores for the twelve other SAT-heavy-use states ranges from 465 to 492 on the verbal and 463 to 489 on the math. Connecticut and New Hampshire do have somewhat higher scores. Compared to most states that make heavy use of the SATs, Indiana scores higher than some, lower than others.

In Connecticut, the SAT verbal score is 506 and math is 503 for B students, and in New Hampshire the scores are 507 and 504. However, Connecticut is the wealthiest state in the union, and New Hampshire has by far the highest proportion of well-educated parents of SAT takers—parents who live in southern New Hampshire but work in high-tech jobs in Boston, Massachusetts, and send their kids to New Hampshire public schools. New Hampshire is a small state that has a number of elite private, college preparatory, boarding high schools, many of whose students come from other states. The College Board, though, counts students as residents of wherever they take the SAT. Thus, in reporting SAT scores, New Hampshire can claim these residents of other states as its own.

The statements about competing with students from other states also perpetuate a myth: The SAT is the lone gatekeeper determining who goes to college where. As has been shown, however, even highly selective colleges, such as Brown, admit students across a 450-point range, from 350 to 800 (Bracey, 1999).

These points might seem technical or even obscure to nonresearchers, but any worthy researcher preparing a report from an objective standpoint would notice them. They are the kinds of ideologically loaded statistical missiles that the public schools' enemies are launching.

Even where the Hudson Institute reports accurate statistics, it gives the numbers a twist to make schools look bad. For instance, the report states that "Socioeconomic status [SES] as defined by the Indiana Department of Education explains *only* 65% of the variability in school passing rates on the eighth-grade ISTEP" (emphasis added; ISTEP is the Indiana state accountability testing program). Statistically, this means that the correlation between SES and passing is slightly better than .80 (variability in scores is given by the square of the correlation coefficient, and .80 squared = .64). This is an enormous correlation.

The Enemy Within

In some cases, the enemy is found within. I cannot speak to the motivations of all the governors, boards, and legislators who have sponsored "standards" and "high-stakes tests." It is clear, however, that the Virginia Board of Education established standards and tests with ludicrously high pass rates in order to make the public school look bad, to make parents nervous about their schools, and, thereby, to ease the passage of voucher legislation. On the first round of tests, 98 percent of all schools failed and on the second round 93 percent. Some high schools have seen dramatic improvements in their algebra I scores to the point where, after four rounds of testing, more than 5 percent of the students passed. Algebra is required for high school graduation. One can only hope that the Commonwealth of Virginia is building sufficient numbers of jails to accommodate all of the kids it seems determined to toss onto its streets.

One group of education officials, the Education Leaders Council (ELC), is in thrall to privatization as well as other reform movements such as charters and vouchers. The council is led by chief state school officers such as Arizona's Lisa Graham Keegan, Pennsylvania's Eugene Hickok,[1] and Georgia's Linda Schrenko, along with Frank Brogan, former Florida Superintendent of Public Instruction and current Lieutenant Governor, and Abigail Thernstrom, coauthor (with her husband, Stephan) of *America in Black and White* and member of the Massachusetts State Board of Education. *The American Prospect* describes Thernstrom as someone "who prefers the usual conservative medicine of vouchers and draconian standards" to improve education (Shatz, 2001).

In September 2000, I "debated" Edison Schools founder Chris Whittle on profit making at the annual ELC conference (debated is in quotes because Whittle presented a 20-minute infomercial on the wonders of the Edison Schools and did not address any of the issues I had raised). Obviously the ELC has no objection to people making money off of schools. After the debate, Keegan thanked me for having the "courage" to appear before the ELC and take on Whittle. I don't think it took courage, just facts, but it is true that I have never had an audience glower at me the way that one did.

These examples could be multiplied many times over. They would all indicate, however, that most of those criticizing public schools are less interested in what the facts really say than in what their ideology demands that the facts say. It's a war, so all's fair.

---

1. Keegan has since resigned her Arizona post to head the ELC, and Hickok is undersecretary of education in the current Bush administration.

2

Dueling Visions

Aristotle argued that education is about the "good life." Because people will always disagree about what constitutes the good life, they will also differ as to what is the purpose of education. At this moment in U.S. history, however, much of the debate has been muted, overwhelmed by a recent shift to a single-minded view about education: Education is about jobs. It is about acquiring skills to keep us competitive in the global marketplace, a contention that thrived even as the economies of Japan, South Korea, Malaysia, Indonesia, and Thailand sank into the Pacific. It is about acquiring skills to compete for what good jobs there are. Back in 1983, *A Nation at Risk* spoke about jobs. Bill Clinton held up the 22 million jobs created during his administration as his leading achievement.

Although the myth is commonly perpetuated that all new jobs are highly skilled and high-tech, as we saw in the last section, the overwhelming majority of them are neither. Despite the glowing rhetoric about prosperity and record low unemployment, there are currently 15 million more families in this country than there are jobs that will support them comfortably (Finnegan, 1998).

Given all this emphasis on jobs, it is not surprising that many people have stopped viewing education as a public good or as something that liberates one from the grind of everyday life, and have started viewing it simply as another market to be exploited. Peter Cookson of Columbia University frames the issues nicely:

> Two competing metaphors will shape the public education system of the future. The first is that of democracy. At the heart of the democratic relationship is the implicit or explicit covenant: important human interactions are essentially communal. Democratic metaphors lead to a belief in the primacy and efficacy of citizenship as a way of life. The second metaphor is that of the market. At the heart of the market relationship is the implicit or explicit contract: human interactions are essentially exchanges. Market metaphors lead to a belief in the primacy and efficacy of consumership as a way of life. (1994, p. 99)

For Cookson, the development of the child into a consumer is a betrayal. He writes:

> We are challenged to choose between the fragmented consciousness of the modern materialistic mind and the humanistic vision of the whole empathetic and productive mind. We need a transcendent view of education, the elements of which include individual responsibility, the centrality of individual worth, equality, peace, and the primacy of the child's physical, intellectual, and spiritual rights. (1994, p. 121)

It is a measure of how far the discourse has changed that Cookson's words, which would have struck most people as vital thirty years ago, seem soft, almost sappy, in light of today's conversations about how the world works.

The words are different, but in his book on school choice, George Washington University's Jeffrey Henig paints a similar picture with a surer brush:

> Rather than simply focusing on the strengths and weaknesses of private versus public institutions as *service-delivery mechanisms*, we need to focus on the differences between private and public institutions and processes as *vehicles for deliberation, debate, and decision making*. The real danger in the market-based proposals for choice is not that they might allow some students to attend privately run schools at public expense, but that they will erode the public forums in which decisions with societal consequences can democratically be resolved. . . .
>
> The market orientation considers education as a *product* of public and private decisions; as such the issues involved are generic ones applicable to other domestic policies. But education also has a special status as a *producer* of the values, perspectives, knowledge, and skills that will be applied in the ongoing enterprise of collective deliberation and adjustment. . . .
>
> While the risk of abuse [from inappropriate socialization] must be acknowledged, public schools have another characteristic that makes this risk potentially manageable. Compared to other forces of socialization—the family, religion, the mass media—the schools are more open to public scrutiny and democratic intervention. (1994, pp. 200–203)

Schools operated as just another for-profit business under the market metaphor do not have this openness. If they become the dominant mode for providing instruction as "service-delivery mechanism," they also constitute a threat to democracy. As Ascher and her colleagues put it, "We will not survive as a republic, nor move toward a genuine democracy unless we can narrow the gap between rich and poor, reduce our racial and ethnic divides, and create a deeper sense of a common purpose" (Ascher, Fruchter, and Berne, 1996, p. 112). Some privatizers have claimed that a market-driven school system can accomplish the first two of these goals, but there is evidence to the contrary. No privatization advocate, to the best of my knowledge, has ever said that a market-driven school system would lead to "a deeper sense of common purpose." How could it? In a slightly different vein, Benjamin Barber of Rutgers University put it this way: "If schools are the vessels of our future, they are also the workshops of our democracy. . . . Public schools are not merely schools for the public, they are schools in publicness: institutions where we learn what it means to be a public" (Barber, 1995).

As we shall see later, to date, market-driven schools have failed to deliver the improvements that market theory claims, even in an entire nation (Chile) that has operated a national market system for almost twenty years. For now, it is important to note that more is at stake here than just a change in a service-delivery mechanism. The war against the schools is a war of two contradictory visions of what the nation should look like and how it should deal with its citizens. Private, for-profit schools will no longer be open to the kind of public scrutiny the public schools receive.

A minor digression: Private, for-profit schools will increase the amount of crime in the education arena. Consider these opening sentences of stories that occurred over a two-week period:

> Providian National Bank, the nation's sixth-largest issuer of credit cards, has agreed to reimburse customers at least $300 million to settle allegations that it unfairly charged and deceived customers. (Chea, June 29, 2000)
>
> About 240 criminal investigations into possible mortgage fraud are underway in 38 states. (Fleischman, July 1, 2000)
>
> The former head of a company that runs group homes for mentally retarded Washington, D.C., residents was accused yesterday of stealing more than $800,000 from the firm and using the money for luxury vacations, furs, and other extravagances. (Miller, July 11, 2000)
>
> One of the world's largest makers of generic drugs tentatively agreed to pay $147 million to settle accusations that it improperly cornered the market on raw materials for two widely prescribed drugs and then raised the price of those drugs, in some instances more than 3,000 percent. (Labaton, July 13, 2000)

These were not an exceptional two weeks in the world of corporate crime. With one exception, they were not even front-page stories. The case of the $800,000 theft made page one, but only in the *Washington Post*—a paper in the city where the theft occurred. People take crime in the private sector for granted. And even where there might not be criminal actions, neglect of standards and quality in favor of profits is the order of the day, as the Bridgestone/Firestone defective-tires case has revealed.

People also take it for granted that most schools are operated honestly, and they are. When the occasional scandal breaks, it is big news simply because such events are so rare in the public schools. A school's books are open to all who might wish to see them. Teachers do not, in most instances, get bonuses for increased test scores. But when the bottom line becomes the most important aspect of an operation, those who run the operation face many pressures to make sure that that line is written in black ink with the largest possible numbers. The temptations to cheat, deceive, and scheme that do not exist—cannot exist—in public schools become much greater.

3

The Master Myth: Money Doesn't Matter

Before examining the various ways in which corporate America is investing in schools and pushing them to serve its aims, we pause to take a closer look at the assumption that underpins so many of these activities—the myth that money doesn't matter. Without this assumption, many privatization efforts would collapse under the weight of their own inconsistencies and contradictions. Several forces sustain the myth: studies that apparently show that there is no correlation between spending and outcomes in districts and states; studies that apparently show that increasing spending over time does not produce increases in achievement; and accusations that the United States spends more money on its schools than any other nation, yet its students do not achieve as well as those in many other countries. We treat each type of study in turn.

The Correlation between Spending and Outcomes in Schools

State Spending

At the state level, the myth can be sustained because, within a given state, schools spend within a fairly restricted range. To be sure, within a given state, the districts that spend the most money spend three to four times as much as those that spend the least, but most districts have similar expenditures. When spending is mostly within a narrow band, it produces a statistical phenomenon known as *restriction of range*, which reduces the possible size of the correlation between money and spending.

We can understand the phenomenon of restriction of range by analogy. Suppose we wish to examine the effect of height on success at basketball. To do that, we calculate the correlation between height and basketball prowess as defined by one or more criterion variables. But suppose everyone we measure is 6'6" tall. Now, our correlation has to be zero because everyone looks the same. Similarly, if we gave a test to predict college success and everyone scored 100 percent correct, there could be no differential predictions based on the test.

School districts don't spend exactly alike, but most districts in a state spend similar amounts, and this limits the size of the possible correlation while also increasing the importance of other variables. For instance, if two districts spend the same but one of them contains a university, it is likely that that district will have higher test scores. Similarly, if one of two equal-spending districts contains the corporate headquarters of an industry that employs large numbers of highly educated workers, that district would have higher test scores.

We can test the limits of the money-doesn't-matter theory by imagining a wider range of spending. Suppose school spending fell to zero. Surely achievement would plummet, as it did in Prince Edward County, Virginia, which once chose to close its schools rather than racially integrate them. Just as surely, if spending rose to $38,000 per student, achievement would soar. This figure represents the average salary for teachers, so, for this amount, we could provide each child with an individual tutor, greatly increasing achievement.

A variation on correlating spending across districts was conducted by former secretary of education William Bennett (Bennett, 1993), who claimed that there was no relationship between spending at the state level and achievement at the state level, as indicated by state SAT averages. Bennett did not actually conduct any statistical analyses on the data; he merely pointed out that some high spenders had low SAT scores and some low spenders had high SAT scores.

The conservative pundit George Will anointed Bennett's "study" in one of his columns, where he noted, as had Bennett, that some of the top-scoring states were low spenders, but that New Jersey, which spent more money per student per year than any other state, finished only thirty-ninth in the Great SAT Race (Will, 1993). What neither Will nor Bennett pointed out was that the top-scoring states had very few students taking the SAT. Most students in these states take the ACT (American College Testing) college admissions battery. In high-flying Iowa, only 3 percent of high school seniors sat for the SAT, whereas in New Jersey, 76 percent did so.

The SATs and State Participation Rates

Will might not have been aware of differences in state participation rates, but Bennett surely was. As secretary of education, Bennett issued "wall charts" that ranked states on a variety of variables. Before states were ranked on college admissions tests, however, the charts divided them into two categories: those that used the SAT and those that used the ACT. The states in Bennett's study that had high SAT scores were those, like Utah, where only a small fraction (in Utah, 4 percent), of the senior class sits in angst on Saturday mornings to bubble in answer sheets for the College Board. These are students who wish to attend Harvard or Stanford or some other institution of higher education outside of Utah that requires the SAT (this was the case at the time of Bennett's report; most colleges now accept either test, although Stanford reports that so few send in ACT scores alone that the scores for those who do are converted into SAT scores for the purpose of creating a profile of incoming classes).

In New Jersey, in the year of the study, fully 76 percent of high school seniors took the SAT. One might wish to applaud New Jersey for encouraging three-quarters of its students to apply to colleges that require the SAT, but when three-quarters of New Jersey's senior class goes up against a 4 percent elite from Utah, there can be no doubt about the outcome.

Since 1993, Bennett's annual report has come to include a number of additional indicators other than SAT scores, such as ACT scores and the NAEP. In the most recent report, Bennett is no longer listed as the author, and some regression analyses have been performed. The message, however, remains unchanged:

> The story they [analyses in this report] write will describe a 20-year period of declining academic achievement accompanied by unprecedented increases in public spending. The characters in this story will include an education bureaucracy that continued to ask for more while delivering less. A generation of children growing up in the world's lone superpower at the end of the millennium who lag behind students in dozens of other, less-developed nations [sic]. . . . What this *Report Card* proves is that the current path is not good enough, and that throwing money at the problem is not the answer. (Haynes, in Barry and Hederman, 2000, p. 1)

It is not clear where Mr. Haynes, a California state senator, found the "dozens" of less-developed nations that have higher educational achievement. In any case, the chapters on "The Master Myth" and "The Condition of Public Education" in this book will refute these contentions.

Puzzled by Bennett's "analysis," Brian Powell and Lala Carr Steelman asked how much of the differences among states could be accounted for by the differences in participation rates we just described. As noted, these rates vary enormously among the states, from 4 percent to 80 percent. Powell and Steelman found that these differences in the proportion of students who take the SAT accounted for 83 percent of the differences in results.

They then asked, "If the states all had the same SAT participation rates, what impact, if any, would differences in spending have?" The participation rate adjustment requires only a simple statistical procedure. When they carried it out, they found that for every increase of $1,000 above the national average for spending, total SAT scores rose by 15 points.

People might debate the importance of a 15-point gain in total SAT scores for every $1,000 spent. However, when one considers that the SAT exam is not directly connected to what transpires in classrooms, the gains seem large.

Studying the Studies: A Closer Look at Methodology

Rather than correlate spending with achievement across districts, an alternative way of analyzing the relationship between money and achievement is to study the studies. That is, if we look at the studies that have investigated the relationship, does such an analysis lead to any generalizations? In 1989, University of Rochester economist Eric Hanushek conducted such an analysis and wrote that "there is no strong or systematic relationship between money and achievement" (Hanushek, 1989). As illustrated by the quoted statement from the latest *Report Card on American Education,* this statement has become a mantra for those who would undo public education.

Researcher Keith Baker quickly pointed out that Hanushek (*a*) did not explain how he reached his conclusion, (*b*) suffered an egregious lapse in logic, and (*c*) was contradicted by his own data (Baker, 1991). In his article, Hanushek merely presented his collection of studies and then baldly drew a conclusion. He made no statement about why the data led to that conclusion, developed no line of reasoning to that end, provided no decision rules.

Hanushek analyzed the data using a primitive "vote-counting" procedure. If a study found that money made a difference, the money-makes-a-difference category got one vote. Obviously, such an unsophisticated technique cannot reveal whether there is a "strong" or a "systematic" relationship between money and test scores. Hanushek's final vote tally looked like this:

Positive and significant:	13
Negative and significant:	3
Positive and insignificant:	25
Negative and insignificant:	13
Unknown:	11

Significant here is used in the statistical, not the practical, sense: Results are statistically significant if the outcomes are unlikely to have occurred by chance. Statistical methods can determine the likelihood of an outcome being due to chance. A study might be highly significant statistically and have no practical consequences. Another study might be statistically insignificant and have large practical implications. Again, Hanushek's primitive technique *cannot* reveal a systematic or strong relationship between money and achievement. But the data he presents clearly show that there are many more positive than negative results. If there really were no relationship between money and achievement, the results could not be so skewed toward the positive side.

Levels versus Changes in Achievement

Baker also pointed out an error in logic Hanushek made that has received little notice: His results have to do with *levels* of achievement, but his policy recommendation—don't throw money at the schools—has to do with *changes* in achievement. Level of achievement is known to be strongly affected by family and community variables, changes in achievement less so. For instance, Paul Barton and Richard Coley of the Educational Testing Service (ETS) found that whereas black students scored lower on the NAEP than white students, the gains for the two groups from grade 4 to grade 8 were virtually identical (Barton and Coley, 1998). Similarly, no matter what one might think of the ultimate value of the "value-added" techniques developed by William Sanders, his analysis finds that gains are not correlated with SES (Bratton, Horn, and Wright, undated).

Hanushek has refused to acknowledge any of the studies that show a positive relationship between spending levels and achievement. In the Summer 1997 issue of *Educational Evaluation and Policy Analysis*, he updated his study and wrote that "there is no strong or consistent relationship between variations in school resources and student performance." There appears to be only a strong and consistent relationship between what Hanushek says at one time and what he says at another, often quite independent of anything the data might say.

An examination of the studies Hanushek included in his analysis leads to substantial doubt about their appropriateness. Many titles have nothing to do with achievement and imply that money is a variable of only minor interest: "Student Perceptions, IQ, and Achievement"; "Instructor Effects in Economics in Elementary and Junior High Schools"; "Selectivity Bias and the Determinants of SAT Scores"; "Children Who Do Exceptionally Well in First Grade"; "Merits of a Longer School Day"; "School District Leave Policies, Teacher Absenteeism, and Student Achievement"; "Do Additional Expenditures Increase Achievement in the High School Economics Class?" (Hanushek, 1997).

Obviously, none of these studies was designed to directly test the money–achievement relationship. Some don't even measure what most researchers typically have in mind when they speak of "achievement"—for example, those using SAT scores. In addition, studies using instruments such as the SAT cannot be generalized to the whole realm of education. Not only does the SAT involve a single class—high school seniors—it also reflects only a nonrandom sample of that class—currently, the 43 percent of the nation's high school seniors who choose to take it because they are interested in attending colleges that require SAT scores.

These questionable studies reflect a problem in econometric research. As Kevin Payne and Bruce Biddle have pointed out,

[N]orms for publication in the field of economics stress the need for careful specification and derivation of structural models but give short shrift to the operational details of empirical studies. Thus, many studies in this literature provide few-to-no details about the sample used, the ways in which the data were collected, the ways in which measuring scales were constructed, the reliability or validity of those scales, the distribution or range of values for variables in the analysis, or even the values of basic correlations among those variables. (Payne and Biddle, 1999)

As the reader might have guessed from these paragraphs, econometric research fails to report virtually everything that educational or psychological researchers hold dear. Ideally, educational researchers who read a study produced by other educational researchers ought to be able to replicate the study's research model. That is, they ought to be able to conduct the same study themselves if they so choose. To be fair, educational research articles do not attain this ideal, but they come much closer than do articles of econometric research, which are often murky indeed.

Does Spending Equal Achievement?

The master myth is also sustained by studies indicating that, although spending for public schools has increased substantially over the years, achievement (test scores) has been flat. Much of the money, however, has flowed into special education services and other targeted areas that would not be expected to increase a school's overall achievement, if that achievement is indicated by test scores. Moreover, the claim that achievement has been flat or stagnant can be made only by selecting data that appear to support the claim. In arguing for stagnant achievement, Hanushek has pointed to results from the NAEP for seventeen-year-olds and, to a lesser extent, to SAT scores (Hanushek, 1999).

The National Assessment of Educational Progress

The argument that increasing spending ought to increase NAEP scores is tenuous at best. For students, chosen at random to participate, NAEP enters their lives only once and disappears that same day (a given student is unlikely ever to participate in more than one NAEP assessment). It has no consequences for the student or for the student's parents, teacher, principal, or anyone else. Until 1988, NAEP was prohibited by law from reporting scores at any level below "region." In 1988, the law was amended to permit state-by-state reporting, and some forty-odd states now participate in such comparisons. But the state level is the lowest level of reporting. The NAEP does not issue district, school, or individual reports.

Moreover, NAEP was not designed to measure a particular curriculum. Its creators viewed it as purely descriptive. It sought to determine what people knew and didn't know. To that end, NAEP was constructed to include some questions that the test makers expected 90 percent of the test takers to get right, some questions they expected 50 percent to get right, and some questions they expected only 10 percent to answer correctly. This procedure has been altered over the years to generate a single score, but NAEP remains only loosely connected to what happens in classrooms.

The question, then, would be why anyone would *expect* spending more money to cause NAEP scores of seventeen-year-olds to rise. As former NAEP executive director Archie Lapointe has said, the big problem with NAEP is keeping kids awake during the test (Lapointe, 1995). This is not just a humorous comment. I once worked in a school district that participated in some field trials for NAEP. In a subsequent "debriefing" meeting, about half of the teachers told me that they had trouble keeping the students, (eighth-graders) on task. It is also well known that students treat low-stakes tests such as NAEP or commercial achievement tests less and less seriously as they get older.

Hanushek could not invoke NAEP scores for younger children because those scores *have* been rising. Nor can he continue to invoke NAEP scores even for seventeen-year-olds, because those scores have been rising as well. Moreover, changes in the average scores that Hanushek uses are attenuated by demographic changes over time in the composition of the NAEP sample.

Simpson's Paradox.   Since its inception in the 1970s, the NAEP sample has contained increasing proportions of minority students. Their scores have been improving, as, for the most part, have the scores of white students, but the scores of minority students remain below those of whites. As minority students become a larger and larger proportion of the total sample, their improving-but-still-low scores mute the changes in the overall average. If this sounds paradoxical, it is, but it occurs often enough to have a name: Simpson's Paradox. We make a small digression to illustrate how it works.

Simpson's Paradox

Time 1	Time 2	
500	510	
500	510	
500	510	
500	510	
500	510	
500	510	
500	510	
500	430	
500	430	
400	430	
490	486	Average

Assume the 500s represent the SAT scores of white students at Time 1, while the 400s represents the SAT scores of minority students. Assume that at Time 2, the 510s stand for whites and the 430s for minorities. Thus, everyone has improved and minorities have improved more, raising their scores by 30 points compared to 10 points for whites.

But at Time 1, minorities constituted only 10 percent of the total sample, and at Time 2 they made up 30 percent of the total. Thus, although everyone improved, and minorities improved more than whites, the average for all students taken together actually declines from 490 to 486. This is solely because the improving-but-still-low scores of minorities are a larger proportion of the total sample.

Table 3.1 shows the changes in NAEP scores over time for all students, for three ethnic groups, for three grade levels, and for three performance levels (until the 1996 assessment Asians were too small a group to be reported separately). Looking at Table 3.1 for all students at the seventeen-year-old level, we do see that the average score (50th percentile) has not moved much over time.

TABLE 3.1 *National Assessment Trends for Seventeen-Year-Olds*

Percentile:	All		White		Black		Hispanic	
Reading								
	1971	1996	1971	1996	1971	1996	1975*	1996
5th	206	213	219	225	165	200	184	198
50th	288	288	293	296	239	266	253	264
95th	356	354	359	358	310	330	321	329
Mathematics								
	1978	1996	1978	1996	1978	1996	1978	1996
5th	241	256	252	266	217	241	224	243
50th	301	308	307	315	268	286	275	293
95th	356	355	358	358	321	333	332	341
Science								
	1977	1996	1977	1996	1977	1996	1977	1996
5th	212	217	231	237	172	192	194	196
50th	291	298	298	309	240	259	262	270
95th	362	365	365	371	310	327	331	340

*Before 1975, Hispanics were too small a group to produce a reliable estimate in the NAEP sampling procedure.

Source: Adapted from *NAEP 1995 Trends in Academic Progress*, National Center for Education Statistics (Washington, DC: Office of Educational Research and Improvement, U.S. Department of Education, 1997).

For reading, it has stayed at 288; for math, it increased from 301 to 308; and for science, it rose from 291 to 298. For low-performing students, (those at the 5th percentile) there is improvement across the board. The only group showing truly "stagnant" scores are high-performing seventeen-year-olds.

As was stated at the outset, however, these scores are affected by Simpson's Paradox: Minorities made up a much larger part of the total in the most recent NAEP assessments than in the earliest ones. If we analyze the NAEP trends by ethnicity, we see virtually nothing but progress. Scores are up for all groups and most performance levels. In math, for instance, the 5th percentile for black students rose 24 points, from 217 to 241, and the 95th percentile rose 12 points, from 321 to 333 (Campbell, Voelkl, and Donahue, 1997). In general, blacks made more progress than Hispanics. The 2000 census found large increases in the number of Hispanics, many of whom do not speak English as their native language. Their progress might well be attenuated by lower levels of English proficiency.

Simpson's Paradox also applies to SAT scores. When a panel examined reasons for the decline of SAT scores from 1963 to 1977, it attributed as much as 75 percent of the decline to changes in who was taking the test: Colleges were opening up to women and minorities; students with relatively weak high school records still aspired to attend college; and people from low-income families set their sights on higher education. A number of the new SAT-takers also were heading now to two-year colleges, not to four-year institutions as had been typical in the past. Students bound for two-year colleges scored substantially lower than those planning for a bachelor's degree.

Demographic Trends and the Iowas

Hanushek and others have refused to acknowledge the NAEP changes, or have ignored test trends that would refute the claim that increased spending has not produced increased achievement. These other test scores cannot be *directly* linked to money, but they have been anything but "flat." The trends in question come from the Iowa Test of Basic Skills (ITBS) and are shown in Figure 1. The Iowas, as they are known, have been around since the late 1920s and are constructed to reflect what happens in classrooms (NAEP, by contrast, is constructed to reflect "best thinking" from professionals in various fields). By Iowa law, new versions of the ITBS must be statistically equated to the previous edition. This equating permits direct comparison of scores at different points in time.

Figure 1 shows trends from 1955 to 2000. The trendlines omit earlier data because in 1955 tests underwent radical content changes. The psychometricians who develop the Iowas at the University of Iowa felt that the test scores prior to 1955 might not be comparable to the later data. By law, new versions of the ITBS must be statistically equated to the old versions.

The scores are presented in grade equivalents, a metric that compares any given student's score to the score of the average (median) student. The score to the left of the decimal in a grade equivalent is a year; those to the right of the decimal are in months. Thus, a third-grader who obtains a grade equivalent of 3.3 in the

FIGURE 1 *Trends in ITBS Achievement: Composite Scores Grades 3–8, 1955 to 2000*

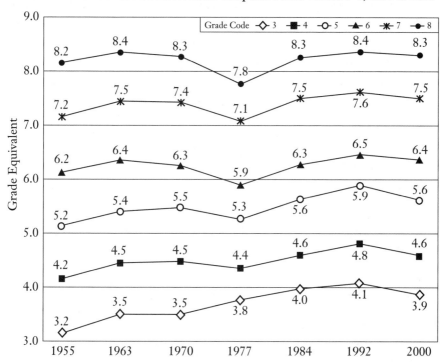

Source: Data provided by H. D. Hoover, Iowa Testing Program (Iowa City: University of Iowa, 2001).

third month of the third grade would be said to be "at grade level." At student with a 3.2 would be one month below grade level, a student with a 3.4 one above.

Figure 1 reveals trendlines that rise from 1955 to 1965, then fall for about a decade and then reverse and head upwards again, reaching record high levels in the late 1980s. The scores obtained when the test was renormed in 2000 show scores that are slightly lower than in the previous renorming of 1992. Most scores have declined by one month, and a couple have declined by two.

Some people remember "the sixties"—more accurately, the period from 1965 to 1975—only in flashbacks. Those ten years, one of the most tumultuous eras in U.S. history, were ushered in by the 1965 Watts riots in Los Angeles. Sparked by the black community's claims of police brutality against African Americans, riots soon spread to virtually every urban area in the nation.

By the 1960s, television had become ubiquitous in American households, and TV brought the military, political, and cultural conflicts of those years into America's homes. Recreational use of drugs, especially marijuana and psychedelic drugs, increased dramatically in the late 1960s, and the rise of a youthful subculture of drugs, rock music, and protest was seen in the so-called Summer of Love in 1967 and in the Woodstock festival in 1969.

At the same time, the Vietnam War was escalating, and a growing protest movement against U.S. military involvement dominated the political landscape. Many groups, including the Black Panthers, Students for a Democratic Society, and the Student Nonviolent Coordinating Committee, took to the streets in protest of U.S. policy in Vietnam and of racial discrimination and inequality at home. The assassinations of public figures, especially Martin Luther King, Jr., Malcolm X, and Robert F. Kennedy, fostered a sense of national crisis. Protests at the 1968 Democratic National Convention in Chicago led to violent confrontations with police; less than two years later, in May 1970, protest turned deadly when four students at Kent State University in Ohio were fatally shot by National Guard troops during an antiwar rally.

Given the immense amount of social disruption, it should not surprise anyone that people's attention might have been focused on matters outside of school. People have also brought forward explanations of the 1965–75 decline in terms of curriculum changes and teacher preparation. It is unlikely at this point that the various causes can be disentangled.

No one knows why scores have edged down in the late 1990s. One possible explanation is the changing demographics of the United States. For example, before 1977, Hispanics were so few in number they were not reported as a separate group in NAEP analyses. Now they are on the verge of becoming the largest minority in the United States and their scores are considerably below those of white students.

Another possibility is that the education reforms of the 1990s, largely imposed by governors, legislators, and other non-educators, have not only not worked but have backfired.

Education Spending in America: Too Much Outlay for Too Little Return?

The third means of trying to show that money doesn't matter is to claim that the United States spends more money on its public schools than any other nation, yet doesn't perform as well on tests. If this is true, then it stands to reason that America's schools are inefficient. However, this is not the case. There are a variety of ways to calculate and compare national school expenditures, and, by any measure, the United States is never the biggest spender.

Calculating Nations' Educational Expenditures

One might think that calculating nations' expenditures for schools would be a straightforward exercise in arithmetic. The arithmetic *is* simple, but the conceptualization is not. We can define a nation's spending on schools in a variety of ways. In one study, which used expenditures as a percentage of per capita income, the United States finished fourteenth of sixteen nations (Rasell and

Mishel, 1988). Another study, conducted by the Organization for Economic Cooperation and Development (OECD), looked at spending as a percentage of per capita gross domestic product (GDP) (OECD, 2000). The United States ranked twelfth out of twenty-three countries in elementary school spending and tied for fourteenth of twenty-two at the secondary level. It ranked fourth in spending on its colleges and universities.

The OECD also calculated how many dollars countries spend per pupil per year.[2] Here the United States attained its highest rank—fifth among twenty-three nations in elementary spending and fifth among twenty-two nations in secondary spending. The United States *was* first in spending at the college level, passing Switzerland for the first time since the OECD started keeping track (OECD, 2000, p. 85).

Which statistic should one use? My preference is percentage of per capita GDP, which seems to me to best represent how much of its wealth a nation is willing to invest in its future.

A Misleading Impression?

At a deeper, more important level, it doesn't matter what method one uses—all of the calculations are misleading. The OECD analyses reveal the United States as the only nation in which nonteaching employees outnumber teachers (OECD, 1993). (Figures from the U.S. Department of Education are slightly different, showing that in 1995 teachers constituted a slight majority, 52 percent, of all employees, down from 70 percent in 1950.) In some nations, by contrast, virtually everyone in a school teaches.

Critics use such figures to claim that American schools are bloated and inefficient, suffocated by an "administrative blob." The spending figures—presented as if all of the money were spent directly on instruction—have led privatizers to claim they can make a profit by cutting out the fat. However, American schools provide many services—food, transportation, counseling and, especially, special education—that other nations either don't provide or provide in reduced amounts. One study, *Where Has the Money Gone?*, analyzed how much new funding had been appropriated for schools between 1969 and 1994 (Rothstein and Miles, 1997). It found that the usual measure of increasing costs, the consumer price index, overestimated the amount of new money going to American classrooms. Using a more accurate index, the study found that spending during the twenty-five-year period had increased by 61 percent. More of this money—over one-third—went to special education than to any other category. Less than one-quarter of the new money found its way into regular classrooms.

---

2. These calculations involve the use of something called *purchasing power parities*, which are designed to equate how many dollars will buy how much of anything across countries. At this point I have been unable to determine how parities are calculated or to assess their accuracy.

Other Justifications for the Master Myth

The master myth is also sustained by the argument that public schools, as a "monopoly," are inefficient, wasteful, and unresponsive to pressures for account-ability. One study, however, indicated that, compared to the various private sectors of the economy, public schools are quite lean (Robinson and Brandon, 1992). They have very few administrators in relation to the number of "front-line" workers (teachers). It is true that the United States is the only country to have more nonteachers than teachers in the workforce, but this results from the wide variety of services that American schools provide.

The master myth also justifies making a profit: If a company can provide "the same" education for less, why shouldn't it be entitled to what isn't spent? Since money doesn't matter, the money that is left over is superfluous to a high-quality education.

To be sure, money per se is not the issue, and the argument should not have been waged in those terms. As Benjamin Barber has pointed out, money per se does not win wars or put men on the moon, but it is the critical facilitator of both (Barber, 1993).

Of course, it is possible to spend money in ways that do not affect outcomes. Consider the debacle of Kansas City, Missouri, a school district that has become the poster child of the political right, which claims it as the definitive case showing that more money makes no difference. Kansas City does provide a classic lesson in how not to spend, but it hardly lends itself to a general rule (Ciotti, 1998).

Kansas City: A Lesson in School Spending

Like many other urban settings, Kansas City became a predominantly minority district as white families moved to the suburbs. And, as in many other cities, African American students achieved at low levels. When a lawsuit sought to address this problem by forcing a union between Kansas City and its surrounding suburbs, a federal judge ruled against that idea but invited the plaintiffs to come up with other means of raising the achievement of black students. The judge and the plaintiffs decided that the best way to raise the test scores of black students was to lure white students back into the city schools. The problem was segregation; once that was cured, raising black students' test scores would be a cinch.

The result was a "Field of Dreams" theory for inducing white students to attend city schools: If you build it, they will come. To this end, Kansas City constructed beautiful facilities with Olympic-size swimming pools. The district built new schools that offered courses in garment design, ceramics, violin, ballet, drama, and foreign languages. They offered courses in Greco-Roman wrestling and hired the former Russian Olympic fencing coach to teach students how to wield an epée. The program spent $900,000 for television advertising to recruit students and $6.4 million for door-to-door suburb-to-city transportation.

The dream was never realized. The programs cost a fortune but managed to attract only about 20 percent as many students as the school district had hoped for. Those who did come seldom stayed for more than a year.

The proposition that the way to raise black achievement was to have black students sit next to white students was dubious from the outset. In any case, the program failed. In addition to programmatic failures, political problems assured catastrophe. The district chewed up ten superintendents in nine years. Many leading candidates for the post took themselves out of contention once they had actually met with the school board.

There seems to have been general agreement that many Kansas City teachers were incompetent. Yet, many in the African American community, especially black clergy, were concerned about a loss of jobs in their communities in a reform effort. As a consequence, getting rid of incompetent teachers was impossible. To encourage teachers to work harder, the city gave all teachers large salary increases. This, too, backfired, as it simply cemented the incompetents in place. Even as Kansas City built new schools, Ciotti found that what he called "rattlingly empty" old schools stayed open, posing a huge financial drain on the system.

From Kansas City, we certainly can extract a clear lesson about school spending: Do not throw money at politically dysfunctional schools with incompetent teachers, administrators, and board members, who are operating under a plan that has little to do with learning and has been constructed by a naïve lawyer and approved by an equally naïve judge.

What Spending Can Achieve

Up to now, we have found flaws in studies claiming to show that money is unrelated to achievement. Studies also exist that clearly indicate that money does make a difference. For instance, the SAT is a test that is relatively tangential to the day-to-day instruction in schools.[3] Yet even results on such a remote test are affected by money, as indicated earlier in the Powell and Steelman analysis.

Howard Wainer of Educational Testing Service noted the absence of a clear relationship between his company's SAT and classroom instruction, as well as the fact that different states have different participation rates and asked: What if we look at a test where the participation rate is the same for all states—for example, the National Assessment of Educational Progress (NAEP), which uses a representative sample of students from each state when it wishes to make state-by-state comparisons. Wainer found a definite relationship between state-level spending and NAEP scores (Wainer, 1993). Another study found that school districts that

---

3. But it is getting less so as schools increasingly choose instruction and assessment that resembles SAT skills. Thus, The Gwinnett County, Georgia, fourth-grade language arts test presents some reading passages, after which come questions in the form of analogies: X:Y as Z:?

spent more money on instructional materials had higher test scores than those that spent less (Lockwood and McLean, 1993).

Ronald Ferguson of Harvard University found that districts that used money to lure more experienced teachers or to reduce class size had rising test scores (Ferguson, 1991). The most elaborate test of money and outcomes is that of Harold Wenglinsky at ETS (Wenglinsky, 1998). In his monograph *How Educational Expenditures Improve Student Performance and How They Don't*, Wenglinsky found that teachers' level of education made little difference, nor did spending on administration at the building level. Spending on administration at the district level, however, paid off. This is possibly because the proportion of administrators in districts has dropped from 2.6 percent in 1950 to 1.7 percent in 1995 (*Digest of Education Statistics*, 1997 Table 82, p. 89). Smaller class sizes also paid off handsomely.

Project STAR

The positive findings for class size have been consistent, with the most important demonstration of class size effects coming from a large-scale study: Tennessee's Project STAR (Student Teacher Achievement Ratio). In the experiment, class size in kindergarten through grade 3 was reduced to an average of sixteen students. The state also appropriated money to give some classes a full-time paraprofessional. And some classes were untouched (Finn and Achilles, 1990; Finn, 1999; many issues concerning class size and Project STAR are discussed in the Summer 1999 issue of *Educational Evaluation and Policy Analysis*, the entirety of which is given over to the topic).

The factor that makes Project STAR so important is this: Classes were randomly assigned to each condition *within each school*. This random assignment is crucial because it eliminates the possibility of selection bias. Without random assignment within buildings, principals who favored small classes might have chosen that option and worked hard to get the results they wanted. Similarly, a principal who liked to use paraprofessionals could bias the outcomes in that direction. Conversely, if a principal chose a condition not favored by the faculty, any positive outcomes could be undermined. Random assignment of conditions within each building eliminates these potential problems.

The classes with teachers' aides produced a small improvement in achievement. Those with fewer pupils produced a larger one. Moreover, the effects were sustained into high school (where the students are currently). Economist Alan Krueger has noted that students who were in small classes in Project STAR have been more likely to take college admissions tests (Krueger and Whitmore, 1999).

In another analysis of the data, Krueger finds that when the same students are tracked over the years, the effects increase with time—they are cumulative. In his paper, Krueger quotes Hanushek as writing of Project STAR's effects (Hanushek has tried often to make them disappear), "If smaller classes [in Project STAR] were valuable in each grade, the achievement gap would widen. It does not. In fact, the gap remains essentially unchanged throughout the sixth grade . . . The inescapable conclusion is that smaller classes at best matter in kindergarten" (Krueger, 1998).

However, Hanushek did not track the same children over time as Krueger did: "For the wave of students who entered [small classes in] kindergarten, the beneficial effects of attending a small class do not appear to increase as students spend more time in their class assignments. For students entering the experiment in the first or second grade, however, the test score gap between those in small- and regular-size classes grows as students progress to higher grades."

Krueger even conducted an analysis comparing different-sized regular classrooms. For students in small regular classrooms (twenty-two students on average), achievement was higher than for students in large regular classrooms (twenty-five students). Most recently Krueger (2000) has issued what might turn out to be the definitive assessment of class size, even though it does not include Project STAR in its analysis. It reanalyzes the set of studies used by Hanushek to prove that class size does *not* matter.

First, Krueger indicates that there is no theoretical justification for Hanushek's treatment of each *analysis* rather than each study as a test of the hypothesis. In Hanushek's approach, each of the analyses receives a vote for whatever hypothesis it supports. That is, if a study simply looked at class size in elementary school and found a positive outcome, the "positive" category would get one "vote." If it analyzed the data for each grade, it would get six votes. If it analyzed the data for each class, for gender, and for the four largest ethnic groups, it would get forty-eight votes. When Krueger analyzed the data after making all studies equal—not weighted by the number of analyses—the data overwhelmingly favor the hypothesis that class size is important.

Perhaps most important, Krueger didn't include Project STAR in his analysis because Hanushek had not. Hanushek has never used Project STAR because, he says, it does not control for family background. Yet Project STAR is one of the few experiments in the history of American education to be able to select randomly what classrooms participated in what part of the experiment. A cynic might conclude that Hanushek has never included Project STAR data because, if he did, he would be forced to reverse his conclusions. Hanushek has testified several times before Congress and before courts in eight states studying school finance issues that class size doesn't matter. Using his technique, he has 277 estimates of class size effects from 59 studies. Project STAR alone would generate over 400 estimates and would swamp the negative analyses in Hanushek's reports.

Project SAGE

A smaller program in Wisconsin, Project SAGE (Student Achievement Guarantee in Education), has found similar results over the three years of its existence. Most SAGE classes contain fifteen or fewer students, and SAGE students consistently have outperformed their counterparts in regular classrooms (Molnar, Smith, and Zahorik, 2000). In an interesting wrinkle, some SAGE classrooms contain thirty students, but two teachers. These classes perform almost as well as the small classes. This could be an important finding because the capital costs of providing small classrooms would be substantial and, in urban areas, nearly impossible because of a simple absence of available space.

SAGE researchers also conducted some case studies and report that, in addition to increased test scores, SAGE classes "dominated by individualization." Small classes permit the teacher to know the students faster and better. They reduce the amount of time teachers spend on discipline and management and, therefore, increase the amount of time available for instruction.

In the small classes, the students participate more, allowing teachers to see if the students fully understand the subject being discussed. Instruction is still teacher-centered but, according to the report, "the use of hands-on activities is growing in frequency." As a consequence, students show more independence and take on more responsibility.

Mandating Small Classes

The impact of small classes is such that President Clinton proposed funds to accomplish it on a national scale. California has mandated small classes and other states are looking to do the same.

It is important to note, therefore, that, as with money, it is not small classes per se that are important. Small classes take some pressure off teachers and allow them to individualize instruction more. People wondered if this would occur under California's mandate. Horror stories abounded as California schools scurried to meet the mandate: Schools hired unqualified teachers, lengthened school days, held classes in closets and restrooms, and so forth. Those are the anecdotes. What has been documented is that thousands of teachers in low-income schools have left to take the new openings in affluent, attractive, high-paying districts. Thus the small-class mandate might have a negative impact on those who could most benefit from it: In Project STAR, low-income and minority students responded more to small classes than did their middle-class peers.

In spite of all this, the first formal evaluation of the class size initiative in California found positive effects (Class Size Consortium, 1999). The second evaluation noted that teacher qualifications continued to decline. It also found that teachers did, in fact, spend more time with individual students. Finally, as in the first evaluation, small positive effects on test scores showed up. In addition, students who had moved from small third grades to regular-sized fourth grades sustained the advantage they had shown in their small classes (Class Size Consortium, 2000).

Both the Master Myth and the spending myth are part of America's popular culture and although they are false, neither myth is likely to disappear from discourse about the quality of schools anytime soon.

4

The Historical Context

In his historical survey of public education in the United States, Arthur Newman noted that criticism of American schools has always been plentiful (Newman, 1978). Over the years, it has had a certain sameness to it: Schools are inefficient; Schools are not preparing students for the jobs of tomorrow; Schools aren't what they used to be (and never were, as Will Rogers observed). Indeed without the constant carping of business and industry, and to some extent, universities, one wonders how much criticism of schools would even exist.

In any case, we must examine the history of such criticism in order to understand how we got to where we are today. What events made Americans nervous about the quality of their schools?

The Factory Model of Schooling

The faultfinding began early in the century. In 1912, Frederick Taylor appeared before Congress to testify about his "scientific management" methods for making factories more efficient. Taylor's timing was impeccable, coming as it did at the height of an era in which the muckrakers had ripped not only corporations, but virtually every American social institution as inefficient or corrupt or both. Taylor's discourse, when applied to schools, affixed an onerous—no, disastrous—vision to them: the factory model of schooling. In 1913, Stanford University's Elwood Cubberly, the most influential educator in the nation at the time declared that

> Every manufacturing establishment that turns out a standard product or series of products of any kind maintains a force of efficiency experts to study methods of procedure and to measure and test the output of its works . . . Our schools are, in a sense, factories in which the raw products (children) are to be shaped and fashioned into products to meet the various demands of life. The specifications for manufacturing come from the demands of the twentieth-century civilization, and it is the business of

schools to build its pupils to the specifications laid down. This demands good tools, specialized machinery, continuous measurement of production to see it is according to specifications, the elimination of waste in manufacture, and a large variety in the output. (Cubberley, 1919, p. 338)

To be sure, this was not a sudden break with some more romantic past. Business early made its presence known in the schools. In 1897, social reformer Jane Addams noted that

> The business man has, of course, not said to himself, "I will have the public school train office boys and clerks for me, so that I may have them cheap," but he has thought, and sometimes said, "Teach the children to write legibly, to figure accurately and quickly, to acquire habits of punctuality and order; to be prompt to obey, and not question why; and you will fit them to make their way in the world as I have made mine." (in Curti, 1961, p. 203)

I do imagine that Addams knew quite well that there were indeed some business-men who said, "Schools, train the clerks so I can get them cheap."

Opposition to the Factory Model

Not all educators acceded to Taylor's claims. John Dewey, for instance, opposed the efficiency movement because he saw children as complex and idiosyncratic beings for whom standardization was inappropriate. Calling for America's educational system to focus on this individual complexity, Dewey said that "It is a change, a revolution, not unlike that introduced by Copernicus when the astronomical center shifted from the earth to the sun. In this case the child becomes the sun about which the appliances of education revolve; he is the center about which they are organized" (Curti, 1961, p. 99).

When the National Association of Manufacturers called for the nation's schools to be reorganized so as to better prepare children for jobs, New York City school superintendent William Maxwell considered the motivation that business and industry might have for such a recommendation. He pointed out that manufacturers had abandoned their costly apprenticeship system and, as a consequence, lacked an adequate supply of skilled workers. They then tried to get the schools to do for free what they had earlier paid for (a condition that prevails today):

> Out of this dilemma the exit was obvious—persuade the State to assume the burden. . . . And as a first step to secure their ends, they and their agents in unmeasured terms denounced the public school as behind the age, as inefficient, as lacking in public spirit. . . . The arrogance of the manufacturers was two-fold—first in condemning the schools for not doing what thinking men had never before considered it the duty of the schools to do and what the traditions of thousands of years laid it upon the manufacturers to do; and, second, in demanding that the state should then proceed to pay the bills for training their workmen. (Maxwell, 1914, pp. 175–176)

Unfortunately for the schools, the Deweys and the Maxwells did not carry the day.

Not only was business held by many as the proper model for schools, the newly emerging field of psychology had utter and complete faith in science as a means to improve man's lot. The early psychologists believed themselves to be doing for psychology what Newton had done for physics: laying down the fundamental laws of the mental universe (even though both the special and general theories of relativity, the twin conceptualizations for unraveling Newton's framework, had already appeared, they were not known to these psychologists). These psychologists also knew something else: they were right. Their writings often took the tenor more of a religious tract than a scientific discourse. The dominant psychology of the day played well into the factory model.

Labor, for its part, was no match for the capitalists. Said economist Roger Babson in 1914, "However successful organized labor has been in many ways, it has never succeeded in directing the education of its children. Capital still prepares the school books and practically controls the school systems" (in Gelberg, 1997, p. 47). As a consequence, William Bagley, another influential educator of the time, noted, "One can see in the mechanical routine of the classroom the education forces that are slowly transforming the child from a little savage into a creature of law and order, fit for the life of civilized society" (in Tyack, 1974, pp. 132–133).

Many educators, especially superintendents, embraced the new efficiency model with a vengeance, producing what Raymond Callahan referred to as a "descent into trivia" (Callahan, 1962, p. 241). The new model changed superintendents from scholars into managers, and nothing was too trivial for their attention. Don't purchase ink as a liquid, wrote one superintendent, make it from a powder. In 1933, U.S. Commissioner of Education William J. Cooper wrote *Economy in Education*, offering school administrators hints on how to save money on paper fasteners, theme paper, colored pencils, and coal. "On the matter of school paper there is always some waste. A sheet may be larger than needed. The best remedy for this is to supply two sizes, one the regular 8 1/2" by 11", the other 8 1/2" by 5 1/2". If the superintendent will study his paper and its uses he will be able to eliminate odd sizes and buy more standard sizes. Toilet paper is frequently a source of waste. I have seen school toilets in which the ceiling and walls were literally coated with paper which had been dipped in water and thrown. As for paper towels . . ." (in Bracey, 1995a, p. 191).

Of course, one might wonder why, instead of studying ways to save money on toilet paper, superintendents didn't investigate why their charges dipped it in water and slung it at the walls.

The Progressive Education Association and the Eight Year Study

Again, there were opposing forces. During the 1930s, some educators, especially those in the Progressive Education Association (PEA), were studying how to make schools more exciting. At their 1932 meeting, PEA members expressed criticisms of traditional high schools and formulated ideas for reform, but also voiced an oft-heard lament: "Yes that should be done in our high schools, but it can't be done without risking students' chances of being admitted to college" (Aikin, 1942; reprinted in Raubinger et al., 1969, pp. 164–169).

Since the formation of the College Entrance Examination Board in 1900, college entrance requirements had emphasized a traditional course of study involving math, languages, literature, history, and, later, natural sciences. The PEA persuaded colleges to waive their usual admissions criteria for some thirty-two schools for a period of eight years. Using a control group of similar traditional high schools, the PEA conducted what came to be known as the Eight Year Study. Generally, kids from these early "break-the-mold" schools outperformed their traditional peers both in terms of their performance in the college classroom and in their involvement with social and political activities on campus. "The guinea pigs wrote more, talked more, took a livelier interest in politics and social problems, went to more dances, had more dates. Especially concerned with campus affairs of the six most experimental schools. There were more dynamos than grinds among them," wrote educator Edgar Knight in retrospect (1952, pp. 114–115). One wonders what educational transformations the Eight Year Study might have accomplished but for the onset of World War II.

The press for efficiency in the early years of the twentieth century had its reprise in calls for higher standards and higher skills in the century's last two decades. The basis for the current upheaval had been laid in the early 1950s, when schools came to be seen for the first time as integral to national defense, as important instruments in the space and weapons races. With numbers supplied by CIA chief Allen Dulles, Admiral Hyman Rickover crossed the country declaring that the schools were producing insufficient numbers of scientists, engineers, mathematicians, and foreign language speakers. "Let us remember," said Rickover, "that there can be no second place in a race with the Russians. And there will be no second chance if we lose" (1956).

Along with the idea that the schools were not making the grade, there now appeared for the first time a nostalgia for some unnamed earlier time when things were better. Arthur Bestor's influential 1953 book, *Educational Wastelands*, was subtitled *The **Retreat** from Learning in Our Public Schools* (emphasis added). It is a nostalgia that persists today and is as misbegotten and erroneous now as it was then (Bracey, 1997a). When the Russians launched Sputnik in 1957, the critics felt vindicated.

Sputnik and the Space Race

Sputnik hit American schools like a tsunami. In early 1958, *Life* magazine launched a five-part series entitled "Crisis in Education." The March 24 cover showed photos of two teenagers, a stern-faced Muscovite, Alexei Kutzkov, and an easy-smiling Stephen Lapekas in Chicago. Inside, photos showed Kutzkov doing complicated experiments in physics and chemistry and reading aloud from *Sister Carrie* in his English class. "Even play has a purpose," commented the text.

Stephen, by contrast, was shown walking his girlfriend home hand-in-hand and dancing in rehearsal for the school musical. One large picture caught him retreating, laughing, from a geometry problem on the blackboard. "Stephen amused his classmates with wisecracks about his ineptitude," said the text.

Novelist and education reformer Sloan Wilson penned a two-page essay that could have appeared in 1998 rather than 1958 with no loss of modernity:

> The facts of the school crisis are all out and in plain sight—and pretty dreadful to look at. First of all, it has been shown that a surprisingly small percentage of high school students is studying what used to be considered basic subjects. . . . People are complaining that the diploma has been devaluated to the point of meaningless-ness. It would be difficult to deny that few diplomas stand for a fixed level of accomplishment. . . . It is hard to deny that America's schools which were supposed to reflect one of history's noblest dreams and to cultivate the nation's youthful minds, have degenerated into a system for coddling and entertaining the mediocre. (Wilson, 1958, pp. 36–37)

For what it is worth: I set out to find Lapekas and Kutzkov. Lapekas became an airforce pilot and is currently a commercial pilot. In spite of enthusiastic assistance from then–National Public Radio Moscow reporter, Anne Garrels, I have been unable to find any evidence that Kutzkov ever existed. On the phone, Garrels said, "There is no way in hell that an American journalist and photographer could have gotten into a typical Moscow high school in 1957." She suggested that *Life* editors might have made the whole thing up. More likely, she thought, the article was a payoff to Kutzkov's father for some extraordinary service to the Communist party.

I did find the photographer of the article. Unfortunately, what I found was a death notice. Since this photographer did do a lot of work in eastern Europe, it seems plausible that *Life* did not construct the story out of whole cloth (the reputation of Henry Luce publications at the time would not rule out this possibility. As teenagers, we had a saying: "*Time* for people who can't think, *Life* for people who can't even read").

The schools never recovered from Sputnik. As years went by, they were accused of many failings. In 1970, Charles Silberman observed that 176 of 186 studies of tests given at two points in time had favored the more recent time. But even though 95 percent of the studies showed progress, Silberman still called his book *Crisis in the Classroom*.

The "Paper Sputnik"

Just over a decade later, secretary of education Terrel Bell went looking for what he called "a Sputnik-like event" that would startle America with revelations of the low state of its schools. Unable to find such an event, a disappointed Bell assembled the National Commission on Excellence in Education. In 1983, the commissioners launched what many referred to as "the paper Sputnik," *A Nation at Risk*. Now the threat that we would be overrun by Russian soldiers was no greater than the fear of being outsmarted by European and Asian workers.

> The risk is not only that the Japanese make automobiles more efficiently than Americans and have government subsidies for development and export. It is not just that the South Koreans recently built the world's most efficient steelmill, or that American machine tools, once the pride of the world, are being displaced by German products. It is also that these developments signify a redistribution of trained capability throughout the globe. . . . If only to keep and improve on the slim competitive edge that we still retain in world markets, we must dedicate ourselves to the reform of our educational system. . . . (p. 7)

One can only hope that the good commissioners are at least embarrassed at having written such foolishness. But, as noted earlier, when the country slipped into recession in the late 1980s, the schools became a very convenient target. Some version of "Lousy schools are producing a lousy workforce and that is killing us in the global market" appeared often and in many places. As noted earlier, some corporate leaders, such as IBM's Louis Gerstner, continue to mouth this criticism.

To be sure, some people saw this foolishness for what it was from the beginning. We have already quoted the distinguished education historian Lawrence Cremin on the topic, but his words bear repeating:

> American economic competitiveness with Japan and other nations is to a considerable degree a function of monetary, trade, and industrial policy, and of decisions made by the President and Congress, the Federal Reserve Board, and the federal departments of the Treasury and Commerce and Labor.
>
> Therefore, to contend that problems of international competitiveness can be solved by educational reform, especially educational reform defined solely as school reform, is not merely Utopian and Millennialist, it is at best foolish and at worst a crass effort to direct attention away from those truly responsible for doing something about competitiveness and to lay the burden on the schools. It is a device that has been used repeatedly in the history of American education. (1989, p. 103)

Even when the U.S. economy recovered in the early 1990s, no one seemed to notice the contradiction between the rhetoric of failure and the reality of success (nor had they earlier: Twelve years after Sputnik, America landed a man on the moon, something attempted but never accomplished by the Soviet Union. No one attributed this triumph to the schools). Indeed, as noted, in February 1994, the Sunday Business section of the *New York Times* carried the headline "The American Economy: Back on Top." Yet, in May 1994, IBM CEO Louis V. Gerstner took to the *Times* op-ed page with an essay headlined "Our Schools Are Failing." When the final-year results from the Third International Mathematics and Science Study appeared to show that American high school seniors looked awful in comparison to seniors in other nations, something the study did not in fact show (Bracey, 2000b, 1998a, 1998b), this writer's phone rang off the hook with inquiries along the lines of "If our kids are so stupid, how can the economy be so good?"

It can be so good because, as James J. Gallagher put it in the title of an article, "Education, Alone, Is a Weak Treatment." It can be so good because the link between schooling and the economic health of a developed nation is also weak. It can be so good because from birth to age eighteen, a child only spends 9 percent of his or her life in school. It can be so good because the things that determine success on the job and economic productivity are not measured by standardized tests. It can be so good because the forces identified by Cremin can overwhelm any connection between schools and the nation's economic health.[4]

Those very government subsidies *A Nation at Risk* admired in Japan turned out to be not an asset but part of a larger problem. Japan's "miracle" was fueled on the assumption that, with a small and finite amount of land, property values would appreciate forever. At one point, the Imperial Palace and its surrounding parks were estimated to be more valuable than the entire state of California. "It was . . . insane," said a Japanese commentator on National Public Radio's *All Things Considered* on August 18, 1998.

But, given the psychology of ever-increasing land prices, Japanese banks made many bad loans, perhaps a trillion dollars worth. No one knows, said another commentator during the same NPR broadcast, because most Japanese banks lack the technology to calculate how bad their plight really is. They simply don't know. The consequence has been, in spite of all those high test scores, a decade-long recession.

Other Tigers had their own problems; some went into an economic freefall from which they still have not landed. Little has been heard from South Korea of late, but in Indonesia, a nation of 2,000 islands and 1,100 dialects, East Timor went through a bloody vote for independence and former President Suharto was accused of bleeding the country for personal gain. On a number of islands there is talk of secession.

Still, business and industry in the 1990s continue trends observed in the 1910s: They push schools to alter their curricula to make students better fit their needs. They call for increases in skill levels even though most jobs do not require highly skilled workers. The Hudson Institute's *Workforce 2020* rightly notes that the proportion of skilled jobs is increasing, but its own tables show that the great majority of jobs do not require highly skilled or highly educated workers (Judy and D'Amico, 1998).

The call for more and more education and higher and higher levels of skills is a blatant attempt by corporate America to drive down the wages of skilled workers. While the Bureau of Labor Statistics projections clearly show an

---

4. This statement would not be so true of a developing nation. Nor would it be true if the schools really were producing generation after generation of idiots, but they are not.

increase in the proportion of skilled jobs between now and 2020, they also show just as clearly that the overwhelming majority of jobs will require an associate's degree or less. Moreover, economist Arnold Packer has noted that while wages for unskilled workers are falling at a faster rate, wages for skilled workers are also falling (Packer, 1999).

In comparison to firms in Europe and Asia, American business and industry also continues to provide little on-the-job training. It was noted in a SCANS (the Secretary's Commission on Achieving Necessary Skills) report, "The Sandia Report," and in *Workforce 2020*, the Hudson Institute's sequel to *Workforce 2000*, that American industry spends the bulk of its training money on people who are already highly skilled (SCANS, 1991; Carson, Huelskamp, and Woodall, 1993; Judy and D'Amico, 1998).

A trend may be developing to provide even less training than the minimal amounts furnished in the past. The waves of downsizing and layoffs due to mergers have diluted mightily any sense of employee loyalty. Firm data are not available, but one hears often that businesses resist spending on employee education because they view it as suicidal: Once employees complete training, another employer will raid the firm and buy them away.

Of late, corporate America has been playing a shell game with education, screaming loudly for more and more highly skilled workers on the one hand, while firing them on the other (Boutwell, 1998). Thus we find IBM's CEO Louis V. Gerstner declaring over and over that "America's education system is broken" and firing 90,000 employee over and above the 183,000 IBM shed before his arrival. Gerstner agreed to leave his position at RJR Nabisco to head IBM for a mere $21 million, including stock options.

Gerstner is only the most obvious and publicity-hungry example of the restructuring of American industry. During the late 1970s and 1980s corporate America had frittered away the nation's competitive edge, blaming the decline, of course, on the schools. What they had actually done was ship 15 million manufacturing jobs to low-wage countries.

Given the task of regaining competitiveness in the global economy, America's corporate elite responded admirably in one sense—they did it, but at a terrible cost. They relentlessly applied technology to replace people. They modified managerial functions under the phrase "reengineering." They internationalized economic interests—investments and ownership and talent and ideas.

One result is that the United States is the most economically stratified nation in the Western developed world. A 1994 study found that the top 1 percent of American families controlled 43 percent of the wealth, compared to 18 percent in Great Britain, the next most stratified country. That study also found that the salary ratio of the top 10 percent of workers in most countries was somewhere between 2:1 and 3:1. In the United States, it was 6:1.

But those ratios don't provide the full picture of the extremes currently existing between corporate lions and their workforces. Gerstner got a mere $21 million to sign with IBM. In 1998, CEO Michael Eisner received around $95 million a year from Disney, and on September 8, 1998, the *Washington Post* reported that Jerry Seinfeld, who received a mere $1 million for each half-hour episode of his television sitcom, would rake in $225 million in *royalties*. These are not rare examples. These are the days of profits without people.

In sum, a historical look at recent criticism aimed at the public schools shows that as the number of nuclear warheads mushroomed after World War II, so did the number of grenades lobbed at the schools. The question, then, is whether the schools deserved such attacks. Clearly, when asked to produce benefits over which they had no control—for example, global competitiveness—the attacks were foolish at best. But another question is whether public schools had failed one of their clear functions, to produce literate Americans. This question is answered in the next chapter.

5

The Condition of American Public Education

It is possible, of course, that the war being waged against the schools is justified. Perhaps it is true, as former secretary of education William J. Bennett claimed, that the longer students suffer through American schools the dumber they get relative to their European peers. Perhaps test scores really are still falling, as we often read. Perhaps most students are leaving school unable to read, do basic arithmetic or even, as is often heard, make change.

We should be suspicious of such assertions, however, because, as earlier noted, each time the United States faces a social crisis of some kind, the schools get blamed for it. They took the hit for letting the Russians get into space first. They were faulted for not integrating the nation ethnically. They were faulted for a temporary decline in international competitiveness.

At present, it is difficult to find anything to blame them for. This doesn't keep people from trying. We earlier noted the full-page ad in the October 3, 2000, edition of the *Washington Post* decrying the apparent poor finish in the final year portion of the Third International Mathematics and Science Study (TIMSS). This appears to be some appeal to patriotism. The end of the Cold War has removed a large source of anxiety that previously education reformers could appeal to. For a while, there was an attempt to replace the Soviet Union with a new enemy, the "Rogue State." Rogue states are too small to wreak global havoc, but can cause localized mayhem. Iran, Iraq, Libya, and North Korea are often labeled rogue states. To some, rogues offer sufficient justification for both a missile defense system and continued reform of schools. The phrase "rogue state," however, was judged undiplomatic and abandoned in favor of "nations of concern."

Currently, there is an attempt to create a malaise by arguing that schools are not, somehow, equipping students to cope with some unspecified "future." The future is always available for scare tactics because no one knows what the future will look like. The popular 1982 futurist book, *Megatrends*, does not mention the Internet (Naisbitt, 1982). Eighteen years later, there are some 50 million sites on the World Wide Web. Schools are sometimes taken to task for somehow not anticipating this trend that no one else foresaw, and not educating sufficient numbers of information technologists to cope with the explosive demand.

The most recent attempt to demean America's schools was George W. Bush's invocation of an "education recession," during the 2000 presidential campaign. As might be expected, the pamphlet contained carefully screened and spun statistics that purported to reveal this recession. The Education Recession, as this is written, appears to have landed with a dull thud, perhaps because the causal allegation behind the charge is so absurd: The Bush camp claimed it was due to eight years of Clinton and Gore. How two men who controlled at best 7 percent of the dollars spent nationally for education could have induced a slide in educational outcomes has not been explained.

For his part, Clinton argued that his policies had produced an "Education Revival." This is more accurate than Bush's claim, but is not really true either: Test scores had started their ascent during the Carter administration (1976–80).

Perhaps the most popular myth in the air these days is Bennett's—and, actually, stated earlier by Clinton as well—that the longer American students stay in school, the dumber they get compared to their international peers. Because of this decline, the nation's Bennetts and Gerstners argue that we need to seek innovations in the form schooling takes, such as charters or vouchers, that will challenge the regular public schools to rise to the occasion. The source of this myth is the Third International Mathematics and Science Study (TIMSS), conducted in 1995 with various data released between 1996 and 1998. American students were above average in both subjects at the fourth-grade level, average in both at the eighth grade, and apparently near the bottom in the twelfth grade. The operative word in the last clause is "apparently." The American secondary school system cannot be compared to those of other nations for reasons to be described shortly.

Compared to students in other nations, American children probably do not learn as much math and science between the fourth and eighth grades as children in other nations. There are several reasons why.

For one thing, American students lug gigantic textbooks around. One survey in Florida found elementary school shoulders bearing as much as nineteen pounds while a similar survey in Pennsylvania found secondary students slumping under as much as twenty-eight pounds (to avoid the weights, some students resorted to the kind of wheeled luggage usually seen in airports) (Maraghy, 1999; Oshrat, 2000). Individually, these are gigantic tomes compared to those of other nations—often three times as thick. Texts in most countries come in reasonable 100–150-page packages. Textbooks in the United States are published for profit by commercial publishers. In the absence of a national curriculum, these publishers must decide which of the various pedagogical approaches they will emphasize. In reality, most take the kitchen sink approach and produce books that are three times the size of those in other nations. And things have recently gotten worse: As states adopt their own, somewhat idiosyncratic standards, publishers have attempted to address them all in a single edition.

Ironically, one of the reasons American children learn less is that their teachers teach too much. American teachers try to cover it all, and, as a consequence, coverage is often brief and shallow. Topics taught one year have to be repeated the next because insufficient time was devoted to them the first time around.

This inefficiency would be sufficient to lower achievement, but there is another reason why American performance might tail off between grades four and eight. American educators have traditionally considered the middle school years as the culmination of primary education. The reviews in grade 7 and, especially, grade 8, are intended to prepare students for the more intense study of high school. Our middle grades look back. Other nations look forward. They treat these middle years as the start of the intense academic study that culminates in graduation from high school. For example, Japanese students receive substantial amounts of algebra in grade 7 and plane geometry in grade 8 whereas most American students must wait for grades 9 and 10, respectively, for these subjects. These circumstances should cause American educators to reflect on what curriculum and instruction should look like in the middle school grades. They are hardly the stuff of crisis.

The European Model for Secondary Education

The European view might be a deliberate decision, but it is likely in part a historical accident as well. Until recently, graduation rates in most other nations were substantially lower than in the United States, and some students ceased their education before high school. A few countries have now caught and even surpassed the U.S. high school graduation rate, but that is an extremely recent phenomenon. For instance, the Second International Mathematics Study reported the proportion of seventeen-year-olds still in school in 1981. Only Japan exceeded the United States' proportion with 92 percent compared to the U.S. 82 percent. No other nation exceeded 65 percent. In Hungary it was 50 percent, in Sweden, 24 percent and in England and Wales, a mere 17 percent (McKnight, Crosswhite, Dossey, Kifer, Swafford, Travers and Cooney, 1987, p. 16).

In addition, only the United States maintains comprehensive high schools. In other nations, after eighth grade, the curricula differentiate. In some nations, over 50 percent of the students enter vocational programs. Others will attend humanities or science and technology programs. The elite in France and Germany will prepare for the *Baccalaureat* and *Arbitur* examinations. Thus, until recently, anything that European nations held to be important to provide to *all* students had to be provided by the eighth grade. The United States could afford to delay algebra or geometry or sciences, knowing that virtually everyone was going to still be in school.

Tables 5.1, 5.2, 5.3, and 5.4 show the countries ranked by the percentage of correct answers their students attained on the TIMSS math and science tests at grades 4 and 8. Different numbers of nations participated in the study at the two grade levels: TIMSS required all countries to test grade 8; grade 4 and the final year of secondary school (so called because it is usually not equivalent to the American senior year of high school) were optional.

Note that most of the nations cluster closely in terms of their percentage correct. The proximity of most nations' TIMSS scores has been obscured for two reasons. First, official TIMSS reports present the data on a 600-point scale. Small differences can seem large when transposed to such a scale. Second, some of the reports have provided only ranks, not scores. Reporting by ranks can be badly misleading, because as seen in these tables, small differences in scores can make large differences in ranks. If American fourth-graders, for instance had gotten 6 percent fewer items correct on the science test, they would have fallen from fourth place to a tie for fifteenth. If American eighth-graders had gotten 4 percent more items correct on the science test, they would have vaulted from nineteenth place to a tie for fifth. In the eighth-grade science results, there are twenty-six nations within plus or minus 6 percent of the U. S. score.

There are occasions when small differences in scores have huge consequences. The difference between a gold medal and a silver in some Olympic events has been as small as .01 seconds. However, it does not seem plausible that

TABLE 5.1 *TIMSS Fourth-Grade Mathematics Results (1996)*

Rank	Nation	Percentage Correct	Rank	Nation	Percentage Correct
1.5	**KOREA**	**76**	14.5	Latvia	59
1.5	**SINGAPORE**	**76**	16	Scotland	58
3	Japan	74	17	England	57
4	Hong Kong	73	18	Cyprus	54
5	Netherlands	69	19.5	Norway	53
6	Czech Republic	66	19.5	New Zealand	53
7	Austria	65	21	Greece	51
8.5	Slovenia	64	22.5	Iceland	50
8.5	Hungary	64	22.5	Thailand	50
11	Ireland	63	24	Portugal	48
11	**UNITED STATES**	**63**	25	Iran	38
11	Australia	63	26	Kuwait	32
13	Canada	60			
14.5	Israel	59		International Average: 59	

Source: Adapted from *Mathematics Achievement in the Primary School Years*, TIMSS International Study Center (Boston: Boston College, 1996).

TABLE 5.2   *TIMMS Fourth-Grade Science Results (1996)*

Rank	Nation	Percentage Correct	Rank	Nation	Percentage Correct
1	**KOREA**	**74**	16	Norway	60
2	Japan	70	16	New Zealand	60
3	Netherlands	67	16	Scotland	60
5	**UNITED STATES**	**66**	18	Israel	57
5	Australia	66	19	Latvia	56
5	Austria	66	20	Iceland	55
7.5	Czech Republic	65	21	Greece	54
7.5	Singapore	65	22	Cyprus	51
9.5	Canada	64	23	Portugal	50
9.5	Slovenia	64	24	Thailand	49
11	England	63	25	Kuwait	39
12.5	Hong Kong	62	26	Iran	30
12.5	Hungary	62			
14	Ireland	61	International Average: 59		

Source: Adapted from *Science Achievement in the Primary School Years,* TIMSS International Study Center (Boston: Boston College, 1996).

TABLE 5.3   *TIMSS Middle School Mathematics Results (1996)*

Rank	Nation	Percentage Correct	Rank	Nation	Percentage Correct
1	**SINGAPORE**	**79**	22	Sweden	56
2	Japan	73	25	England	54
3	Korea	72	25	Norway	54
4	Hong Kong	70	25	Germany	54
5.5	Belgium (Fl)	66	25	New Zealand	54
5.5	Czech Republic	66	**27.5**	**UNITED STATES**	**53**
8.5	Slovak Republic	62	27.5	England	53
8.5	Switzerland	62	29.5	Scotland	52
8.5	Hungary	62	29.5	Denmark	52
8.5	Austria	62	31.5	Latvia	51
11.5	France	61	31.5	Spain	51
11.5	Slovenia	61	33	Iceland	50
14	Russian Federation	60	34.5	Greece	49
14	Bulgaria	60	34.5	Romania	49
14	Netherlands	60	36.5	Lithuania	48
17	Canada	59	36.5	Cyprus	48
17	Ireland	59	38	Portugal	43
17	Belgium (Fr.)	59	39	Iran	38
19	Australia	58	40	Colombia	29
20.5	Thailand	57	41	South Africa	24
20.5	Israel	57	International Average: 55		

Source: Adapted from *Mathematics Achievement in the Middle School Years,* TIMSS International Study Center (Boston: Boston College, 1996).

TABLE 5.4 *TMSS Middle School Science Results (1996)*

Rank	Nation	Percentage Correct	Rank	Nation	Percentage Correct
1	**SINGAPORE**	**70**	19	Germany	58
2	Korea	66	23.5	Thailand	57
3	Japan	65	23.5	Israel	57
4	Czech Republic	64	25.5	Switzerland	56
6	Bulgaria	62	25.5	Spain	56
6	Netherlands	62	27	Scotland	55
6	Slovenia	62	28	France	54
9	England	61	29.5	Greece	52
9	Hungary	61	29.5	Iceland	52
9	Austria	61	31	Denmark	51
11.5	Belgium (Fl.)	60	33.5	Latvia	50
11.5	Australia	60	33.5	Portugal	50
14	Slovak Republic	59	33.5	Belgium (Fr.)	50
14	Sweden	59	33.5	Romania	50
14	Canada	59	36	Lithuania	49
19	Ireland	58	37.5	Iran	47
19	**UNITED STATES**	**58**	37.5	Cyprus	47
19	Russian Federation	58	39	Kuwait	43
19	New Zealand	58	40	Colombia	39
19	Norway	58	41	South Africa	27
19	Hong Kong	58		International Average: 56	

Source: Adapted from *Science Achievement in the Middle School Years*, TIMSS International Study Center (Boston: Boston College, 1996).

such small differences on paper and pencil tests taken by nine- and thirteen-year-olds would have *any* practical consequences.

It is worth noting that when the eighth-grade results of the TIMSS were released, only two newspapers of the many that the author saw, *Education Week* and the *New York Times*, reported the American finish as "average." All of the rest deemed our performance "mediocre." However, "average" is a statistic, while "mediocre" is a judgment. The runners who finish fourth and fifth in the final heat of the 100-meter dash in the Olympics are average but hardly mediocre. One story about the results ran for fifteen paragraphs. Fourteen of them were devoted to the below-average math score. One acknowledged that the science score was above the average.

After the TIMSS eighth-grade data appeared, the U.S. Department of Education commissioned ETS to statistically link the TIMSS data to our NAEP data (Johnson, 1998). The link puts both studies on a common scale and permits a direct comparison between the forty-one nations in TIMSS and the forty states that take part in the NAEP state-by-state analyses. Only six of the forty-one nations outscored the highest scoring states in math, and only one outscored the highest states in science,[5] but only three scored lower than the lowest scoring state. These results give some idea of the great variability of academic achievement in the United States.

Those who were responsible for the release of the TIMSS Final-Year Study now contend that it compares the different outcomes of different *systems*. They claim that it doesn't compare students at all, except insofar as different systems produce different outcomes. This claim cannot be substantiated because of flaws in the study (Bracey, 1998a, 1998b, 2000b) and it is certainly not how the study was presented when released. At that time, the study was taken as showing that our seniors went up against their seniors and got trounced. This is not what happened at all, but consider these characterizations of the study:

"American high school seniors have scored far below their *peers* from many other countries on a rigorous new international exam in math and science," declared Rene Sanchez in the *Washington Post* (emphasis added). One could wonder how Sanchez knew that the test was rigorous since he had not seen it.

"American high school seniors—even the best and brightest among them—score well below the average for their *peers* participating in TIMSS," said Debra Viadero in *Education Week* (emphasis added).

"U.S. twelfth graders rank poorly in math and science study," said Ethan Bronner in the *New York Times*.

"American twelfth-graders scored at the very bottom of the rankings," reported William Raspberry in the *Washington Post*.

"Hey! We're No. 19!" according to John Leo in *U.S. News and World Report*.

The study, however, did not compare apples to apples, or even apples to oranges—it was more like apples to aardvarks. Some twenty-two nations administered one or more of the Final-Year Tests, of which there were three: a math–science literacy test, an advanced mathematics test, and a physics test. TIMSS officials, through Statistics Canada, chose a representative sample of all students in their final year of study for the math–science literacy test. Nations could choose which students to test in physics and advanced mathematics.

Most nations do not have a culture of public self-criticism like that found in the United States. Indeed, in some countries such criticism can get citizens jailed, tortured, or executed. Left to their own devices, most nations would choose to test students who will do well and make the country look good. As a consequence, the various nations were not permitted to select their students for the general tests (they did choose whom to test in Advanced Mathematics and Physics). An Ottawa company, Statistics Canada, was provided with lists of all schools in all nations and a set of demographic data to describe those schools. Statistics Canada then drew a representative sample for each nation.

---

5. The six nations with higher math scores were Singapore, Japan, Korea, Hong Kong, the Czech Republic, and the Flemish-speaking part of Belgium, which was treated as a separate country from the French-speaking part. Only Singapore had a higher science score.

TIMSS authorities could not, of course, force the participating nations to accept the lists from Statistics Canada, and many of them did not. They excluded some groups or even some regions. Russia, for example, tested only Russian-speaking schools. Italy lopped off whole provinces. Some chosen schools refused to participate. The TIMSS directors established criteria for participation rates and exclusions below which the data would be considered not to have met criteria for a valid result.

Only five nations met the participation criteria. One can truly wonder, then, why the study was published in the first place. It likely has to do with the enormous bundle that U.S. taxpayers put up for the study—$53 million overall.

Many other problems afflict the data. When I happened to ask some of the TIMSS directors why we had administered the advanced mathematics test to students in precalculus classes, I received a nonchalant answer: "Just to see how they'd do." Well, they did awful. Their performance hardly came as a surprise: Twenty-three percent of the items on the advanced mathematics test *presume* that the test taker has taken calculus. American students who had actually taken such a course scored right at the international average, whereas those in the precalculus classes scored 100 points—a full standard deviation—lower. If American calculus students' average score is taken to represent the 50th percentile, then the precalculus kids attained only the 16th percentile rank.

Those of us who have lived abroad will never have any confidence in the international comparisons. There are too many cultural variables that affect scores but cannot be quantified. Do other nations experience a "senior slump" as severe as that in the United States? U.S. secondary schools generally don't give low-stakes tests to seniors. Some will simply refuse to take them, others will make pretty designs on the answer sheet, and nobody tries very hard. Nevertheless, U.S. students took the TIMSS tests in May of their senior year.

As mentioned earlier, after the eighth grade, other nations' curricula differentiate. This affected test results. For instance, Sweden and Norway had the highest scores on the physics test. The students these countries test had studied physics for three years. Most U.S. high schools offer only one year of physics. Some affluent districts offer two—a "regular" physics course for able juniors followed by Advanced Placement physics when they become seniors. Should American high schools offer multiyear sequences in the natural sciences? That is a legitimate question (although one wonders where the teachers would come from). It is not legitimate, however, to compare students who have studied a subject for three years with those who have studied it for only one year—unless one makes note of that difference.

The differentiated programs in other nations also produced another difference. On average, the international students taking the math–science literacy test were over a year older than American students—in one nation they were the same age as American *college* seniors.

The Connection between Students, Work, and Performance

Sometimes, in an international comparison, a cultural variable that affects the scores will come to light. In the case of TIMSS, one such variable became visible in connection with how many hours students spend working at paid jobs. In most countries, a person is either a student or a worker, not both. The United States, however, has a culture that encourages teenagers to work (and which also views the teen years as including dates, cars, malls, and extracurricular activities).

Does working affect school? Yes, the research done in this country is clear: Students who work up to twenty hours a week achieve better in school than those who work longer hours and better than those who do not work at all (D'Amico, 1984; Gottfredson, 1985; Schulenberg and Bachman, 1993). This effect appears to happen independent of social class. That is, one could predict that students from poor families, who tend to have lower grades, would also have to work longer hours to help sustain the family and would also have fewer resources at home. But even when this is factored out, the relationship between work and school performance remains the same.

Table 5.5 shows the profile for a typical nation and that for the United States. In parentheses are the percentages of students working the number of hours shown at the top. Fully 55 percent of American seniors taking the TIMSS tests said they worked more than twenty-one hours a week at a paid job. Twenty-eight percent said they worked more than thirty-five hours a week. Students who worked twenty-one to thirty-five hours a week were below average, and those who worked more than thirty-five hours a week scored far below average. American students who worked a moderate amount scored at the international average.

When we look at subgroups of American students who most resemble their foreign counterparts, the scores remain average among the nations. However, the TIMSS Final-Year data are so flawed that they are best not considered at all.

TABLE 5.5   *Hours Per Week at a Paid Job and Math/Science Literacy Scores*

Hours Worked	<7	7–14	21–35	>35
United States	484 (39%)	506 (7%)	474 (27%)	448 (28%)
Sweden	563 (84%)	541 (5%)	511 (5%)	497 (3%)

(Overall, Sweden had the second-highest score among the twenty-one nations in this part of the study, the United States had the sixteenth.)

Source: Data adapted from *Mathematics and Science Achievement in the Final Year of Secondary School*, TIMSS International Study Center (Boston: Boston College, 1996).

Misleading Impressions

Americans get the wrong impression about their schools not just from careless handling of data by both researchers and the media, but from deliberate attempts to mislead. Americans tend to have negative perceptions of public schools partly because the Reagan and Bush administrations painted them that way. Both administrations advocated vouchers and tuition tax credits for people spending money on private schools. One strategy for achieving this agenda was to accentuate negative findings about public schools and ignore positive findings. Where these administrations could suppress positive data, they did, and when they could not actually prevent the data from being seen, they ignored them as best they could.

Thus, in 1990, a 176-page report from Sandia National Laboratories concluded that "there are many serious problems in American public education but there is no system-wide crisis."[6] The political appointees of the U.S. Department of Education deemed the report too positive and killed it (Carson, Huelskamp, and Woodall, 1990; the report was finally published in 1993).

When the Sandia engineers presented their findings in Washington, D.C., David Kearns, former CEO of Xerox and then Deputy Secretary of Education, told them: "You bury this or I'll bury you." (An *Education Week* article on the meeting states only: "Administration officials, particularly Mr. Kearns, reacted angrily at the meeting.") James Watkins, secretary of the Department of Energy, which funds Sandia, called the report "dead wrong" in a letter to the *Albuquerque Journal* (Miller, 1991).

The *Education Week* article also quoted a source saying that the Sandia researchers "were told that [their report] would never see the light of day, that they had better be quiet. I fear for their careers." Although none of them actually lost their jobs, at one point the researchers were forbidden to leave the state of New Mexico to talk about the report.

The "official story" of the report's languishing maintained that it was undergoing peer review. Previously, the peer review of a report from one federal agency by another was unheard of. The Bush administration never cleared the report. Compiled in late 1990, the peer review never approved it for publication. It did appear after Clinton became president, constituting the entirety of the May–June 1993 issue of the *Journal of Educational Research*.

The fate of the Sandia Report (officially titled *Perspectives on Education in America*), was not an isolated event. One study was commissioned by the U.S. Department of Education in 1983 to prove that people who become teachers are not very bright. When the report found teachers to be about as smart as anyone else in college, the report was buried. I uncovered it only through a chance comment made by David Imig of the American Association of Colleges of Teacher Education.

---

6. This sentence did not appear in the published version.

If positive reports were buried, negative reports were hyped. Thus, in February 1992, when an international comparison in mathematics and science found American ranks mostly (but not entirely) low, the Department of Education held a well-attended press conference. The study received wide coverage in both print and electronic media. "An 'F' in World Competition" was the headline over the story in *Newsweek.*[7]

Five months later, in July 1992, an international study of reading skills was published. There was no press conference, no coverage. Over two months elapsed before *Education Week* found out about it, and then only by accident: A friend of then–*Education Week* reporter Robert Rothman sent him a copy of the study from Germany. *Education Week* carried the story on page one (Rothman,1992). *USA Today* played off the *Education Week* article with its own front-page story (Manning, 1992). The *USA Today* story, however, had a curious aspect to it—a quote from then–deputy assistant secretary of education Francie Alexander *dismissing* the study as irrelevant.

The study disappeared from view, so much so that four years later, then–secretary of education Richard Riley rereleased the results. *USA Today* again heralded the results on page one. The only other notable coverage, however, came from the Washington Bureau of the *Los Angeles Times.* I inquired of *Times* reporter Josh Greenberg why his paper was interested in four-year-old data. He advised that he and others had been suspicious when Riley had called them over to discuss the results. But he also said that when he checked around, he found that no one knew about the study, so it was still news.

By that criterion, it still is. In speeches, I always ask for a show of hands of those who know of the study. Even in a room full of other researchers, it is rare to see more than three or four arms in the air. In audiences of teachers or administrators, there is almost never a single one.

The handling of this story also reflects two other factors that bear on our perceptions of the condition of public education: We have a neurotic need to believe the worst about our schools, and good news about schools serves no one's education reform agenda. I have already mentioned the translation of "average" in the TIMSS results to "mediocre." As for the reading study, conducted by the same organization that conducted TIMSS, the story ran in the *American School Boards Journal* under the headline "Good News: Our 9-year-olds Read Well; Bad News: Our 14-year-olds Don't."

The "good" news about the study was that American nine-year-olds finished second among twenty-seven nations, outscored only by Finland. The "bad" news was that American fourteen-year-olds had finished eighth among thirty-one nations. However, if one looked not at the ranks but at the actual

7. *Newsweek* seems constitutionally incapable of saying anything positive about schools. When the eighth-grade TIMSS data arrived, *Newsweek*'s headline was "The Sum of Mediocrity" (Wingert, 1996). American ninth-graders were average. When the TIMSS fourth-grade data showed American students near the top, *Newsweek* had no story.

scores, one found the American fourteen-year-olds as close to first place as the nine-year-olds and significantly outscored only by Finland.

These results are shown in Tables 5.6 and 5.7. It is important to keep in mind the distinction between ranks and scores. From ranks alone, one can know nothing about performance. To return to the Olympic dash analogy, in that race, or any other, someone *must* rank last. He is still the eighth fastest human being on the planet that day (see chapter 9 of Bracey, 2000a, for more discussion of ranks versus scores).

The good-news-is-no-news aspect of the story applies to more than the media. Conservatives advocate vouchers and privatization. One way of furthering that aim is to accentuate the negative about the existing public school system in order to make people nervous about public schools. Liberals want to preserve and improve public schools, but their improvement efforts often involve pointing to problems in the schools and, therefore, to the need for money to solve them.

Thus we found Bill Clinton repeatedly saying that only 40 percent of American third-graders can read independently. This is really not a valid claim, only a misinterpretation of the NAEP data of proficiency levels, a scale that has been rejected by everyone in the psychometric community—most recently by the National Research Council, which called them "fundamentally flawed" (National Research Council, 1999). Even so, these are the same kids who are second in the world. In theory, we could be in the midst of a worldwide literacy crisis, but that is not what I hear people saying.

TABLE 5.6   *How in the World Do Students Read? Results for Nine-Year-Olds*

Rank	Nation	Score	Rank	Nation	Score
1	Finland	569	14.5	Spain	504
2	**United States**	**547**	16	Germany (W)*	503
3	Sweden	539	17	Canada (BC)	500
4	France	531	18.5	Germany (E)*	499
5	Italy	529	18.5	Hungary	499
6	New Zealand	528	20	Slovenia	498
7	Norway	524	21	Netherlands	485
8	Iceland	518	22	Cyprus	481
9	Hong Kong	517	23	Portugal	478
10	Singapore	515	24	Denmark	475
11	Switzerland	511	25	Trinidad/Tobago	451
12	Ireland	509	26	Indonesia	394
13	Belgium (Fr.)	507	27	Venezuela	383
14.5	Greece	504			

*Germany not unified at the time of the study

Source: Data adapted from International Association for the Evaluation of Educational Achievement (1992).

TABLE 5.7   *How in the World Do Students Read? Results for Fourteen-Year-Olds*

Rank	Country	Score	Rank	Country	Score
1	Finland	560			
	Countries above this line significantly higher than the United States				
2	France	549	17	Norway	516
3	Sweden	546	18	Italy	515
4	New Zealand	545	19	Netherlands	514
6	Hungary	536	20	Ireland	511
6	Iceland	536	21	Greece	509
6	Switzerland	536	22	Cyprus	497
8.5	**United States**	**535**	23	Spain	490
8.5	Hong Kong	535	24	Belgium (Fr.)	481
10	Singapore	534	25	Trinidad/Tobago	479
11	Slovenia	532	26	Thailand	477
12	Germany (E)	526	27	Phillipines	430
13	Denmark	525	28	Venezuela	417
14	Portugal	523	29	Nigeria	401
15.5	Canada/BC	522	30	Zimbabwe	372
15.5	Germany (W)	522	31	Botswana	330

Source: Data adapted from International Association for the Evaluation of Educational Achievement (1992).

Like the liberals, the research universities accentuate the negative to pry money from governments and foundations. As noted earlier, Susan Fuhrman, dean of the School of Education at the University of Pennsylvania, drew no reaction in a roomful of academics when she said: "If you want money you gotta say the schools are lousy. So what else is new?" What, indeed?

As observed earlier, business and industry criticize the schools to persuade them to do for free what business and industry pay for in on-the-job training. Only the armed forces, long faced with having to make do with whatever recruits they can obtain, seems to accept quietly whoever comes along, although until recently they did insist on people with at least a high school diploma. And, of course, we don't know what the military's "per pupil expenditure" is for its recruits (except that it's significantly above the national average for those recruits' children who attend Department of Defense schools).

Domestic Data on the Condition of Education

We have already examined much of the domestic test score data in the chapter on the "master myth." There we noted that achievement test scores are at all-time highs and that NAEP scores have been rising, especially when examined by ethnicity. Even when one looks at the aggregate averages, NAEP scores in reading, math, and science are at record levels.[8] SAT scores have also risen and, again, the changes are obscured by demographic changes in who is taking the SAT. The Sandia Report, for instance, found that SAT scores would have risen in the period between 1975 and 1990 if just the students' rank in class had stayed the same. Instead, more and more students in the fourth and fifth quintiles of their classes were aspiring to college and taking the SAT.

Interpreting SAT Scores

The decline of the SAT "elite"—usually defined as those scoring above 650 out of a possible 800 on each test—has been touted by school critics as reflecting declining school rigor. Once again, this is a statistic that is so much a part of the popular culture that it augments the believe-the-worst tendencies, even in institutions that should know better and be more careful, such as *Education Week*.

In February 1993, *Education Week*, noting that April 1993 would mark the tenth anniversary of the publication of *A Nation at Risk*, began a multipart series, later combined into a book, titled *From Risk to Renewal*. In an opening editorial essay, the authors asked in general what had happened in the tumultuous decade since *Risk* appeared. Their answer was, essentially, not much:

> The proportion of American youngsters performing at high levels remains infinitesimally small. In the past 10 years, for instance, the number and proportion of those scoring at or above 650 on the verbal or math section of the Scholastic Aptitude Test has actually declined. (February 10, 1993)

In a table near the text's margin, *Education Week* provided the following figures for the number of students scoring above 650 on the SATs.

	Verbal	*Mathematics*
1982	29,921 (3)	70,352 (7)
1992	22,754 (2)	58,662 (6)

The figures in parentheses are the proportions represented by the numbers, and it certainly appears that both numbers and proportions fell in the period from 1982 to 1992. For some reason, these numbers looked suspicious to me, so I checked the figures against those given in my collection of "Profiles of College

---

8. The NAEP scores for seventeen-year-olds in science might be an exception to this statement. "Might be" because the earliest NAEP science assessments were not intended to provide longitudinal data. The NAEP science assessments prior to 1977 are extrapolations from the 1977 assessment. Perhaps for this reason, the U.S. Department of Education provides trends data now only from 1977 forward. The most recent NAEP score is 296; the extrapolation back to the 1970 and 1973 assessment yield scores of 305 and 296, respectively.

Bound Seniors," an annual College Board publication the provides information about those who take the SAT along with the year's latest SAT results.

I determined that the figures for 1982 were correct. So were the figures for 1992—as far as they went. But the figures for 1992 were incomplete. Whereas the numbers for 1982 included everyone who scored from 650 to 800, the numbers for 1992 were only for the students scoring between 650 to 690 (the College Board arranges the results in a table using 40-point intervals). When the results for students scoring between 700 and 800 are added to the 1992 results, Table 5.8 takes on a quite different appearance. Over the decade the proportion of students scoring above 650 on the verbal section remained steady at 3 percent. This is less than half of what it once was, and no cause for joy. For the math section, however, the proportion rises from 7 percent to 10 percent. I wrote *Education Week* and asked for a front-page correction. The editors printed no correction, but only published my letter in the usual letters section. They did, however, affix an editorial note to my letter that said, yes, but it's still a tiny proportion.

Thus I had to write a second letter, pointing out that when the SAT took its modern form in 1941, its developers imposed a normal, bell-shaped distribution and that it is inherent in bell curves that few people score at the extremes (an SAT score of 650 corresponds to the 93rd percentile). More important, the standardization of the SAT test that took place in 1941 remained in place until 1996, when the test was "recentered" (any other testing organization would have said simply "renormed").

This raises the question: What students formed the standardization group? The answer is 10,654 students living mostly in the northeast. Ninety-eight percent were white, sixty-one percent were male, and fully forty-one percent had attended private, college-preparatory high schools. They were an elite. It was to this elite's average raw score that the average scaled score of 500 was affixed (Donlon and Angoff, 1971).

The comparison between the standard-setting group and any other group is valid only to the extent that the second group has the same demographics as this academic aristocracy. But, of course, by 1992 it did not. The group formed

TABLE 5.8 *Number of Students Scoring between 700 and 800 on the Scholastic Aptitude Test (SAT)*

	Verbal	*Mathematics*
1982	29,921 (3)	70,352 (7)
1992 (*Ed Week*)	22,754 (2)	58,662 (6)
1992 (Actual)	32,903 (3)	104,401 (10)

Source: Adapted from data supplied by the College Board (1982, 1995).

by the 1,034,133 seniors who sat for the SAT in 1992 contained 29 percent minority students, 52 percent women, and 82 percent public school students (46,000 students did not report what type of school they attended). For 42 percent, their parents had a high school diploma or less. Some 30 percent reported annual family incomes of $30,000 or less. Even if one allows for inaccuracies in teenagers' knowledge of parental incomes, it is clear that the SAT pool became greatly democratized between 1941 and 1992. Given the statistical properties of the normal curve, we know that 6.68 percent of the standard-setting group got 650 or better. In 1992, the verbal proportion had fallen to only 3 percent, but the mathematics proportion had grown to 10 percent.

I included this statistic in a *Washington Post* op-ed essay in late 1995. In the spring of 1996, the Heritage Foundation published *Issues '96: The Candidates Briefing Book*, a document that Heritage puts forth in every presidential election year. In this edition, Denis Doyle wrote the chapter on education and took me to task over my analysis of the SAT high scorers: "[Bracey] does not tell the reader who is pushing the SAT scores higher: mostly Asian and Asian American students" (Doyle, 1996).

Asian Americans, the SATs, and the "Math Gene." Doyle's comments are typical of school critics when confronted with positive data about the schools: There must be some special or unusual circumstance behind the statistics, because such data couldn't possibly come from the typical American school. In this case, the special circumstance is the consequence of the immigration of students with a "math gene."

Doyle presented no evidence to back up the claim, meaning that, at best, he had formulated a hypothesis. I tested Doyle's hypothesis by obtaining SAT scores by ethnicity from the College Board. Over the period from 1981 to 1995, (the latest year for scores at the time of the analysis) the results for all students are shown in Table 5.9. If Doyle's hypothesis were valid, removing Asian American students from the sample should reduce the 74.6 percent substantially. In fact, when Asian American students are removed, as shown in Table 5.10, the

TABLE 5.9 *Students Scoring above 650 on the SAT-M (All Students)*

	1981		1995
Number	70,307		132,898
Percent	7.1		12.4
Change		74.6%	

Source: Adapted from data supplied by the College Board (1982, 1995).

TABLE 5.10   *Students Scoring above 650 on the SAT-M (Excluding Asian American Students)*

	1981		1995
Number	65,672		118,879
Percentage	6.8		10.7
Change		57.3%	

Source: Adapted from data supplied by the College Board (1982, 1995).

growth does decline, but it remains substantial.[9] In 1981, students reporting their ethnicity as Asian represented 3 percent of the total pool of SAT test takers, and in 1995 they constituted 7.5 percent. From this alone, one would predict a higher proportion of high scorers, since Asian students do score much better on the SAT-M than members of any other ethnic group. However, with Asian students removed from the sample at both years, one still sees a 57 percent increase for black, white, Hispanic, and Native American students. The Doyle hypothesis is rejected.

With the recentering of the scale in 1996, individual researchers cannot calculate these proportions on the old scale.[10] However, Educational Testing Service and the College Board were considerate enough to do this for me. In 1997, the proportion remained at 12.4 percent, but by 2000 it had climbed to 13.2 percent.

Interestingly, the SAT's verbal scores have also been creeping up. In one 1995 essay, I predicted a further decline in verbal scores because of the emerging "iconic" culture in which pictures and graphic images played a larger and larger role. That prediction has also failed. The proportion of students scoring above 650 on the verbal test bottomed out in 1983 at 2.9 percent, but had climbed back to 4 percent by 1997 and is at 3.7 percent for 2000.

Results from the SAT are included here because, since the 1977 analysis of the decline of the SAT average score, they have been a part of our popular culture, worthy of front-page treatment in the eyes of many newspapers (Wirtz and Howe, 1977). The fact is, however, that the SAT test-taking pool is an ever-changing one of self-selecting students that is gradually increasing—currently 43 percent of the entire senior class.

---

9. These figures are not based on precisely the same numbers as those for all students. Some 99,000 students reported their ethnicity as "other" or did not report it at all.

10. If one is working only with SAT math scores and only with the proportion scoring 650 or higher, it does not matter whether one uses the original scale or the recentered one. The proportion is the same on both. Some students get slightly higher scores with the recentered scale, and some actually get lower scores with the recentered scale than they would have on the original. The difference is no more than 10 points on any part of the scale, but is nonexistent at the threshold point of 650.

Standardized Test Scores and College Admissions

Changes in college admissions procedures have made the numbers even more squishy, and generalizations drawn from SATs could easily be wrong. Formerly, colleges in the Northeast, Atlantic Seaboard South, and California were "SAT schools." Institutions in the Midwest, Northwest, Southwest, and non-Atlantic South were ACT schools. More and more, most colleges now accept either test.

In some states, college admissions tests represented only a "second chance." In Iowa, for example, students with GPAs that put them in the upper half of their high school classes can attend any institution in the state system. It is not clear what that does to Iowa averages, but one can imagine that those in, say, the top 20 percent of their class wouldn't bother to take college entrance exams if they plan to attend a state school.

Other states have recently adopted similar systems as a means of getting around affirmative action prohibitions. Thus California high school students with a B-average GPA are assured admittance to their state university system, as are Texas students with a high class rank, no matter what school they attend. The impact of all these changes is impossible to calculate but they do make generalizations more difficult.

The National Assessment of Educational Progress (NAEP) avoids the selection problems of using SAT and ACT scores because it draws a national probability sample of students. The NAEP has its own difficulties as a national barometer, however. It is not tied to any specific curriculum. Until recently, it had no consequences for the test takers, their teachers, parents, or anyone else. Now, a few states have started to use the NAEP or changes in the NAEP for "bragging rights," eliciting worries that the NAEP's integrity might be at risk.

When the states that have the largest increases in NAEP scores also have the largest increases in students given special education exclusions, one wonders if the gains are legitimate. Making the NAEP anything like a high-stakes test certainly brings to mind Bracey's paradox, formulated around 1979: Test scores mean something only when you don't pay any attention to them.

With these considerations in mind, the reader's attention is drawn to the discussion of NAEP scores in Chapter 3. There it was shown that the average scores for reading, math, and science assessment have risen. It was also shown that the scores for minorities have risen more than the scores for whites, but that these rises are partially masked by Simpson's Paradox.

Summary

If we look at international studies, we find American students near the top in reading and in the middle in mathematics and science. The best U.S. readers score higher than those of any of the thirty-one other nations in the study. The performance of American students in math and science is an improvement over earlier international studies. National data are mostly positive: Standardized test scores including the proportion of SAT-M high-scorers (with the proportion of high-scorers on the SAT-V rising) and NAEP scores, are at all-time highs.

The actual test data from U.S. schools do not point to a crisis in K–12 education. These data cannot be used legitimately to make parents nervous about their schools or to justify the creation of charters, vouchers, or education management organizations. More extensive reviews of the data that bear on the condition of American education can be found in Bracey, 2000a, Bracey, 1997b, and Berliner and Biddle, 1995.

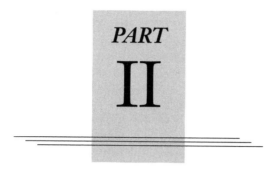

PART

II

Invasion of the Privatizers

The data presented in the preceding sections strongly call into question the widely held idea that American education is in a state of crisis. This is not to say that reform is not needed; schools could be substantially improved, particularly in cities and poor rural areas, where many schools really are in crisis. The spring 2000 administration of Virginia's Standards of Learning Tests revealed that some city schools had Algebra 1 pass rates of less than 5 percent—and this represented an improvement from the previous year. In urban schools, other standardized tests had pass rates of less than 20 percent. Of the forty-one nations participating in the TIMSS, only South Africa scored lower than the District of Columbia in both math and science (compared to the highest-scoring U.S. states, recall, only six nations performed better in math, and only one in science).

There are, in addition, many qualities of a school that cannot be captured by test scores. Without naming them all, this concept was captured well by a committee of the National Academy of Education after reviewing recommended changes in the NAEP:

> [Many of] those personal qualities that we hold dear—resilience and courage in the face of stress, a sense of craft in our work, a commitment to justice and caring in our social relationships, a dedication to advancing the public good in our communal life—are exceedingly difficult to assess. And so, unfortunately, we are apt to measure what we can, and eventually come to value what is measured over what is left unmeasured. The shift is subtle and occurs gradually. (Glaser, 1987)

The domestic and international test results, however, constitute the great bulk of the cross-country data that exist. These are the data that have been spun or

63

selected or, in the case of the reading study, ignored, in order to "prove" American public schools have failed.

We now turn to an examination of the various incursions of the private sector into public schools. Charter schools, vouchers, outsourcing, and Educational Management Organizations have all been put forward as means of improving the public schools or, as some privatizers like to say, the "government schools." For charters and various privatization efforts, advocates have put forth claims about how and why such restructuring should or will bring increased achievement, efficiency, responsiveness, and other qualities. In general, the conclusions drawn here about the need for these reforms, as well as advocates' claims, can be summarized in the title of a song from George Gershwin's *Porgy and Bess:* "It Ain't Necessarily So."

6

Charter Schools

What is clear from the Arizona and Michigan experiences with charters is that without rigorous accountability, both students and taxpayers suffer.

Thomas Toch

—*U.S. News & World Report*, April 27, 1998

It is simply not yet clear whether charter schools will lead to the revitalization of the traditional public education system or its evisceration.

—Henig, Moser, Holyoke, and Lacireno-Paquet, 1999

Are charter schools part of the war on public schools? In some places the answer is yes, in some it is no, and in others it's not clear. Certainly some advocates of charter schools are also advocates of public school generally. In May 2000, President Bill Clinton, a public school advocate, announced the release of $16 million in new grants for charters and $121 million in continuation grants. His stated goal was to take the number of charters from 1,700 to 3,000. He observed that in some states, charter laws were too lax, in others too restrictive. Clinton apparently saw charters principally as a means to provide education to children who have had difficulty in the public schools. But for some charter school advocates, just as certainly, the ultimate goal is the privatization of the educational system.

Some see charters as a means of fulfilling an educational vision; others see them as a means of making money. TesseracT, Inc., for instance, having had its school management program drummed out of Baltimore, Maryland, Hartford, Connecticut, and Dade County, Florida, set up fourteen charters in the "Wild West" charter-friendly state of Arizona. The collapse of these schools was staved off at least through the fall of 2000 when TesseracT convinced a creditor to hold off on an overdue loan until the end of December. Sometimes these two versions of charters are sequential: The visionary opens a charter without the practical management skills to operate it, burns out, and turns the school over to a private, for-profit school-management firm.

Therein lies the rub. Even ardent charter advocates have had to admit that no one is watching the store. Former assistant secretary of education Chester E. Finn, Jr., and his colleagues Louann Bierlein and Bruno Manno, all charter advocates, acknowledged in their first Hudson Institute study that they had "yet to see a single state with a thoughtful and well-formed plan for evaluating its charter school program. Perhaps this is not surprising given the sorry condition of most state standards-assessment-accountability-evaluation systems generally. The problem, however, is apt to be particularly acute for charter schools, where the whole point is to deliver better results in return for greater freedom" (Finn, Bierlein, and Manno, 1996).

Accountability remains, however, the one quality charters most commonly lack. Four years after Finn and his colleagues expressed accountability worries, Finn returned to the scene, observed the inadequate accountability measures for charters, and proposed "accountability via transparency" (Finn, 2000). The charter schools would report on student achievement, their organizational viability, and their compliance with the law. Achievement should be reported in absolute terms in reference to the school's standards, in value-added terms—how much more do they know at the end of the year than at the beginning—and in comparative terms, in relation to district, state, or national norms or standards.

Needless to say, charter school operators have not rushed to adopt this approach. First, as outlined by Finn, the system seems at least as onerously complex as the bureaucracies the charters were invented to escape. Second, the seeming rationality of Finn's approach is undercut both by the motivation of some firms and by the absence of any oversight agency in any state that could competently ensure that all the data Finn proposes be collected is, in fact, collected and reported. Any such agency would need to be much larger than current state departments of education because it would have to deal directly with individual schools, not districts.

Finally, it is now clear that a number of charter schools simply wouldn't fit under Finn's rubric. For some, for instance, the goal is getting dropouts back into school. Why should these schools be required to provide absolute, comparative, and value-added reporting of test scores?

Still, accountability *is* the point. In theory, charter school proponents promise to improve student achievement. In return, they receive a "charter" from some agency (the granting agencies differ in different states) that frees them from many state and local regulations. In states with "strong" charter laws, the charter puts the school largely beyond the power of the local school administration and school board (in the lingo of charters, "strong" laws are those containing the fewest limits on charter schools and the least oversight). Looking at the two most active charter states, Arizona and Michigan, Toch concluded that the point has been missed.

The Genesis of Charter Schools

Ray Budde, a Massachusetts teacher, now retired, tinkered with the idea of charter schools in the 1970s and found zero interest. Budde based his concept on the Charter Between Henry Hudson and the Directors of the East India Company in 1609. That document lays out the purpose and vision of Hudson's trip, the risks entailed, what Hudson must do to satisfy accountability requirements, how he will be compensated, and the rewards for productivity. Would that charter schools had followed this model (the entirety of which can be placed on a single sheet of paper).

In the years that followed *A Nation at Risk*, interest in the charter idea grew slowly. In 1987, the Northeast Regional Laboratory for Educational Improvement circulated drafts of Budde's *Education by Charter Within a Ten-Year Plan*. Budde also circulated the draft at a school reform conference in 1988 (Budde, 1988). It was popularized, however, only when embraced by Albert Shanker, then president of the American Federation of Teachers (AFT). Shanker had endorsed the idea in a National Press Club speech (Shanker, 1988a) and urged the AFT to press it. At their annual convention, the AFT adopted the notion of charter schools, and Shanker then championed it in his weekly paid advertisement-column in the *New York Times* (Shanker, 1988b). Three months later, Shanker again proposed the idea at a Minnesota conference on school improvement; two years later, Minnesota enacted the first charter school law.

In theory, once schools were free of bureaucracy, creativity would flower, energy would deploy, and learning would soar. If there is a single word that characterizes charter school advocates, it is "hope." Hope pervades Shanker's column: "Over time we can expect charter schools to stimulate a different and more effective school structure." Indeed, Joe Nathan, a long-time charter advocate, titled his 1996 book *Charter Schools: Creating Hope and Opportunity for American Education.* Early paragraphs in his preface provide an excellent summary, an anthem actually, of how and why charter school advocates hold out hope:

> The charter school idea is about the creation of more accountable public schools, and the removal of the "exclusive franchise" that local school boards presently have. Charter schools are public, nonsectarian schools that do not have admissions tests but that operate under a written contract, or *charter,* from a school board or some other organization, such as a state school board. These contracts specify how the school will be held accountable for improved student achievement, in exchange for a waiver of most rules and regulations governing how they operate. Charter schools that improve achievement have their contracts renewed. Charter schools that do not improve student achievement over the contract's period are closed. . . .
>
> The charter idea is not just about the creation of new, more accountable public schools or the conversion of existing public schools. The charter idea also introduces fair, thoughtful competition into public education. (Nathan, 1996, p. xxviii)

In theory, this is how it is supposed to work, but in practice, things are a bit messier. In retrospect, it is clear that the early pronouncements about what charter schools would accomplish fall into the long line of miracle cures and magic bullets people have proposed for what they see as education's ills.

Budde and Shanker were both properly skeptical in warning people to stay away from quick fixes, but while their names are still invoked, their admonitions are not. Both saw charters as having two great advantages over other school improvement programs: Because a *school* contracted with another organization for the charter, the people at the school would feel that they had ownership of the program; and because the charter was for a specific timeframe, the program was protected from the whims of a new administration that might wish to sweep out all previous innovations.

Opposition to the Charter Movement

Not everyone has welcomed the charter concept. Some people have suspected all along that charters were simply the first stage of a process that would lead eventually to vouchers and other forms of privatization. Indeed, in commenting on Bill Clinton's first call for increasing the number of charters from 1,700 to 3,000 (in his 2000 State of the Union address), the *Christian Science Monitor* characterized charters as a warning to public schools to shape up or get ready for vouchers: "Charters inject a stirring element of competition to public education. But they are still an experiment to see if the public schools will really respond. If they don't, then that argues for taking the bolder step of giving vouchers to parents to send their children to private and parochial institutions" (Weir, 2000).

Jeffrey Henig of George Washington University, one of the most dispassionate observers of the various incarnations of school choice, worried that it will be difficult to evaluate the "stirring element of competition" posed by charters because they show no interest in such evaluations. Henig noted that charter schools "show few signs of interest in systematic, empirical research that is ultimately needed if we are going to be able to separate bold claim from proven performance. Premature claims of success, reliance on anecdotal and unreliable evidence are still the rule of the day" (Henig, 1994, p. 234).

Alex Molnar of the University of Wisconsin at Milwaukee is both more skeptical and more trenchant:

> Charter schools will fail, fraud will be uncovered, and tax dollars will be wasted. But just as certainly, glowing testimony will be paid to the dedication and sacrifice of the selfless teachers and administrators at some "Chartermetoo" school who transformed the lives of their students and proved the success of charter school reform. Free-market zealots will either claim vindication or argue that their revolutionary ideas need more time to work. Supporters of public education will call the experiment a costly failure and marvel at the willingness to spend large sums on unproven alternatives while cutting resources for the public system that serves most children. With an absence of any uniform standards, the war of educational anecdotes and

misleading statistics will remain "subject to interpretation." And all the while, the desperation of America's poorest children and their families will grow. (1996, p. 167)

Molnar resurrects the two visions mentioned earlier in connection with all incursions into public schools: "The struggle is not, at its root, between market-based reforms and the educational status quo. Rather it is a battle over whether the democratic ideal of the common good can survive the onslaught of a market mentality that threatens to turn every human relationship, inside and outside the classroom, into a commercial transaction" (p. 167).

The Popularity of Charter Schools

For whatever reasons, charters have become popular. In 1992, there were no charters; by 1995, there were 100, and as 2000 began, 1,700. Still, this represents a tiny proportion of America's students. In the twenty-seven states where charters were operating in the 1998–99 school year, charter school enrollment accounted for only about 0.8 percent of all students. Almost 25 percent of charter schools are in four states: Arizona, California, Michigan, and Texas (Office of Educational Research and Improvement, 2000, p. 11). If one were to remove Michigan and Arizona from the list, the proportion would be smaller still. Estimates are that

Seeing through a Graph

The first third of *Bail Me Out: Handling Difficult Data and Tough Questions about Public Schools* (Bracey, 2000a), is titled "Principles of Data Interpretation, or How Not to Get Statistically Snookered." It shows some of the common flaws in how data are reported. One principle is "Try to 'See Through' Graphs." It discusses and illustrates how graphs might mislead. Sometimes a picture is worth much less than a thousand words.

Page 19 of the Department of Education's Fourth-Year Report on charter schools is a classic illustration of how graphs that do not present the full range of possible data can mislead (Office of Educational Research and Improvement, 2000). The graph on that page shows the percentage of students in charter schools for each of the states operating charters. Several of the states have lines that run almost from the left border to the right border of the page. Graphically, it looks like they have huge charter school populations. However, a look at the scale at the bottom of the graph shows that the graph only runs from 0 percent to 5 percent. If the graph had been scaled to go from 0 percent to 100 percent, it would be seen that no state has more than 4 percent of its students in charters (the District of Columbia has 4.4 percent, but many people consider D.C. enrollment figures of all kinds suspect).

only about 10 percent of all charter schools are privately operated, giving them .05 percent of the student population.

Smaller Classes

The same Fourth-Year Report finds that charters differ from regular schools in some significant respects. For instance, the median-sized charter school contains 137 pupils compared to a median of about 475 for public schools. Sixty-five percent contain fewer than 200 students (p. 20).

Descriptions of charters often speak of their small classes as well. The U.S. Department of Education's survey found the desire for small classes a major reason for creating charter schools. The survey finds charter schools with smaller classes at virtually all levels, with an overall class size of 16.0 for charter schools and 17.2 for public schools. However, the results from this survey in all likelihood misleadingly show the class sizes in charter and public schools as closer than they really are.

The department's survey used pupil/teacher ratio as a proxy for class size. This is highly inappropriate for public schools but probably less so for private schools. Pupil/teacher ratios includes anyone who has a certificate. Thus special education, English As a Second Language (ESL), and other specialists are included. The average class size in public schools is twenty-four for elementary schools and thirty-one for secondary schools (National Center for Education

Make Sure the Level of Aggregation Is Appropriate

Calling attention to the proper level of aggregation should have been a principle in *Bail Me Out!*, but it eluded me at the time. The department's survey, while containing many useful descriptive characteristics of charters, has some statistics that are aggregated at inappropriate levels. It reports percentage by ethnicity and percentage of students with disabilities, both aggregated to the state level.

The state, however, is not an appropriate unit of analysis for these two pieces of data. In Michigan, for instance, there are many charters in the largely African American area of Detroit but many others are in largely white, rural parts of the state. Averaging them does not give a good indication of the segregation or integration of charters: It's like averaging a very hot summer with a very cool one and reporting that temperatures over the two-year period were normal.

Similarly, some charters are started for the purpose of educating students with learning disabilities. Even though the report does show that there are smaller percentages of students with disabilities in charters than in public schools (8.4 percent versus 11.3 percent), if these specialized schools were factored out, the differences would be even larger. The same might well be true of limited English proficiency (LEP) students, where reports show that charters and public schools contain almost equal percentages.

Statistics, 1998). Since charters provide fewer or no services for special education students or students with limited English-language skills, the pupil/teacher ratio is likely to be much closer to the actual class size.

School and class size data could be important in evaluating charters. Many people think that small schools produce better results (e.g., Gladden, 1998, Gottfredson, 1995; and Wasley et al., 2000), and the research is clear that small classes do (Finn and Achilles 1990, 1999; Krueger 1998, 2000). Therefore, improved achievement, if it occurs, might well derive from these factors, not from some putative effect of "choice" or "charterness."

Private corporations might well increase their share of charters beyond the current 10 percent. One *Education Week* story in late 1997 began with a vignette of people who started charter schools and then gave up (Schnaiberg, 1997). "It was a burnout situation," said one founder of Northlane Math and Science Academy in Freeland, Michigan. The school opened in 1995 and although quite small, had exhausted its founders by 1997. They gave the keys to Mosaica, a private for-profit firm. The myth that anyone can teach is currently complemented by the myth that anyone can start and run a school: It's not all that tough, especially if you have a "vision" of what good education should look like.

Turning the Charter "Vision" into a Reality

The reality is, as many people discover, that operating a school requires hard work, long hours, and a multitude of skills many people do not have. Most people are not familiar with budgets, payrolls, and financing, among other things. Money and personnel issues are usually not active parts of a vision. No doubt this is, in part, why the *Washington Post* reported that "a large number of the city's 27 charter schools have failed to comply with a wide range of regulations addressing finances, record keeping, and police background checks" (Blum, 2000). Many charters have failed to fill out forms and papers that public school administrators would look on as routine.

Idyllwild

In Idyllwild, California, described as a mountain town "where artists and intellectuals dwell among the pines," those artists and intellectuals decided to operate a charter school. In part, their desire came from a vision of using the community's talents to enrich high school education. They also hoped to eliminate the need to send their kids to the nearest public school, "a 45-minute bus ride, and a world away, in cultural terms."

According to the author of the story, the charter starters did not face a hostile board. The problems started only *after* the charter had started operations (Brennan, 2000b). Although a number of teachers hired by Idyllwild had taught at the university level, they lacked teacher certification and, apparently, the skills to get the bureaucracy to provide emergency credentials. A computerized attendance system failed. Staff fingerprinting "baffled administrators." "School officials acknowledged that they had little experience running a school and were stumped by the obstacles they faced." The local school board revoked the charter but encouraged the charter school officials to come back with another proposal once the problems had been worked through. The officials say they might be too tired to make a renewed effort (Brennan, 2000a).

The Idyllwild saga is not an isolated one and it has implications for the control of charter schools. The lack of skills, coupled with the long hours, will likely influence trends in who opens and runs charter schools. The U.S. Department of Education study of charters listed "to realize an alternative vision of education" as overwhelmingly the major reason for starting a charter (75 percent of respondents, compared to 30 percent for the next most cited reason, "serving a special population." Numbers do not equal 100 percent because categories are not mutually exclusive). A number of seers have found their visions dimmed by the harsh realities of managing a school. As with Northlane Academy, other founders of what one evaluation called "mom-and-pop" charter schools could hand control over to private managers of what the same evaluation called "cookie-cutter" charter schools.

The greatest difficulties in starting and maintaining a charter school, by all accounts, involve finance and facilities, areas with which the for-profits presumably have more experience. Jack Clegg, CEO at Nobel, a chain of upscale private schools, contends that good business practices are good business practices whatever the setting. His attitude is probably shared by a number of entrepreneurs.

Three Case Studies: Arizona, California, and Michigan, and a Glimpse at Ohio

Three states, Arizona, California, and Michigan, have led the nation in creating charter schools, and Ohio is rapidly gaining on them. Evaluations produced in the top three states indicate that Nathan's idealistic aims are not being realized. It is too early for evaluations of Ohio schools to have occurred, but a series of articles in the *Akron Beacon Journal* reveals what happens when educational goals such as those expressed by Nathan get woven in with political ambitions and the desire to make a profit (Oplinger and Willard, 1999a, 1999b, 1999c; Willard and Oplinger, 1999a, 1999b, 1999c). Let us now examine the results to date in these three states and take a peek at what seems to be happening in Ohio as well.

Arizona

At the outset of this chapter, I quoted Thomas Toch emphasizing the need for accountability in any charter school. In Arizona, thanks to powerful charter advocates, Toch's point might have deliberately been overlooked.

Getting Started.   Arizona's charter system actually developed out of a failed voucher movement, one initiated by the state's then-superintendent of education, Lisa Graham Keegan. Keegan favored vouchers, but in 1995, the Arizona senate narrowly defeated her voucher proposal that had passed earlier in the house. Keegan, then chair of the senate education committee, banded together with Beverly Harmon, her equivalent in the house, and called a special session of the legislature to deal solely with the voucher issue. Vouchers were discussed, but were soon replaced by bills providing for charter schools.

Whereas the voucher bills had been divisive, the charter bill elicited broad bipartisan support. The bill contained the fewest restrictions of any in the nation. "Anyone who could stand up and breathe got a charter," observed one legislator.

Keegan thus entered the state superintendency very much an advocate for charters. She has protected them from all harm, helping form the Charter School Board, an independent entity whose function was to fend off interference by those perceived to be opponents. When, in 1997, the Arizona Department of Education launched an investigation of the charters after receiving many complaints, Keegan withheld the resulting report for a year, releasing its findings only after the state school board association's lawyer filed a freedom-of-information-act request. Before releasing the report, Keegan had her top aide remove the evaluators' handwritten notes, an act permissible under Arizona law.

The *Arizona Tribune* was not amused. In a seething editorial, the paper said, "What is especially outrageous is that Keegan killed a monitoring program with charter schools that was starting to uncover some serious problems. After some charter school owners complained, the monitoring program was scrapped and the complaints were buried in department files" (August 25, 1998, A12). Two days later, the *Tribune* was back with another editorial essay titled "Wake up, Keegan" (August 27, A14). It accused her of having been a tireless cheerleader for charter schools but "now that problems have surfaced, she's got all fingers pointing in other directions."

While the *Tribune* editors were outraged at Keegan for killing the monitoring program, some observers might find another episode more troubling. Paul Street, a former district administrator, was recruited to the evaluation team. "We did every school in the state," he said. When the evaluations were completed, he turned all of his notes in to the Department of Education. However, the department's folder marked "Street" contained a single scrap of paper.

Meeting the Standard.   Arizona state law requires only that high school students attend class four hours a day. As a consequence, some charter "high schools" operate in two or three four-hour shifts, not a bad strategy for increasing profit. Standards are often low. When the monitoring program did exist, Marilynn Henley, a deputy associate superintendent and former curriculum director of the Arizona Department of Education visited more than 100 of the 241 schools operating in Arizona. She found many courses in these high school lasted only a few weeks. Rarely did they prescribe homework.

Computer coursework at these high schools consisted of seventh- or eighth-grade-level drill-and-practice worksheets transferred to computers. At one school that paid faculty bonuses for rising enrollments, thirty students sat through a course called "American Literature Through Cinema." When Toch visited, the class was studying *The Last of the Mohicans*. The film was not being shown, however; the students merely listened to its soundtrack. Except, notes Toch, those who were asleep.

Henley and her team of evaluators found that a majority of the schools were not living up to the terms of their charters. A *Tribune* article said that while Henley and her team of "monitors were supposed to focus on whether schools were complying with laws and charters, those with education backgrounds found it hard to ignore such things as out-of-control classrooms or the absence of instruction" (Todd, 1998a, 1998b, A1). Keegan, who according to Toch, contends that charter schools not be held to higher standards of achievement than the public schools, reassigned Henley and shut her monitoring group down. Henley is now a curriculum consultant in private practice.

Irregularities in Charter Administrations. Henley's study of charters also turned up a number of instances where the enrollment figures submitted to the state were considerably higher than average daily attendance. In addition, according to one article, "it's nearly impossible for the state to recover money in the event a charter school fails." (Donohue, 1998, p. 63). This was true even in one case where the owner of a failed charter had used school money to buy her mother an expensive home.

Given such staggering problems, we might expect that a number of Arizona charter schools have lost their charters. Not so. Going into the 1999–2000 school year, only six operators had lost the privilege to operate schools. Some forty others deemed by the report as "bad enough to close," writes Toch, "were left alone on the grounds that they weren't physically endangering students or defrauding taxpayers" [author's note: ?].

Why such a hands-off attitude? It is directly attributable to Keegan's politics and ideology. As mentioned earlier, before becoming the state superintendent, Keegan was a state legislator and wrote school voucher legislation, resorting to charters only when that failed.

Keegan appears unconcerned. Commenting on the evaluation report, she said "I would prefer that everything [the monitors saw] was wonderful. But if it wasn't, OK. In the main, I'm pleased, far and away with the quality of the public charter schools. . . . How much monitoring do you think is going on in the traditional system?" One could wonder what criteria she is using to judge "quality." As noted, she and the heads of the State Board of Education and the State Board for Charter Schools have halted any further systematic study of Arizona's charter schools. For her part, Marilyn Henley says "I resent [Keegan] and others who say charter schools are just like or no worse than district schools. Charter schools are *way* worse" (Todd, 1998a, A1).

We can note here that a similar evaluation-free situation has prevailed in Milwaukee, Wisconsin, in regard to that city's voucher program, and, thus far, in Florida as well. In Milwaukee, publicly funded vouchers afford about 11,000 students an opportunity to attend private schools. Initially, the state required an annual evaluation of this program. The fifth annual evaluation stated that the voucher students showed no advantage in terms of achievement. Shortly thereafter, another analysis claimed that the voucher students actually did gain more benefits from their education, but the advantage showed up only after four years. The matter is still in dispute and is discussed in Chapter 8. For the moment the important thing to note is that voucher advocates have succeeded in having the evaluation requirement removed from the legislation. In Florida, which in 1999 became the first state to finance vouchers statewide, the private schools attended by voucher students do not have to administer state tests or report on any tests that are administered. It is more than a bit ironic that choice advocates, claiming the public schools need to be more accountable, have thus far largely succeeded in avoiding accountability for their own endeavors.

For her part, Keegan has become more adventuresome in her public statements. At a September 1998, conference sponsored by the Children's Educational Opportunity Foundation (an organization providing vouchers for children to attend private schools, discussed in Chapter 8), Keegan recalled that a woman had shouted at her that "'You're killing public education as we know it.' I told her, 'Every night, I pray that this is true.'"

Building Accountability into the Law. The *Tribune* editorials mentioned earlier were occasioned by the findings of a five-part series, "Guinea Kids: Arizona's Charter School Experiment." The editors concluded that "Arizona's charter school experiment is well worth salvaging. And the first step is for state officials to stop shrugging and pointing fingers and to start building some accountability in the law" (August 27, A14).

In this they appear to have the support of Arizona's governor, Jane Hull. In an interview following the five-part series, Hull said she would support charter-school reforms that would require the submission of sound business plans, prohibit schools from stacking their boards and schools with family members, heighten the monitoring by either the Board for Charter Schools, the Arizona Board of Education, or an outside agency, restrict charters to five to seven years instead of granting them for the current fifteen-year period, and establish a clearinghouse to provide parents with easy access to reliable data about the schools, data too often now out of date and inaccurate (Nowicki, 1998, A1).

The *Tribune's* series itself was very much a good-news, bad-news collection of articles. Some charter schools appear to be doing excellent work ("appear" because no one is actually conducting the needed evaluations), some appear to be awful, and a few have closed. The school closures had a common characteristic: The kids, especially those requiring special education services, were left stranded and out of school for some period of time. When businesses go bust, the owners, creditors, and investors take the hit. When charter schools fail, the burden falls on the state, the parents, and the children.

A new testing program, Arizona's Instrument to Measure Standards (AIMS), was introduced on a pilot basis in the spring of 1999, with "for real" testing to begin the following spring. According to the *Tribune*, this will permit comparisons between charter schools and public schools. It won't do that, of course, unless how the charter schools select their students is factored in. In the first administration of AIMS, 90 percent of *all* children failed the test. Charters had some of the lowest scores. Again, however, without knowing the students' scores before they entered the charter or tracking their growth over time at the charter, there is no way to determine if these low scores actually represent failure. As of early 2001, the AIMS program is in limbo. Its quality has been impugned and some legislators have called for a delay in its further administration until these issues can be resolved.

A doctoral dissertation at Arizona State University strongly implies that the charters will perform well on standardized tests, and that this showing will not necessarily have to do with their quality of instruction: Many charters are selecting highly able students and offering them college-prep curricula (Cobb, 1998). At least, those with predominantly white students fit this category. Charters with a majority of minority students typically offer vocational programs. This is discussed in detail below.

It is all very reminiscent of the 1970s experiences with Performance Contracting. Books were cooked, test scores confabulated, and the whole thing went down in flames. Asked by the *Tribune* what kind of society he thought the charter schools movement would lead to, Arizona State University School of Education dean David Berliner replied, "Bosnia" (Van Der Werf, 1998, p. B3).

While Berliner used hyperbole to make his point, evaluations in California and Michigan make a similar case more quietly (Wells, 1998; Horn and Miron, 1999). Some parents clearly use charters to find schools serving families "like them." Thus, ironically, although charters might produce more variation in the types of schools across districts, the students of a given school might well become more homogeneous in terms of ethnicity, socioeconomic status, the values of their parents, and the curriculum received. Some suggest that charters could cater to religious extremists or skinheads or other radical groups. Even without such extremes, one can see how charters could produce more *pluribus* and less *unum* in society.

The Threat of Resegregation.   Three other evaluations have examined Arizona charter schools. The right-slanted and charter-favoring Goldwater Institute asked *Who Is Choosing Charter Schools?* (www.cmbe.org/publications/02_who.html). The answer?

The report concludes that charter schools are attracting diverse students from several districts. The data also put to rest accusations of "white flight," showing that more than four times as many minority students than white students have sought variances from the Phoenix Union High School District to attend charter schools in this area. . . . There is concern of charter schools causing resegregation among all public schools. The data clearly demonstrate that charter schools are providing a variety of choices for parents, not forcing resegregation.

Unless we assume that Goldwater Institute analysts suffer deficiencies in logical reasoning, we must take the above statement as one of sophistry: The claim that "charter schools are providing a variety of choices for parents" does not conflict with the conclusion that these schools are in fact resegregating the schools, while not "forcing" resegregation. Data presented below show that this is happening.

In fact, the Goldwater report itself hints at resegregation: "The data show there are higher percentages of students who are white, black and Native Americans in charter schools, and a smaller percentage of Hispanic students." Given that blacks and Native Americans together only constitute 11 percent of the students in Phoenix, but that 31 percent of the students are Hispanic, this alone points to resegregation. The proportion of Hispanics in charter schools is about half of what it is in public schools. The report concludes that, "Charter schools have more white students than district schools do, but after accounting for county of location, the charter factor becomes negative."

Curiously, the report provides even more statistics pointing toward resegregation, but fails to notice their import. First, charter schools are likely to locate in areas with high test scores. Second, the Goldwater Institute found, "When we look at racial composition based on the numbers of students rather than numbers of schools the data show something different. The data show that there are more charter school students in schools that have a very high proportion of white students or a very low proportion of white students."

Thus, charter schools are often not established to attract a representative sample of the entire state, but rather to serve a particular clientele. On occasion, this clientele is largely minority, but mostly it is white. The state's charter might require a school to accept all applicants or use a lottery system if the school is oversubscribed, but this mandate can be subverted by specifying the goal of the school—for example, serving at-risk students or providing an Afro-centric curriculum. This is seen most particularly in the charter schools established on Native American reservations. An Arizona State University study, discussed below, found that in Arizona, charter schools with high proportions of white students had college-oriented curricula, while those with higher proportions of minorities had vocational criteria or were aimed at students who had dropped out of or been kicked out of other schools. However, when one averages across schools or students, these differences get washed out.

The Goldwater Institute, through its Center for Market-Based Education, returned to the charter scene in 2000 with its *Five-Year Charter School Study*, (Gifford, Phillips and Ogle, 2000). This study is closer to a self-report than a formal

evaluation. In regard to achievement, it found that although some charter operators considered the state-mandated tests to be good indicators of achievement,
most did not (p. 11). Moreover, "more than half of the schools report that students
are coming in working below grade level, but get closer to grade level the longer
they are at the charter school" (p. 13). Apparently, Goldwater researchers made no
attempt to verify this claim, nor does the report state what the remainder of the
schools reported about student achievement over time or vis-à-vis grade level.

The Demographic Makeup of Arizona's Charter Schools.   Casey Cobb took a
more detailed look at resegregation trends in Arizona's charter schools in his
doctoral dissertation at Arizona State University. Even at the state level, Cobb
finds data suggesting a trend toward resegregation. For 1995, 1996, and 1997,
Cobb found these percentages of white students in charter schools: 64.8 percent,
67.0 percent, and 68.4 percent, respectively.[11] Cobb, Glass, and Crockett (2000)
reported that "More Arizona students attended ethnically and racially stratified
charter schools in 1998 than they did two years prior [the year of the original
study]" (p. 11).

To get a more precise read on the figures, Cobb matched pairs of schools
geographically. He asked, What is the proportion of white students in a charter
school? Then he asked, What is the proportion of white students in the geographically closest public school? Cobb conducted this analysis on all charters in
the metropolitan Phoenix area, which contains 62 percent of Arizona's population (U.S. Census, 2000).

At the extreme, Cobb uncovered large differences. One public school contained 12 percent white students, while the nearest charter had 82 percent white.
In the seventeen pairs of schools where the proportion of whites in charter
schools was at least 20 percent greater than the proportion in the nearest public
school, the percentage of white students in public schools exceeded 50 percent
only three times; only once did it exceed 60 percent. That is, in most of these
pairs, whites constituted a minority in the public schools, a substantial majority
in the charter schools. In the seventeen charter schools, the percentage of white
students never dropped below 50 percent and only three times did it fall below
70 percent.

Cobb found eight charter schools where the proportion of white students
in public exceeded the proportion of white students in charter schools by at least
10 percent, reaching a maximum difference of 23 percent. However, these
schools were *all* predominantly white. In the case of the 23 percent difference,
the public school was 90 percent white and the charter school *only* 67 percent
white. Cobb also found that three of the four charter schools placed in what he

---

11. In 1998, the most recent year for which data are available, the proportion of white students
declined in both public and charter schools. Associate Dean of Education at Arizona State University
Gene V Glass reports though that there is reason to suspect the accuracy of this data.

calls the least prosperous and most ethnically diverse area of Scottsdale had higher proportions of white students than did the proximal public school. For the most part, Cobb found that where the proportion of whites in charter schools was the same as in the public schools, all schools were located in overwhelmingly white residential areas.

Critics have complained that Cobb's procedure is unfair because charter schools draw students from a number of districts. This criticism does not seem to mute the point that the charters contain a large proportion of white students.

Getting the Word Out. It is not clear from information obtained in any of the studies what attempts the charter school founders made to apprise the general population about the presence and nature of their particular schools. Earlier work by Amy Stuart Wells found that people in economically depressed areas were unlikely to know anything about any schools beyond those in their own neighborhood. (Wells, 1993). Six years later, a survey found that not much had changed. Not only did the general public know virtually nothing about charter schools (and vouchers), even parents living in areas "rich with charters" knew little about them (Public Agenda, 1999). According to free-market theorists, a free market can function to the benefit of the consumer only where the consumer has access to quality information about the product. This is unlikely to have happened in Arizona.

In Chapter 3, I quoted Payne and Biddle (1999) on the murkiness of econometric research, a model of which appeared in early 2001 from the Center for Market-Based Education at the Goldwater Institute in Phoenix (Solmon, Paark, and Garcia, 2000. The report can be accessed at www.goldwaterinstitute.org.) Arizona has the capability to track students no matter what school they attend, cause for researchers to smile and libertarians to shudder. The center's report alleges that students who spend multiple years in charter schools make bigger gains on achievement tests than do those who stay in public schools. Gene V Glass, associate dean for research at Arizona State University, has commented, "Those who have spent time with it [the study] still don't feel they understand what was done" (personal communication, May 30, 2001).

Whatever the numbers might say, the report's philosophy is clearly biased toward charters, as when claims are made that students who start in a charter and switch to a public school gain more academically than those who start in a public school and switch to a charter. One might conclude, given some of the charter anarchy described by Toch and others, than getting out of a charter improves the student's learning situation whereas going from a public school to a charter causes confusion. One might even take this as indicating the superiority of public schools. The report, however, credits the gain to the superiority of the charter schools: "Whatever deficiencies a student brings with him upon enrolling in a charter school may be remediated by the charter school, thus preparing the student to perform better when returning to a TPA [traditional public school]" (p. 13). The public schools cannot win.

California

In 1992, California became the second state to pass charter legislation (Minnesota had enacted its law a year earlier). As with Arizona, it is relatively easy for an individual or groups to start a charter school. Chartering authorities include local boards of education and the state board of education. Initially, the number of charters was capped at one hundred. The cap rose to two hundred fifty in 1998–99, with an additional one hundred schools permitted every year thereafter. Charters are supposed to enroll anyone who applies and to use a lottery in the event of too many applications. They may give preferences based on residence and other siblings in the school. Public schools, start-up schools, and home schools can be chartered, but private schools cannot convert to charter school status. A charter denied by a local board can be appealed first to a county board and then to the state board of education.

When SRI International looked at about one hundred charter schools in California in 1997, it concluded that, overall, ethnicity did not matter much in charter school enrollment (www.lao.ca.gov/sri_charter_schools_1297-part1.html). Even so, 48 percent of students in charter schools were white, compared to 40 percent in public schools statewide, and 34 percent of students in charter schools were Hispanic, compared to 40 percent statewide. African American students comprised 9 percent of both charter and public schools.

Examining the data by district rather than at the state level appeared to show more segregation. However, SRI International did not compare the ethnic makeup of the schools with that of residential areas, so no firm conclusions can be drawn. Nevertheless, in 67 percent of the schools, the proportion of white students in charter schools exceeded the proportion in noncharter schools, with the difference exceeding 10 percent in 39 percent of the schools. Conversely, in 77 percent of the charter schools, the proportion of Hispanic students was less than in the noncharter schools, and in 37 percent of the charter schools the difference exceeded 10 percent.

Charter Schools and Homeschooling.   Although the charter legislation did not consider homeschooling, the law permits home-based charter schools. These tend to be tiny and, according to the report, have little impact on the picture of charter schools overall. Still, it is noteworthy that these schools are 81 percent white. It is not clear at this time if more people, having now realized that the home-based option is available, will choose it.

As a minor digression, we can note that 2000's Proposition 38, which would have provided all California children with charters, was opposed by the Home School Association of California. They felt that vouchers would inevitably lead to home schools being designated as a specific kind of school and subject them to much more state regulation than is currently the case.

Charter Schools and Socioeconomic Status.   SRI International found a class factor operating in California charter schools. Seventy-four percent of the charter schools report fewer students eligible for free or reduced-cost lunches than in non-charter schools. In 36 percent of the schools, the difference exceeds 20 percent.

When it came to achievement, the SRI International report came up empty:

> Measuring student achievement is made difficult by the diversity of assessment practices, philosophies, and available data among charter schools. . . . Some charter schools performed better than comparable noncharter schools when compared to national averages, with all noncharter schools in their sponsoring districts, and with comparable noncharter schools within their districts. Others did not. Likewise, comparisons of charter schools; performance over time yielded mixed results.

The report then cautions that an above-average performance must be evaluated against the population from which the charter school students were chosen. That is, the charter school students might score well because the school chose them from high-scoring samples. In the few cases where SRI International matched charter schools to public schools, some charters scored higher on tests, some lower. Some charters showed larger gains in test scores compared to their matched public school; some showed no gains. No attempt was made to determine which features of the schools might determine which outcomes.

Evaluating Charters: The Wells Study. An appropriate evaluation of the impact of a charter school on test scores can be accomplished in one of two ways: First, it could start with the test scores of the students *before* they enter the charter school. If the charter draws students from many schools, this could be difficult, logistically, but in many places it is possible. Second, tests could be administered over time to chart growth. Thus far this has not happened in California.

More recent evaluations of charter schools have been undertaken by Eric Rofes at the University of California at Berkeley, and by Amy Stuart Wells and colleagues at the University of California at Los Angeles (Rofes, 1998; Wells et al., 1998). The Wells study is of particular interest because of its scope and organization. Rofes limited his inquiry to how public school districts were reacting to both charter school laws and the schools themselves.

The Wells study is illuminating because it examines the charter schools in the light of claims made by charter advocates, like those presented by Joe Nathan a few pages earlier. These claims can be stated briefly as follows:

1. *Accountability:* Because charter schools are more accountable for student outcomes, charters will work harder to meet their stated goals.
2. *Efficiency:* Freed from the shackles of bureaucracy, charter schools will be more efficient and/or will be able to do more with fewer resources.
3. *Competition:* By creating competition for the other schools in the district, charters will force change in the public schools.
4. *Innovation:* Charters will create new models of schooling and serve as laboratories of innovation from which public schools can learn and adopt.
5. *Choice:* Because charter schools will develop new models, they will provide parents with a wider range of choices.

6. *Autonomy:* Because charter schools are freed from bureaucracy, they will be empowered to better serve students and their families.

These are the common claims of charter school advocates. What did the UCLA study find regarding them?

Accountability.   In theory, this is the simplest prediction to examine. In his book, Joe Nathan wrote, "Hundreds of charter schools have been created around this nation by educators who are willing to put their jobs on the line, to say, 'If we can't improve students achievement, close down our school.' That is accountability—clear, specific and real" (Nathan, 1996, p. xxx). And nonexistent.

In reality, accountability is much more complex, largely because the "goals and outcomes are often vaguely written and ill-defined; they frequently cover a wide range of desired outcomes, such as the goal of 'enabling pupils to become self-motivated, competent, and lifelong learners.'" (Wells et al., 1998, p. 20). These are noble goals, but all but impossible to assess. Most educators, it must be said, cannot write clear goal statements in the first place, much less decide in advance how they will be measured.

Indeed, most educational practitioners are not in the habit of thinking about program evaluations, nor are they trained to conduct them. Practitioners typically start a program either because it has some kind of validity on its face for them, or because the political climate in the district rewards innovation and change. Several years after the program has been started, someone will get the idea that it might be a good thing to evaluate the program. By then, of course, it is too late. The time to plan for the evaluation of a program is the year or so before it begins.

The UCLA investigation was hampered by the fact that, during the study, California was revamping its assessment system; it had no state assessment system against which the charter schools, or any public schools for that matter, could be measured (the system currently in place, though, is still inadequate for such evaluations). But even if such a system had been in place, it would not have been applicable to all charters. Some of the charter schools in the UCLA study were "back to basics" schools that featured basic skills, drills, memorization, and the mastery of discrete pieces of information. Such schools usually favor the use of standardized, norm-referenced tests.

On the other hand, some charter schools had project-based, thematic curricula that emphasized learning through experience and interdisciplinary units. Some charters wanted to improve student and staff attendance rates, to increase parent participation, or to offer new opportunities for professional development of teachers. Not only were such goals not directly tied to student achievement, the sections of the chartering documents containing the goals were often "extremely vague."

We can note again that the program evaluation statements of Chester Finn and Joe Nathan seem naïve when held against the reality and complexity of charter schools. Charter schools are started for many reasons, with many different aims. A single test would not be appropriate for all of them. Still, one must wonder why granting agencies paid so little attention to achievement outcomes or to what kind of instrument *would* be appropriate if a test were not. Why were so many charters granted with so little attention to what *would* be appropriate instruments of observation to evaluate the school's goals? Why have so many charter schools neglected one of Budde's central tenets? Why have so many chartering agencies let them?

Looking around the nation, a partial answer to this question appears to be short-staffed and weak granting and oversight agencies. Sometimes the agencies' shortcomings appear to have been deliberately imposed to give charters as much leeway as possible. We saw this in Arizona, Michigan, Ohio, and Texas. As its governor, George W. Bush "touted Texas's charter schools." But between the time that Bush left the governorship and assumed the presidency of the United States, a panel of the Texas legislature called for a moratorium of charters. Noting that the state educational agency gave an "unacceptable" grade to over one-quarter of the 103 charters it evaluated, committee chairman Jim Dunnam said, "I think that the expansion of any program that is suffering from such admitted and recognized lack of oversight is not responsible government whether it is a state park or a charter school" (Associated Press, 2000). These considerations make it even less likely that something like Finn's "evaluation via transparency" will ever transpire as a viable model.

Wells found that accountability in the charter schools involved money, not achievement. The schools that lost their charters did so because they misappropriated or misspent public tax dollars. Schools with clean books had their charters renewed, even though they had not met the academic goals specified in their charter contracts.

The UCLA study was not unsympathetic to the accountability plight of charters:

> Charter school reform in its purest sense is about community-based groups trying to respond to dissatisfaction with the public schools by creating alternatives to what they perceive to be an unresponsive public system. In many cases, the value of these alternatives will not be accurately measured by a state-imposed assessment. While a centralized, common state test causes many problems in the regular public educational system, it is particularly problematic for charter school educators, many of whom assume that their schools are anything but standardized and that they know more than politicians in Sacramento about how to serve their particular students. (Wells, 1998, p. 24)

Still, "as long as finance, not learning, is the central focus of the accountability arrangements, the promise of student accountability may be deceptive" (p. 24).

To complicate matters, there is confusion about whom the charter is accountable *to*. Clearly, the market theory of charters puts the parents in charge; if the charter does not respond to their needs, the parents will "vote with their feet" and leave. Good schools will flourish, bad schools will close. Yet charters also have accountability responsibilities to the chartering agencies and, in some states, to the public school districts in which the charters reside.

The charters' accountability to parents had a side effect of discouraging some parents from enrolling their children. Some charters were started with a particular vision of education, one clearly communicated to interested parents. "This means that charter school communities—parents and educators alike— often try to send clear signals to prospective families about who is welcome and who is valued in the school. Sometimes, families who are not a good fit are encouraged to leave" (Wells, 1998, p. 27).

An earlier study of California charter schools had found that some charter schools required parents to sign contracts concerning parental involvement (Becker et al., 1996). The evidence indicated that some schools used the parents' willingness to sign such contracts as a means of selecting students. The schools were thus holding the parents accountable. The UCLA study likewise found - evidence that "the schools are holding their 'clients' accountable" (Wells, 1998, p. 27).

The advantages claimed for charter schools including accountability and responsiveness, are also held out as reasons for private school superiority. Yet one study that compared public and private schools failed to find that the private schools were more accountable (Rothstein, Carnoy, and Benveniste, 1999). This study found that community characteristics overwhelmed differences in school governance: Public schools in affluent communities resembled private schools in affluent communities. Public schools in poor communities resembled private schools in poor communities.

In fact, in affluent communities, the public schools were substantially *more* accountable to parents than were the private schools. Affluent parents felt they had both a right and a responsibility to participate in their children's education, and bombarded teachers with questions and suggestions about what to teach and how. Affluent private schools, by contrast, had been more successful in advising parents that curricular and pedagogical decisions lay within the realm of the school's faculty and administrators. They were able to tell parents essentially, "If you want to send your child here, you must accept our verdicts on curriculum and instruction." One school had reduced its accountability program to a motto: "Caveat emptor." The researchers found that the proprietors had maintained a clear policy of discouraging parental involvement to prevent interference in the school's operation. Until recently, and for most of the school's twenty-eight-year existence, there had been no parent association or other parent advisory group and no invitations for parents to assist in classrooms.

In poor neighborhoods, both public and private schools struggled to get parents more involved and make them more responsible for their children's academic proficiency and their nonacademic behavior. In effect, these schools were trying to hold the parents accountable for their children's achievement. Private schools were somewhat more successful in this arena than public schools because they could make parental involvement a condition of admission. This involvement, however, was typically nonacademic, having to do with activities such as fund-raising or decorating the school for some special event.

The accountability issue will remain important and perhaps become more so. As we shall see in the discussion of charter schools in Michigan, most of that state's charters are run by educational management organizations (EMOs)—some located in Michigan, some not. All bring with them a curriculum prepared elsewhere. This makes them unresponsive to parental input. Indeed, one evaluation of charter schools in Michigan refers to them as "cookie-cutter schools" (Horn and Miron, 1999).

Efficiency. While advocates claim that charter schools will be more efficient, and thus require fewer funds, the UCLA study found they actually require more money. To survive, charter schools must rely on private sources of income, and their ability to tap into such sources varies greatly. The greatest factor in a school's financial health was its leadership. "We learned that charter schools are highly dependent on another critical resource: a visionary and well-connected leader." The study found some schools functioning without heat, adequate plumbing, science labs, or any athletic facilities. "These schools did not seem efficient, just poor" (Wells, 1998, p. 60).

Competition. Competition failed to develop in the public schools apparently because public school officials felt that the charters had an unfair advantage. Their ability to require parent contracts, or a certain number of hours of involvement, their ability to select students and limit enrollments, their greater hiring autonomy and less paperwork meant that the playing field was not level. Charter schools did not have to accept children after the school year started. As a consequence, they had more stable enrollments: Not having to adjust class activities to the arrival of new students or attend to their needs gives the charters a considerable advantage.

In Rofes' study some teachers and administrators saw competition as a positive development, but most did not. Districts that did respond to charters had "reform-minded leaders who seized on charters as a strategic tool to step up reforms in their districts" (p. 18). That is, the charter school became an instrument that permitted the administrators to accomplish what they had wanted to do all along. On the other hand, one teacher responded to competition this way: "I don't do my job based on thinking I have a competitor. I do it based on knowing what the child needs to grow and have a good education to get somewhere. That's what motivates me" (p. 21).

Innovation. That charter schools will be laboratories of innovation is tightly linked to the idea that they will provide competition. Joe Nathan again: "The charter school movement attempts to promote widespread improvement in public education both by allowing people to create new kinds of schools and by encouraging existing school systems to improve in order to compete effectively with these new schools" (p. 18). For charter advocates, innovation in the individual schools was only the start. Charter advocate Ted Kolderie had this to say:

> Too often those asking "What's happening?" (in regard to the impact of a charter law) look only at the schools created and the students enrolled: the first-order effects of a law. There are also second-order effects: changes/responses in the mainline system when laws are enacted and schools created. An evaluation needs to look for these. . . . Despite what the words seem to imply, "charter schools" is not basically about the schools. For the teachers who found them and the students who enroll in them, true, it is the schools that are important. But for others, from the beginning, "charter schools" has been about system-reform, a way for the state to cause the system to improve. The schools are instrumental. (1995)

This does not appear to be happening much in California—or elsewhere. The 1998 survey from Eric Rofes found that "The majority of districts had gone about business-as-usual and responded to charters slowly and in small ways." At one level, this would be expected if the public schools felt that the charter schools were both in competition with them and had an unfair advantage. It would be hard to imagine that the two groups would voluntarily engage in collaborative activities.

Indeed, Rofes's major finding was that

> Certain innovations and changes in school districts and traditional public schools [that I hypothesized would take place] had rarely occurred: Few superintendents, principals and teachers in district schools were thinking of charter schools as educational laboratories or attempting to transfer pedagogical innovations from charters to the district schools; districts were still building large school facilities and were rarely creating smaller schools; the large urban districts studied rarely had responded in meaningful ways to charter laws and charter schools. (p. 13)

Wells and her research team would not be surprised at Rofes's conclusion. They found that "there are no mechanisms in place for charter schools and regular schools to learn from each other." As a consequence, "all but two of the public school educators we interviewed reported that they had very little information about what was going on in the charter schools, and nearly all of the educators we interviewed said they saw little if any direct impact of charters schools on their schools" (p. 54). Beyond that, the feeling that charters operated with better conditions led to a sense of resentment that further inhibited cooperation. Even the charters' presence was taken by some as "a slap in the face." The very existence of the charter implied to people in public schools that they were doing something wrong.

For their part, few charter educators saw informing public school colleagues about their charter schools as part of their mission. And even if they did, most charter school personnel lacked the time and resources to get involved in meaningful collaboration with their public school counter parts. More recently, Roy

Romer, superintendent of the Los Angeles unified school district, has approached area charters, but not seeking innovative curricula and pedagogy; Romer is searching for seats to relieve the crowding in his packed schools.

If charter schools turn out to be the catalyst for systemic reform, it will be the first time in the history of education that this has occurred. Too often, one finds what I call "the pathology of envy" that seems to prevent the spread of good ideas (1993). A RAND study of federally funded educational innovations found that few of them became institutionalized even at the schools or districts that invented them (McLaughlin, 1990). So fragile have been educational reforms that the U.S. Department of Education created an entire organization, the Joint Dissemination and Review Panel, to help other schools "adopt and adapt" successful innovations. Congress recently killed the panel.

A few focused programs such as Success for All (SFA) have gotten wider distribution, but it might take an "educational entrepreneur" such as SFA's Robert Slavin to ensure that it happens. Other successful alterations in schools can ooze into wide practice if they require no programmatic change on the part of teachers or administrators—for example, the findings from Project STAR that small classes result in higher achievement.

Fads come and go, of course. Their trajectory is so predictable that Slavin was able to describe their path clearly (Slavin, 1989). They are usually the product of some entrepreneur, such as Madeline Hunter, whose concept of "Teach More, Faster," was embraced enthusiastically by practitioners in the absence of any data. When the data eventually do begin to appear—Hunter's program was developed in 1969 but no research data were produced until 1984—they are usually disappointing and the fad, likely already being replaced by something new, fades.

Choice. Charter schools did offer more programmatic choices, although, as the report concludes, often not to those parents who had the fewest options to begin with. Requirements for parents and students alike allowed the schools to do some choosing of their own. Because few of the charter schools provided transportation, only parents with a car and a flexible schedule could reasonably send their children to those schools.

As we shall see in the Michigan charter evaluations, many of their charter schools could not be differentiated from public schools in terms of offering meaningful choice.

Autonomy. The UCLA study found mixed results here. The area of greatest autonomy, and the area that administrators reported as the most important, was teacher hiring. Otherwise, they often used—even depended on—the bureaucracy of the school district in which they were located.

This led Wells to conclude: "It is time to rest the tired rhetoric that all bureaucracy is bad and all autonomy from bureaucracy is good. There are many charter schools in California that could not exist without the ongoing support of their local school districts. In fact, policy makers and educators have a lot to learn from charter school operators about which aspects of autonomy are most important . . . and which aspects of bureaucracy are most supportive" (p. 6).

However, as we shall see in the next section, this last conclusion is contingent upon how the charter law is framed. In California, the charter schools are part of the school district and operate through it. In Michigan, charters receive grants directly from the charter authorities, mostly Michigan state universities. Wells's conclusion is no doubt true—not all bureaucracy is bad, but the Michigan system does provide charters a great deal more autonomy.

Michigan

The intent of Michigan's charter law is fairly typical. As summarized at the beginning of an evaluation report on Michigan charter schools, those schools should:

- Improve student achievement for all pupils, including but not limited to educationally disadvantaged pupils, by improving learning environments.
- Stimulate innovative teaching methods.
- Create new professional opportunities for teachers.
- Achieve school accountability for pupil education performance by placing full responsibility for performance at the school-site level.
- Provide parents and pupils with greater choice among public schools.
- Determine whether state education funds may be more effectively, efficiently, and equitably utilized by allocating funds on a per-pupil basis directly to the school.

The law does not limit the total number of charters, but limits the number of schools chartered through state universities to 150, and no one university may have more than half of this total. An individual or any legal entity may apply for a charter through a number of authorizing agencies: local school boards, intermediate school boards, community colleges, and state public universities. The great majority of Michigan charter schools, locally called Public School Academies (PSAs) are chartered through one of the state universities—150 of 173 at the moment. Public and private schools can convert to charter status or schools can start from scratch. Home-based schools are not allowed. According to a November 1999 article in the *Detroit News*, over one hundred applications are awaiting approval. This backlog is being used to lobby the Michigan legislature to raise the cap on universities.

Schools cannot have entrance requirements and, in case of oversubscription, must select students by lottery. In those charter schools authorized by universities, all students in the state are eligible for enrollment; for charters authorized by other bodies, only students in the district where the school is located are eligible.

As part of other legislation, the Michigan legislature authorized two charter school evaluations. One was conducted by the private consulting firms Public Sector Consultants and MAXIMUS (hereafter, PSC), focusing on schools in major urban areas—Detroit, Flint, and Lansing (Khouri, Kleine, White, and Cummings, 1999). Western Michigan University (hereafter, WMU) conducted the other evaluation which looked at PSAs in the rest of the state (Horn and Miron, 1999). Several colleges of Michigan State University (MSU) collaborated in a third, independent, examination of charters.

How well has the Michigan charter school venture thus far realized the goals of its legislation? We take each goal in turn.

Stimulate Innovative Teaching Methods.   Many of the "innovations" listed as such by the schools' teachers and administrators will not strike the reader as especially new:

- Community activity experience for students
- Time set aside for reading
- Multiage classrooms
- Before- and after-school activities
- Individual Education Plans (IEPs) for all students
- Small class size
- Greater individualization
- Teaching assistants and volunteers in classrooms
- Cooperative learning
- Chicago Math and Saxon Math
- Learning labs
- Foreign-language instruction
- Outcomes-based learning
- Direct instruction
- Montessori methods
- Curriculum with specific focus—for example, Native American or African American culture, arts, or ecology, and so on.

Although none of this is in itself new, one could certainly argue that by including only a homogeneous group of parents with shared beliefs, instruction would be more effective. That is, if all the parents sending their children to a school believe in the efficacy of, say, direct instruction, such instruction might work well for the children in that school. Or, if children are learning something they would not otherwise be, such as a foreign language, then the instruction is improved. And, although these various pedagogies do not represent innovations in the field, they might well be innovative to the parents in a particular school.

Overall, however, WMU found that "there is little evidence that these practices have a positive impact on the achievement of the students or the overall success of the school" (p. 77). Furthermore, the extent of the innovations seemed small. "Based upon school visits and documentation provided by the PSAs, we conclude that there are limited innovations being developed and applied in the PSAs. In fact, the charter schools were remarkably similar to the regular public schools, with the notable exceptions of generally smaller student enrollments, the presence of additional adults in the classroom, governance, and span of contracted services" (p. 99). The evaluations did find PSAs quite innovative in how they ran the schools. This is discussed later in this section.

Improve Student Achievement.   Here, all evaluations concluded that it was really too early to measure achievement levels and that the specification of proper evaluation instruments was difficult. The only instrument available in both the regular public schools and the charters were the Michigan Education Assessment Program (MEAP) tests. Other than the MEAP, charter schools used some twenty-one different tests—some nationally normed standardized tests, others oriented to specific curricula.

All three evaluations concluded that the MEAP could not serve as an appropriate evaluation instrument for all schools. For instance, some schools focused on getting dropouts back into an academic setting. Because dropouts generally have low test scores, they would not stack up well against students in a regular high school. Yet the school could still be meeting its goal; namely, to keep students in a school and off the street.

None of the evaluations was able to use what would be appropriate test score data: The scores of students in the charter schools compared to the scores of those same students before they entered the charters. The PSC evaluation noted this and pointed out as well that the state would have to restructure its data storage in order to make such comparisons possible.

The PSC evaluation did attempt to measure progress in achievement. The Michigan assessment formula has a means for determining if a school made adequate yearly progress. The evaluators matched a PSA with a district public school that had similar characteristics and then compared test results. The evaluators found that charters outperformed the public schools considerably in math, and somewhat in reading. Fully 83 percent of the PSAs made satisfactory progress in math compared to 58 percent of the public comparison schools. For reading, the figures were 63 percent and 46 percent, respectively. In 71 percent of the schools evaluated, charters made greater gains in math than in the matched public school. Only half of the charter schools made greater gains in reading.

Why should the math improvements be better than the reading gains? We cannot know, but one possibility is that, in the elementary grades, mathematics tests have computation items on them, and computation can be drilled to high levels of automaticity. However, to score well on reading tests, students must read independently. A student can be drilled on addition, but not to read text he or she has not seen before; namely, reading passages on standardized tests. It might not be the kind of reading students engage in when reading a book, but it is reading of a sort.

The PSC evaluation also found that PSAs had larger gains on MEAP scores. As noted earlier, most Michigan charters are quite small in overall enrollment and contain small classes. One could expect that they would achieve more for this reason alone.

The evaluations found the most striking differences between the charters and the regular schools in how the boards and administrators managed the schools. PSAs contracted for services from profit-making and nonprofit companies. Some schools contracted for instructional services rather than hiring teachers. PSAs required parents to provide transportation. People from the same family often held different, and key, management or instructional positions in a given school, a practice either avoided or forbidden in many public service sectors.

It should be noted, however, that nepotism is common in the private sector and often is touted as a productivity multiplier: People from the same family will work harder towards a common goal—profitability—than will unrelated people. The WMU evaluators concluded that some of these practices might be undesirable in the PSAs. For instance, if a school employed members of the same family, would accountability be compromised?

The evaluators also wondered if the requirement that parents provide their own transportation would amount to a selection criterion (especially when coupled with an absence of free or reduced-price lunches supplied by public schools). The UCLA evaluation of California charters indicated that transportation did function as a selection factor. The WMU evaluation provided no data one way or another, but the evaluators concluded that "there are no convincing arguments or evidence that all of these [innovations] are legally or ethically desirable (p. 74).

The MSU evaluation also noted little educational innovation and much management modification:

> The most significant innovations associated with charter schools are found in the area of school governance and management. These are basic innovations and should be recognized as such. The most important charter school innovations are not about teaching and learning, but rather about control over school operations. Of particular significance in Michigan is the emergence of the EMO as a new and important actor in the management and governance of charter schools. (Horn and Miron, 1999, pp. 67–71)

EMO stands for Educational Management (or Maintenance) Organization, so named because some people consider them analogous to the Health Maintenance Organizations (HMOs) found in the field of health care. This analogy would give some people pause in terms of whether or not EMOs are desirable. EMOs vary greatly in the kind of services offered. Some have a limited scope, while others take over an entire school, providing the curriculum and instructional program as well as food service, physical plant management, and other noninstruction-related services.

Just why EMOs should be flourishing in Michigan, in contrast to many other states, is revealing. In the first place, not all state charter laws even permit EMOs; Michigan's does. Second, PSAs get set amounts of state funding and do not negotiate their financing with the school district, as in some other states.

Third, Michigan offers very little in the way of start-up funding; working through an EMO allows the new schools access to much-needed private capital.

Michigan's law permits school districts to grant charters but, as noted, virtually all charters are provided through universities. The university connection increases the autonomy of the charters in relation to the public school system and lowers the influence of teachers' unions. Finally, if a school hires employees through an EMO, it does not have to contribute to the Public School Employee Retirement system. The amount saved more than offsets the management fee charged by the EMO—no small matter.

As noted earlier, Michigan's law permits private schools to convert to charter status and receive public funds. This has served to increase competition—but between the formerly private schools that converted to charter status and those that remained private. Given the amount of money that Michigan provides for each pupil, the former privates can drop their tuition (which, by law, they must), and get by nicely on state funds whereras those that remain private must continue to charge tuition in order to survive.

The general way that Michigan finances schools should influence competition as well. At one point, the richest Michigan districts spent about three times as much as the poorest (this ratio is typical for most states). A change in the law removed from district control the amount of money a district received from both state and local coffers. The law did not reduce any district's funding level, but it increased the levels of the poorer districts. Thus, when a student transfers from one school to another, or one district to another,[12] the district loses all of the funding for that student. In most states, only the state portion of the funding would be lost. If the 100-plus applicants for charter schools are able to get the cap lifted, this could well affect the responsiveness of districts to charters.

Just how EMOs will be held educationally or fiscally accountable for their services is a process still in flux. We have observed that the whole issue of educational accountability is complex. In terms of keeping books, while public schools regularly publish detailed budgets, EMOs have provided little information about where their money goes. They justify this on the grounds that they are, after all, private organizations. The tension between "private organizations" and funding agencies and the public expecting accountability is likely to rise.

If charters such as those in Michigan persist and grow to control a sizable share of students, we could see the evolution of a system similar to those found in much of Europe. There, most countries fund private as well as public schools, but hold both to the same rules for accountability. The students in private schools must study the same curriculum and take the same tests as those in public schools; the teachers must meet the same professional requirements and be paid the same, and so on. In some countries, the state even dictates the instruc-

---

12. Michigan provides for interdistrict transfers. Any student may transfer into any district, space permitting. In general, students using this form of choice are moving from less affluent to richer districts.

tional techniques that private schools must use. The major difference between public and private schools in most of Europe is the freedom of the latter to offer specific religious instruction.

Like the other evaluations, the MSU study concludes that charter schools will *not* be a source of major innovations in curriculum and instruction. It points out that, overall, parents are quite conservative when it comes to such innovations. There appears to be a "not-with-my-kid-you-don't" attitude toward change in this country's schools. Parents figure that their schools did okay by them and want the same for their children. "Insofar as this is what parents want, PSAs have little to gain and much to lose from experimentation with innovative practices" (p. 57).

In addition, although increased scores on the MEAP are not goals of all charters, the PSAs face strong pressure to perform well on MEAP tests. As in other states, MEAP results show up as "box scores" in newspapers. Such comparisons might very well be unfair—comparing, say, scores from poor urban areas to those in affluent suburbs with no adjustment for wealth—but they are influential nonetheless.

The MSU study also observes that many innovations are costly. A well-financed program like the Edison Project might be able to afford them, but the small, independent charters cannot and are more likely to take something "off the shelf." (In fact, Edison, after spending a great deal of money trying to develop new curriculum, adopted the Success For All reading program and Chicago Math, two off-the-shelf programs; even so it has yet to turn a profit, and founder Chris Whittle does not expect one before 2004.)

Accountability via Responsibility Placed at the School-Site Level. The swing to EMOs in Michigan has numerous ramifications. It further reduces the opportunities and incentive for innovations because the EMOs bring with them curricula packages developed elsewhere, packages that they do not want to modify. Although individual EMOs differ from one another, within an EMO, the schools are alike. According to some people, some chartering agents steer charter applicants toward EMOs rather than a small, idiosyncratic "mom-and-pop" charter model. The agents do this partly because they contend that if every charter were unique, they would have too many models to oversee well. It also helps prevent some scandalous story popping up in a newspaper describing some particularly inept or corrupt school; at least the EMOs are known quantities.

To some extent, using an EMO also removes accountability from the school site and moves it to some remote corporate headquarters. If parents or the Michigan Department of Education complain about the lack of achievement at a particular school, one can foresee a dispute over who is responsible or who dropped the achievement ball. The school officials might well claim they were not properly supported in their endeavors; the EMO might argue that the school faculty and staff did not properly implement the EMO's program, which certainly would have produced the desired results if implemented correctly. In fact, just such a blow occurred in California, as discussed earlier. We should point out, too, that using an EMO removes money from local neighborhoods and gives it instead to a corporation.

When *Michigan Alive* reporter Karen Schultz looked into her state's charter issues, she found little accountability, and officials split over whether there should be more (Schultz, 1999). Schultz's paper had found that in 1997–98, twenty-one management companies in Michigan had received $16.7 million in public money. "A key worry about management companies [which operate 70 percent of the charters in Michigan] is that once public money is handed over to the companies, how it is spent suddenly becomes a private rather than a public concern." Because companies are not required to divulge how much of that money they pocket for themselves, they don't, and no one knows how these funds are distributed.

Some commentators told Schultz that such lack of disclosure doesn't matter as long as the parents, teachers, and taxpayers are satisfied. However, David Arsen of Michigan State University, and one of the authors of the Michigan State evaluations of charters, said, "Just because people are happy doesn't mean we should spend taxpayer money on it." Several companies "refused repeated inquiries about their schools" [from Schultz].

Create New Professional Opportunities for Teachers.   It is not clear that schools lacking in true innovations can attain this goal. It might be, however, that the choice of different schools does provide teachers an opportunity to gravitate to schools whose pedagogy they prefer. A charter school focused on phonics and back-to-basics math is not likely to recruit or attract teachers who wish to use whole language and the National Council of Teachers of Mathematics standards. Indeed, in one California Edison school, when teachers expressed the desire to make changes, they were told, "Maybe our model is not for you." This is discussed in more detail in the section on Edison schools.

Beyond that, the teachers in PSAs are younger, have less experience, and receive lower salaries than public schools teachers. The PSC evaluation found that PSAs teachers received average salaries of just over $29,000, compared to $47,000 for public school teachers. When one remembers that charter teachers also receive no contributions to the state retirement fund, this difference becomes even larger. PSA teachers generally do not have tenure. The low salaries and lack of tenure have further implications: One could not imagine Michigan evolving into an all-PSA state under such conditions. There would be insufficient numbers of teachers willing to work under such conditions.

The PSC evaluation found that administrators often deliberately recruited younger teachers, not only because were they cheaper, but because school administrators felt they were better trained, not "set in their ways," and had more energy for the long hours that charter schools often require. Teachers not set in their ways would also presumably be more amenable to using the "canned" curricula offered via EMOs. On the other hand, the opportunities for mentoring from veterans is diminished.

The Rules Matter. The MSU study is subtitled "The Rules Matter" (Arsen, Plan, and Sykes, 1999) and it lists areas in which different rules will produce different outcomes:

- Procedures for student selection and admissions
- Parents' access to information
- Teacher certification
- Curriculum and assessment
- Criteria for granting or refusing charters
- Restrictions on the location of charter schools
- Duration of charters
- Criteria for review and revocation of charters
- Charter school governance structure
- Funding level and access to start-up and capital funding (p. 14).

We have already observed how the charter-granting procedure itself produces differences between Michigan and California. In California, the charters come through the public school system, building, for better or worse, a connection between the two entities. In Michigan, the schools are largely bypassed, with most charters issuing from universities. As a consequence, the Michigan charters enjoy more autonomy.

The Horn and Miron Evaluation: A Clearer Picture. Subsequent to the production of the above material, a more summative examination of the charter schools movement in Michigan has become available. Although dated July 2000, the document was not available until late fall. The rumor, unverified, was that it was being withheld until after the presidential election because its portrait of charter schools was so unflattering. True or not, the new evaluation by Jerry Horn and Gary Miron of Western Michigan University does present a warts-and-all picture. The investigators put their findings into categories and we address each one in turn. Not all conclusions are presented here. The report can be found at http://www.wmich.edu/evalctr.

Impact and Mobility. Charter schools did cause some public schools to offer new services such as before- and after-school programs, all-day kindergarten, foreign languages in elementary grades, clearer school mission statements, and more open and receptive relationships with parents. Some districts reported large losses of students, but statewide the net impact is nearly zero. Most charter school growth is occurring from the entry of students into kindergarten. Smaller districts and districts with no growth potential are most heavily affected. The impact has been felt mostly as a reduction in support services.

Some districts reported that charters would hold students until "count day," the time at which state aid is determined. They would then send the students back to the public schools, keeping the money but forcing the public schools to educate the children without compensation.

While charters have provided additional options for parents, in many cases, the options are illusory. Most charters do not provide transportation and most parents cannot find the time or the money to fill this gap, putting charter schools out of their reach.

Special Education.   The charters provide little special education, even in the categories one most often sees, such as learning disability. Some 12.5 percent of public school students are classified as receiving special education services. Only 3.7 percent of charter school students have such classification, with about half of the charters reporting no special education students at all. A few cater only to students with disabilities.

"One of the most striking and perhaps surprising aspects of the Michigan charter school movement is the growth in and number of schools operated by education management organizations (EMOs)" (p. iv). Some people will find this the most disturbing aspect as well. In 1995–96, 16.7 percent of Michigan charters were operated by EMOs. In 1999–2000 the figure was 71.4 percent. Nationally it is 10 percent. The growth of EMOs is shown in Table 6.1.

Only 5 percent of the EMOs are nonprofits. State universities in Michigan are refusing to grant charters except to schools that have contracted with an EMO. Horn and Miron state that this is because the EMOs have financial resources and business acumen that individual applicants do not. As noted earlier, chartering a known quantity also reduces the potential embarrassment to the university. This would seem to negate one of the fundamental purposes for charters: to increase diversity and innovation. Because charter schools search for desirable communities in which to place their schools, in fact, charter schools are choosing communities, not vice versa.

"While charter schools emphasize that they are a new form of public schools, they are increasingly appearing and behaving like private schools" (p. 93). Employ-

TABLE 6.1   *Growth in Educational Management Organizations: State of Michigan*

Year	Number of Companies	Percentage of Charter Schools Operated by EMOs
1995–96	6	16.7
1996–97	10	27.4
1997–98	21	52.8
1998–99	25	60.6
1999–00	38	71.4

EMOs manage 122 schools. Five percent of EMOs are nonprofit. It is estimated that because EMOs tend to work with larger schools, they account for more than 80 percent of charter school students.

Source: Data adapted from Jerry Horn and Gary Miron, *An Evaluation of the Michigan Charter School Initiative: Performance, Accountability, and Impact* (pp. 44–45), (The Evaluation Center, Western Michigan University, 2000).

ees in charters are private, not public, workers. Facilities, equipment, and furniture are privately owned. And, perhaps most significant, the student bodies look more and more like private schools: Fewer minority and special needs students are enrolled. Requirements for parent participation, preapplication interviews, and the absence of transportation all help structure or shape the student body.

Michigan Educational Assessment Program (MEAP) Results. The authors note again that while regular schools outperform charters in a given district, the comparison can be inappropriate because some charters concentrate on serving at-risk students. MEAP passing rates for charter schools declined from 1995–96 to 1996–97, rose the next year, then declined again. Over the entire period there was little change in the passing rates. Public schools in the host districts, however, showed a gain from 49.4 percent to 68 percent over the same time period. Schools run by Edison Schools, Inc., the Leona Group, and Charter Schools Administrative Services were consistently among the poorest performers, both in terms of absolute scores and trends over time. This finding casts doubt on the claims by Edison for large test-score gains, at least at the national level. The MEAP results for each grade and subject area are shown in Table 6.2.

Charter schools reported using twenty-nine different tests and assessment instruments other than the MEAP. They did not put the results from these assessments in their annual reports or school improvement plans, nor did they respond to requests from Horn and Miron for the results.

In their conclusions, which might well have triggered the rumor that some wanted to withhold the report, Horn and Miron have this to say: "After nearly five years of operation in Michigan, we conclude that (i) the state's charter

TABLE 6.2 *Summary of MEAP Results*

Assessment	4-Year Average Pass Rate by Percentage	Range of Pass Rates by Percentage	Trend
4th-grade math	45.2 (63.9)*	33–35 (49–68)	mixed/stable (mixed/up)
4th-grade reading	35.8 (51.7)	33–38 (38–55)	stable (mixed/up)
5th-grade science	20 (30)	14–22 (19–37)	stable (down)
5th-grade writing	43 (56)	36–57 (49–69)	mixed/down (mixed/down)
7th-grade math	33.8 (47.3)	25–36 (32–51)	mixed/up (up)
7th-grade reading	30.5 (37.9)	19–34 (33–44)	mixed/up (up)
8th-grade science	9 (18)	8.6–9.4 (15–20)	stable (stable)
8th-grade writing	46 (59)	37–62 (50–72)	mixed/down (mixed/down)

*Values for host district are in parentheses

Source: Data adapted from Jerry Horn and Gary Miron, *An Evaluation of the Michigan Charter School Initiative: Performance, Accountability, and Impact* (p. 80), (The Evaluation Center, Western Michigan University, 2000).

schools are producing few and limited innovations; (ii) few schools are implementing comprehensive accountability plans; and (iii) the extensive involvement of EMOs is creating new "pseudo" school districts in which decisions are made from great distances rather than at the school level" (p. 93).

If these conclusions are valid, then Michigan's charter schools appear to be doing largely just the opposite of what Nathan, Finn, and other champions claimed they promised to do. As noted earlier, however, "the rules matter," and a similar summary study in Arizona or California might reach different conclusions.

Ohio and Elsewhere

The evaluations thus far reported do not reveal charters as laboratories of innovation for improving the public school system overall. True, it is early in the game and more time must pass to really evaluate what is happening. It is also true that the evaluations discussed above are all done by academic institutions and are rather sterile when it comes to discussing what is really happening. Only the *Arizona Tribune* descriptions provide some feel for the various political, ideological, and fiscal manipulations that are sometimes involved.

Ohio's charter schools are too new to have been the subject of a formal evaluation. Dennis Willard and Doug Oplinger, reporters at the *Akron Beacon Journal*, however, have done an excellent job in ferreting out some of the shenanigans involved in establishing charters in that state (Willard and Oplinger, 1999a, 1999b, 1999c; Oplinger and Willard, 1999a, 1999b, 1999c). These journalists bring the issues "up close and personal" in a way that academic evaluations cannot.

Here, let me just present a few of the opening paragraphs from the first article in the series:

> Ohio, already No. 1 in the 1990s for putting public dollars into private schools[13] and last in the nation for placing children in safe and sanitary buildings, is on course to earn a new distinction in the next decade.
>
> The state is ready to rival Arizona, California, Florida and Michigan for funneling state and local tax dollars to a new class of schools—charter schools—that are public in some ways and private in others.
>
> Now, less than five months into the second year [of charter school funding]—as charter schools move from concept to reality—serious questions and disturbing problems are starting to arise.
>
> • Private, profit-minded companies, known as education management organizations, are making strong inroads into the state. In doing so, these EMOs are concentrating school ownership in the hands of a few and brushing aside the people who were to be given control of their local charter, or community, schools—parents, teachers, and community members.

---

13. This is a true statement, but it is not due to the recent trend toward charters, vouchers, and other forms of privatization. Ohio has a long history of state support of private schools, support that is substantially larger than in any other state.

- The Ohio Board of Education, responsible for oversight, is rubberstamping contracts as fast as it can without thoroughly reviewing the written proposals or hearing from a single charter school representative. One reason: Most board member say they have almost no authority to reject a proposal.
- Lawmakers did not fund an oversight office for charter schools until the program's second year and after more than 60 contracts had been approved and 15 schools had opened. The undermanned office is hard-pressed to complete routine checks for fire safety and criminal backgrounds, and is barely monitoring academic progress.
- Children are bearing the brunt of the charter school problems. The state has allowed charter schools to open without textbooks or indoor toilets. Students have attended class in unsafe buildings that lacked sprinklers or fire alarm systems. And local police in Columbus were called 12 times in two months to one charter school to investigate disturbances, including one case of sexual assault.
- Most charter schools are not models for reform. First-year test scores indicate students in charter schools are doing dramatically worse than public school-children, and the new schools are not incubators for innovation as proponents promised they would be.
- Profits are being reaped, but there is no evidence that charter schools are reducing education costs or saving Ohio taxpayers money—despite lower pay for teachers and exemptions from 191 state mandates that hike the cost of education in public schools (Willard and Oplinger, 1999a).

As mentioned earlier, taken alone, low test scores do not necessarily mean the charters themselves are flunking. In some cases, the charters cater to at-risk students who were not performing well in public schools either. This is particularly true in Ohio, where a first-year evaluation of fifteen charters found them to enroll a higher proportion of poor and minority students (but a lower proportion of special education students) than public schools in the district where the charters were located.

The appropriate data for evaluating the impact of charters have not been collected or do not yet exist. In the first instance, we would need some index of how the students did in the charter schools paired with the same information on how they were performing in public schools. In the second case, we need trend data of the students in charter schools compared to the same growth trends for students in public schools.

Still, these few paragraphs give a flavor of the situation in Ohio. Ohio looks a bit like Michigan all over again, with one additional component: The charge for charters is being led by David Brennan, one of Ohio's political powers, and a man who has been considered a serious candidate for chairman of the Republican National Committee. The *Akron Beacon Journal* series depicts Brennan using his influence with the governor and the state legislature to get favors and favorably written laws from which he benefits. At least one such favor violated Ohio's constitution.

At other times, Brennan's behavior simply looks like an entrepreneur in action. When Cleveland set up its voucher program in 1995, Brennan started two new schools. When the charter legislation became law, Brennan quickly converted his schools to charter status. The tuition he receives for charter students is about three times the value of the former voucher. It looks like the bottom line, not scholastic achievement, is a driving force in Brennan's pedagogy.

All of this harkens back to Molnar's prediction concerning fraud, greed, and corruption. If anything, Molnar underestimated what the desire to turn a profit might cause. In Texas, *Houston Press* reporter Stuart Eskenazi heard some rumors about the Renaissance Charter School there. The school had been considered a model by state officials, who obviously had not actually visited the site. When Eskenazi did, he found

> A decrepit, two-story gray stucco office building that sat woefully along a busy commercial street. The City of Arlington [Texas] had declared the second level of the vacant building unsuitable for habitation, so the school set up shop in two large rooms on the ground floor. The building had no heat. The classrooms had no desks, no chairs, no textbooks, no chalkboards, no trash cans, no gymnasium, no lunchroom, no vending machines, no functioning toilet. (Eskenazi, 1999)

All of this came to light after frustrated teachers instructed students to write the Texas Education Agency about the conditions of the school. Children could write only if they brought materials from home—there were no pencils or paper at the school. One letter said simply, "If you name it, we don't have it."

The evaluation of Ohio's charter schools, conducted by the nonpartisan Legislative Office of Education Oversight, is gentler in its conclusions (2000). It did find, however, that most of the charters failed to provide evidence of how they met their educational goals or evaluated student performance. Although required by law, most did not provide annual reports to parents, and most school directors claimed they were not even aware that such reports were required.

Recall that one claim for charter schools is that they will be more accountable than normal public schools. As has been seen in other states, this accountability is not being met in the academic realm. Because the evaluation was of first-year operations and the original charters are good for five years, fiscal accountability has not yet surfaced as an issue.

The Ohio evaluation also turned up some other findings that are important when thinking generally about charters. The teachers in charter schools had an average of 4.2 years of experience and were paid an average salary of $22,070. Teachers in the public school districts where the charters were operating had an average of 14.8 years of experience and were paid on average $43,162. Class size in the charter schools averaged eighteen students. Thus the Ohio charters have less experienced teachers and smaller classes than regular schools. Teachers are paid barely half of what the typical public school teacher receives. One wonders what possibilities the charter school teachers have for mentoring from more experienced teachers.

It is unlikely that the number of charter schools could be expanded substantially with these characteristics. Although we cannot know how many teachers would work for so much less than a regular public school teacher, the available pool of inexperienced teachers willing to work under these conditions is not likely to be large. Note that the charters contain two factors that operate in opposite directions in relation to academic achievement: a relatively neophyte teacher corps, and small classes.

Charter Schools and Public School Funding

Information on how different states fund charter schools and how funding for charter schools affects public schools has been slow to arrive, perhaps because it is so complicated and variable.

Some contended early on that charters would not adversely affect the public schools because the public schools could reduce services commensurately. This view did not reflect the reality of how charter schools operating over a wider geographical area than a single school district, obtain students. Even where a charter restricts membership to students in the "host" public school district, it draws from many schools. Thus a charter school third grade made up of twenty-five students is highly unlikely to have drawn them from the third grade of a single public school. If it did, the public school could dismiss a third-grade teacher, although that would not recoup all costs—building operation, transportation services, and so on—associated with educating children.

Eric Rofes, while at the University of California at Berkeley, surveyed twenty-five charter schools in eight states and the District of Columbia as well as personnel in the public school districts where the charters were located (Rofes, 1998). He found that the impact of charters varied a great deal depending on other conditions affecting school attendance. In rapidly growing areas, students who departed for charter schools were replaced by new arrivals. In stable or declining areas, however, the impact was felt immediately. Holland, Michigan, for example, lost over $1 million. The district coped with the reduced revenue by putting off capital purchases and improvements, sacrificing the tidiness of the school and the condition of the buildings and grounds. At the time of Rofes's survey, however, Holland's school district had not fired any staff or eliminated any positions.

Other data put dollar figures on public school losses. As noted previously, EMOs in Michigan received $16.7 million. According to one report, the 4,000 students who attend charter schools in Cincinnati, Ohio, will cost that city $21 million in the 2000–01 school year.

The funding arrangements for charters vary greatly from state to state. A study conducted by the research department of the American Federation of Teachers for the U.S. Department of Education revealed a dazzling array of funding formulas (Nelson, Muir, and Drown, 2000). Some states fund charters based on the host district's revenue, others on the host district's spending, and still others a state average or a district formula. In Connecticut, state-authorized charters receive the state average, but district-authorized charters make unique funding arrangements with their host district (Nelson et al., p. 32)

Some states give more money to urban districts, some to remote, sparsely populated districts. Some adjust for cost of living. States that fund districts based on district expenditures typically fund charters with similar amounts. Thus, if a charter enrolls a student population similar to the district's, it gets no advantageous funding. If the charter's population is different from the district's it might be advantaged or disadvantaged. Most charters are elementary schools, which cost less than secondary schools. Funding formulas usually include both elementary and secondary schools. Elementary charters could thus have "extra" money even as a secondary charter suffered from insufficient funds.

Sometimes the advantages and disadvantages offset one another. An evaluation of charter schools in Texas found that they had about twice the percentage of low-income students as did public schools, but only about one-third the proportion of special education students and one-half the limited-English proficient students (Texas Education Agency, 1998). In other states, people have alleged that students requiring special education services are counseled out of attending privately run charters. Why? These students cost more and cut the profit margin.

The AFT study attempted to compare the funding of charters to the funding of host districts in twenty-five states and two cities. It found that, in general, charters received less funding than the hosts when they were secondary schools or contained many special needs or low-income students. They also received less for facilities and other capital expenditures. Charters received more money than host districts when they were elementary schools or enrolled few special needs students and low-income students.

A full discussion of the AFT study is outside of the scope of this book, but the interested reader is encouraged to examine this comprehensive, detailed, and clear report.

7

Private Schools and the Private Management of Public School Programs

In the war on the schools, two of the three most powerful weapons are private schools and the private companies that manage public schools (the third is the voucher). Some charter school arrangements do not directly drain away either students or money from the public system. This is not true of private schools or public schools that are managed by private, for-profit companies. Their impact is direct and immediate. Private schools absorb public school students and, because funding is tied to daily attendance or membership money. The private management companies, usually referred to as Educational Management Organizations, or EMOs, take some percentage of a school's funding for its own employees and officers. Not only does the money leave the school system, it usually ends up far away from the community. When Edison Schools Incorporated operates a school in San Francisco or Kansas City, at least some of its management fee flows to corporate headquarters in New York.

To date, private schools have been less active than EMOs. Where they exist, they have generally aimed for niche markets, such as Nobel Learning Communities, which targets upwardly mobile, becoming-affluent families. EMOs have appeared in a variety of locations. Some, like National Heritage Academies in Michigan, aim to attract a white, middle-class, religious sector. Others, like Advantage Schools, Inc., put their resources into urban schools. And still others, like Edison, appear in a variety of socio-economic strata.

How one feels about such arrangements depends largely on where one's eyes are fixed on the dueling visions discussed in Chapter 2. If one sees education as simply the provision of service, then these developments might be viewed with equanimity, even enthusiasm. If one sees education as a public good, as, in

Benjamin Barber's words, workshops of democracy, these trends are seen with a jaundiced eye.

General Trends

By 1994, sufficient numbers of school districts had begun to use private firms to manage programs previously provided by the district itself that the National School Boards Association (NSBA) surveyed 3,000 districts to determine who was doing what for (or to) whom. Districts which reported using contractors and consultants are listed by category of service provided in the NSBA publication, *Private Options for Public Schools* (National School Boards Association, 1995).

At the time of the survey, which has not been updated since 1995, contractors overwhelmingly provided some kind of management service. The districts reporting that they use such services occupy thirty-seven pages of the report. Those reporting private provision of some type of instructional support occupy only eight. The proportion of schools using the most-often reported instructional management, special education, was barely half of that reported for the least reported use of administrative management, vehicle maintenance, 14 percent and 24 percent, respectively.

Without question, private companies are primarily sought out by schools as a means of saving money, although the savings might turn out to be a Trojan horse. Of the four most commonly given reasons for using private firms, only one—the improvement and maintenance of buildings—is not about saving money. Forty-five percent of responding districts listed cost reduction as a reason, 29 percent listed improved efficiency, and 21 percent listed declining resources. Twenty-eight percent listed building improvement.

Among the listings of districts, the NSBA has placed comments from the respondents. Although it cannot be determined how representative these are, the most common message they send is, "approach with caution": "Give deep consideration to the value of private contractors, but don't sell out on quality for lower costs." Or, "Seek first to understand! Get the facts before jumping into it. Get all the stakeholders into the process."

Contracts for instructional programs fell mostly in one of three categories: at-risk children, special education, and technology in education. Some contracts were for driver education, and a few were for either science or foreign language instruction. A pair of districts reported using consultants for instructional design; one to teach curriculum design to the teachers, and the other to assist teachers in designing integrated curriculum units. This has likely changed. Berlitz now offers more foreign language programs and Sylvan Learning Systems has obtained many contracts to provide Title 1 remedial instruction.

The number of these programs has no doubt increased since the NSBA conducted its survey in the 1994–95 school year. In and of themselves they do not appear to loom large on the horizon of privatization, but they could well have a "fooling the frog" impact. An analogy of accommodation (for some reason much loved by conservative school critics), holds that a frog tossed into boiling water will immediately jump out, while one in a pan of water that is then slowly heated will not try to jump until it is too late. To mix metaphors, the privatization of management services and small instructional programs might serve as the camel's nose under the tent, to be followed shortly by the whole camel. At least one theorist, Paul Hill of the University of Washington, has argued that the camel should be welcomed (Hill, 1995).

Results on choice from abroad show, at best, mixed outcomes. It has become fashionable in some quarters to point to results from privatization in the schools of Chile as proof that private schools are inherently more efficient than public schools. A recent study of Chilean data from 1984 to 1996 by Patrick McEwan and Martin Carnoy of Stanford University casts doubt on this conclusion. McEwan and Carnoy found that Chile's private schools were not more efficient producers of achievement than public schools. The private schools did cost less, but this was due more to constraints on how public schools could allocate funds than on an inherent efficiency (although some would likely contend that that is the point: With government control comes nonessential constraints that drive up costs and lower efficiency). The achievement gap is due at least as much to the selection bias favoring the admission of high-income children into private schools as to any greater efficiency. This gap between public and private schools in Chile has been closing since 1990, but McEwan and Carnoy conclude that this is more due to increased spending by the Chilean government than from any response on the part of public schools to their private competition (see pages 165 to 168 for details; McEwan, 2000; McEwan and Carnoy, 2000a, 2000b, 1999).

Private Management Companies

In America, the predominant private-sector model of ongoing school management is that of larger organizations which propose to manage entire schools. Some of these corporations provide firm-developed curriculum (Sabis and Nobel), while other don't (Edison, which decided that it was too much work). Many of these companies do not provide EMO services exclusively. Edison, for instance, manages a combination of existing public schools and new charter schools. Nobel, whose major line is a group of private schools, has also recently entered the charter market.

We consider each of the major players in turn, excluding those who provide daycare services, college-level services, or services in the rapidly burgeoning "post-education" sector that concentrates on job improvement skills. First, however, is a look at the Association of Education Practitioners and Providers, something of a maverick for championing a smaller, entrepreneurial school management model.

The Association of Education Practitioners and Providers (AEPP) (Formerly, the Association of Educators in Private Practice)

The Association of Educators in Private Practice was started in 1990 in Watertown, Wisconsin, by Milwaukee native Chris Yelich. Yelich served as a medical technologist for many years before becoming a teacher. Perhaps her medical background gave her the perspective to view teachers and other educators as skilled practitioners who should be able to market themselves in the same way medical professionals do. She was rankled by the limited ways she had to show her skills as an educator: Work in a school system or find some other line of work. Her initial goal in founding AEPP was to open more career paths to educators, so they could pursue opportunities to be businesspeople and entrepreneurs, not just employees of a school system. The organization has about seven hundred members, the bulk of whom are indeed individuals in private practice.

For her part, Yelich has broadened the scope of what she sees as desirable for schools, now favoring a model very much like that presented by Paul Hill, who argues that schools should be managers, not providers, of education. (Hill, 1995). Yelich and Hill believe schools should contract out to the providers but should remain public entities.

Yelich bases her arguments in part on efficiency concerns, but mostly in terms of learning differences among children. One size doesn't fit all. She believes that there are people who know how to teach all children, but that we can't expect them all to be in a finite-sized school.

AEPP's EDventures.   AEPP's major venture beyond the local level is EDventures, an annual conference that now extends beyond the Yelich–Hill focus, although Hill was the keynote speaker at EDventures'98. Many featured speakers have had agendas beyond schools-as-managers. The following spoke at EDventures'98:

> Howard Fuller, Marquette University (and former superintendent of Milwaukee Public Schools)
>
> Deborah McGriff, Edison Project (and former Assistant Superintendent of Detroit Public Schools)
>
> Mike Ronan, Beacon
>
> Jack Clegg, Nobel
>
> Jeanne Allen, Center for Education Reform
>
> John McLaughlin, Education Industry Group
>
> Chester E. Finn, Jr., Hudson Institute (and former assistant secretary of education)
>
> Janet Beales, Kids1, Inc.

Ted Kolderie, Center for Policy Studies

Dwight Evans, Pennsylvania state assemblyman (and sponsor of Pennsylvania's charter school legislation)

Bruno Manno, Hudson Institute

Eric Rofes, University of California at Berkeley

There is no overall sponsorship of EDventures. Attending the conference in 1998 cost $140 for members, $190 for others. Everyone pays, and no one gets an honorarium. Some events—receptions, dinners—are sponsored by organizations to cover some expenses. A correspondent told me that there are many good people in AEPP—and some hucksters.

AEPP is a small undertaking at this time, but it could become much larger in general, if not through the specific organization. As noted, it subscribes to Paul Hill's notion that schools should manage education not provide it. It is, in some ways, the converse of an Edison or TesseracT (discussed below). These organizations move in and take over whole schools. AEPP seeks to build from the bottom up, creating an infrastructure of individual entrepreneurs who can provide various educational services. If a school or district wishes to operate in the manner espoused by Hill, it is AEPP's hope that that school or district would be able to find the service providers already in place in its community.

The TesseracT Group
(Formerly Education Alternatives, Inc.)

Of those who work in the area of privately managing public schools for profit, two names dominate: Chris Whittle of Edison Schools, Inc. and John Golle of TesseracT. Hoover's Capsule refers to Golle as "a pioneer in for-profit schools" (Mattern, 2000a). An article in the *Arizona Republic* described him as the man credited with inventing for-profit schools. In spite of this distinction, by early 2000 TesseracT faced ever-increasing economic woes. Golle, who had retired, came back to try to straighten things out. He did not succeed.

Golle is hardly a newcomer to education, free or for profit, but he did enter the field from an unusual corner. Most of the early developers of educational computer software, although touting their products as instruments to improve educational outcomes, really saw schools as just another market. One of the few who didn't was William C. Norris, for many years the CEO of Minneapolis-based Control Data Corporation (CDC). Norris was genuinely interested in schools and learning and promoted a computerized interactive learning system called PLATO. He poured millions into PLATO development; unfortunately, because it was such a drain on the parent company's resources, his devotion ultimately cost him his job. He has kept the faith through the Williams C. Norris Institute and the Norris Education Innovations, Inc.

CDC's financial problems in the 1980s forced it to unload twenty-two companies, including the PLATO-based USSA Private Schools, Inc. USSA's goal was a national chain of private schools. Capital Dimensions bought USSA and Capital's head, John Golle, changed the company's name to Educational Alternatives, Inc. (EAI). EAI, along with the Edison Project, was one of two for-profit educational services organizations that were being closely watched by Wall Street. When EAI acquired a technical college (Academy of Business College in Phoenix, Arizona), and then merged with Sunrise Services, Inc., an operator of thirty-three Arizona preschools, the company was renamed again and became the TesseracT Group.

The Rise of EAI.   EAI attracted a lot of attention from the "education industry" watchers, including Michael Moe, then with a branch of Lehman Brothers, now the director of Global Growth Research at Merrill Lynch. These industry observers viewed education as analogous to the health maintenance organizations that were beginning to dominate the delivery of essential medical services and preventive health care in the United States, breaking the hold of more traditional insurance companies. "Industry" advocates in both fields were convinced that privately managed companies could provide services more efficiently and at lower costs to large numbers of people, improving on the performance of existing infrastructures. By 1994, EAI was singled out by the education industry as the leader in its field. Although financial analysts acknowledged that it was a largely untested investment arena, many touted education as a potentially lucrative market for investors unafraid of speculating with their funds. Left unaddressed was the fact that this emerging view of education—from a public service to a profit center—represented a radical shift in attitude with profound implications for public schools in America.

Bouyed by Wall Street's confidence in this new approach to education, EAI landed contracts (now defunct) in Baltimore, Maryland, Hartford, Connecticut, and Dade County, Florida. EAI enjoyed some early success, in large part because its methods of keeping books made its pockets seem deeper than they actually were. Most of the money given to EAI under its contract with Baltimore city schools, for instance, had to be used to pay teachers and to cover other expenses. EAI's books showed these funds as unrestricted income, a rather unusual bookkeeping practice. EAI also invested substantial amounts of the money in high-risk derivatives. For a while, the "profit" EAI was showing was actually interest on these investments. When interest rates declined, so did EAI's fortunes, literally and symbolically.

The interest from the stocks and the practice of counting obligated money as unrestricted income caused EAI's stock to rise, after which Golle and other EAI officers sold large portions of their shares at large profits. Some people became skeptical. *Barron's* noted that "Education Alternatives has been more successful at issuing stock than at any of its other competencies." Disputes flared. Lawsuits followed.

Education Alternatives, Inc. in Baltimore. EAI's Baltimore contract was for five years, beginning in the fall of 1992. In August 1993, EAI announced that students in its nine Baltimore schools had gained an average of .88 grade levels compared to a .30 gain that would be expected under "normal" circumstances. Shortly thereafter, it had to admit that this figure was an error. EAI blamed its partner, Computer Curriculum Corporation (CCC, now owned by Paramount which, in turn, is owned by Viacom; CCC grew out of research conducted from the early 1960s onward by Patrick Suppes of Stanford University). CCC blamed EAI. Stock prices plummeted. Baltimore contracted with the University of Maryland, Baltimore County (UMBC), for an external evaluation.

The UMBC report, issued in the summer of 1995, concluded that there had been no improvement in test scores in the nine EAI schools since 1991–92, the year before the contract (Williams and Leak, 1995). This was true for the district as a whole. The UMBC team also found that teachers at the EAI schools spent more time teaching in small groups and a great deal more time preparing students to take standardized tests. This makes the finding of no improvement actually look negative: It is not that hard to influence test scores. Without such attention to test preparation, the scores might well have been lower than those in a matched group of public schools.

Although EAI had touted its CCC computer software, the evaluation team also found that "there is little about the computer-using experience [at EAI schools] that can be considered preparation for an 'age of technology'" (p. 100). The UMBC team did find that EAI had been successful in mainstreaming a number of special education students, but concluded that, despite establishing parent activities in the schools, the level of parent involvement did not differ from that in the control schools.

EAI abolished most paraprofessional positions in Baltimore schools, replacing them with low-wage interns, many of whom stayed only one year. The paraprofessionals tended to live in the school's neighborhood; the interns did not. This action thus removed both wealth and community resources from an impoverished area. Molnar has observed that contracting with EAI to run poverty schools assures that money moves from minorities in the neighborhood to whites living outside of the area (1996).

A detailed analysis of spending in Baltimore schools led researchers at the Economic Policy Institute to conclude that it was not clear how Baltimore school officials arrived at the per-pupil allowance provided to EAI (Richards, Shore, and Sawicky, 1996). What was clear was that this amount was more than was spent on a matched control group of schools. Matched public elementary schools spent $4,464 for each pupil compared to $5,474 for EAI. Only 14 percent of all Baltimore elementary schools exceeded the EAI figure, and some of those were schools with particularly high costs for special education or other targeted programs. At the middle-school level, Baltimore spent $3,808 compared to EAI's $5,474, and no public middle schools exceeded the EAI average costs (p. 111).

EPI also looked at how EAI and the Baltimore schools allotted their dollars. EAI spent more on facilities and teacher training and less on general instruction. EPI's general conclusions and recommendations bear noting:

- Do everything possible to encourage competitive bidding.
- Carefully check the backgrounds, track records, and corporate structure of private voucher companies, especially their financial stability.
- Do not turn large sums of cash over to private providers who are likely to invest the money in ways that are riskier than your district's policies. Rather, schools should invest funds themselves and release them as needed to meet obligations.
- Collect good baseline data on student performance and school expenditures using both the privately managed schools, a group of control schools, and district averages for comparison.
- Require private providers to disclose both detailed expenditure reports that use line items which parallel those used in the school district, and relevant personnel and student data in a timely fashion.
- Write contracts that include accountability and performance standards.
- Establish per-pupil cost comparisons by school type (for example, K–6, elementary, grades 6–8 middle schools, grades 9–12 high schools, special education schools, alternative schools, and vocational technical schools).

"Though these recommendations will not guarantee a positive outcome, they should dramatically reduce the risks associated with private contracting" (p. 126).

EPIs call for would-be-contractor districts to look at "track records" is a source of some controversy. Good business practice would require such an examination, but for most of the companies involved—Edison, EAI, Beacon—there was no prior track record. A legitimate defense for using new companies in inner-city settings, however, is that there already exists a long track record of failure.

EPI also concluded that, independent of the quality of the schooling provided, "EAI has yet to show that it can make a profit by managing schools. To the extent that it does make a profit, the profit comes from interest earnings and speculation on the price of EAI stock" (p. 85). This does not mean that some of the individuals in EAI and other companies did not make money, drawing their salaries out of the commissions paid.

There has been no examination of the Hartford and Dade County programs to equal EPI's look at the situation in Baltimore, but as noted at the outset, all the contracts are now defunct and were cancelled under less-than-friendly circumstances (EPI's scrutiny of the funds EAI received from Baltimore and how it spent that money takes some fifty pages).

The Move Westward.   With the collapse of contracts in Connecticut, Maryland, and Florida, Golle abandoned the East Coast and EAI's original mission. He headed for the freer clime of the West, notably Arizona. He changed the corporation's name to The TesseracT Group, borrowing from Madeleine L'Engle's fantasy book, *A Wrinkle in Time*. A TesseracT is a fifth-dimensional corridor that leads to places otherwise unattainable. In its eastern venues, EAI had worked in poverty-ridden schools. Now it swung to the other extreme, opening private schools that cost as much as $8,000 a year in tuition. By the time the crisis loomed, EAI had three private schools, thirteen charter schools, and twenty-two private preschools. In March 1999, Golle moved TesseracT's headquarters from Minneapolis to the toney Phoenix suburb of Scottsdale.

TesseracT headed for Arizona in an upbeat mood. The company would no longer take over existing schools or open its charters in trailers or church basements; now, it would build the schools. TesseracT's initial application to the Arizona Charter School Board proposed building twelve elementary, middle, and high schools in the state over a three-year period that would enroll around 6,600 students.

TesseracT's troubles seemed to burst on an unsuspecting company and clientele alike. As late as 1999, Golle was still talking about expansion plans. "TesseracT Charter School Schedules Signup" was a headline in the May 1, 1999, *Arizona Republic*; "TesseracT Group Plans High School" was another, on August 3, 1999. Yet at the same time some sources of money had been closed off. Some of TesseracT's charter schools received as much as $1.95 per mile for student transportation, but reimbursed parents only 5¢ a mile. In just three months in 1999, TesseracT collected $760,000 in such fees. Legislators then closed the loophole that allowed such profit-making on student transportation.

TesseracT expanded too rapidly and found itself with cash flow problems that soon exacerbated its general condition. Unable to pay rent and construction costs, TesseracT borrowed $5 million from Benjamin Nazarian of the Pioneer Venture Fund. The loan agreement permitted Nazarian to convert the unpaid principal to 3.5 million shares of TesseracT stock. The company's shareholders rejected this deal, however, causing the loan's interest rate to jump from 12 percent to 18 percent annually. In early February 2000, TesseracT CEO Martha Taylor Thomas and CFO Richard Yonker both resigned. No reasons were ever given (*Arizona Republic*, 2000).

The shareholders' rejection of Nazarian's offer was a stroke of good luck for him as TesseracT stock soon plummeted. In early February 2000, the stock that had peaked at $48.50 traded for 56¢ a share and was dropped from its NASDAQ listing. "The worst is behind us," said Golle (Mattern, 2000a). It was not.

By May 2000, TesseracT's debt totalled $48.9 million and it was losing money at the rate of $12 million a year (Mattern, 2000b). To stanch the flow of money, TesseracT sold several schools and its business college. The schools were bought by Nobel Learning Communities (Mattern, 2000c), discussed later in this chapter.

For their part, parents of TesseracT students fretted over possible closures. Some said they were willing to pay even higher tuition. According to an article in *The Arizona Republic*, children in TesseracT schools move at their own pace and receive lots of individual attention. The schools don't have "the rigidly academic atmosphere of some college-prep private schools. Instead, parents say there's also emphasis on building life skills and emotional intelligence that will give their kids an edge in the world" (Gonderinger, 2000). For instance, first-graders learn to be comfortable speaking in front of large groups by participating in daily meetings where students address the entire school.

As noted, Golle said, "The worst is behind us." The *Arizona Republic* wasn't certain that this comment would hold up. "Golle, the man credited with creating the for-profit school industry, has been making a lot of promises and apologies lately" (Gonderinger, 2000, p. A1). A substantial amount of TesseracT's income came from overcharging for transportation. In at least one school, TesseracT had been collecting about $4,400 per student through its $1.95 a mile transportation charge. This year the schools get a flat fee of $174 per pupil. "'We don't know what the impact is going to be,' Golle said" (Mattern, 2000a, p. A1).

TesseracT limped into the 2000–01 school year having trimmed its administrative staff by 80 percent. It sold two schools to Nobel. Nazarian agreed to restructure their now-overdue loan, making it payable at the end of 2000. These efforts have proven insufficient to shore up the organization. On October 9, 2000, a school holiday (Columbus Day), TesseracT filed for Chapter 11 bankruptcy protection. Although the company has been visibly floundering financially since early 2000, Lucian Spataro, then TesseracT CEO, described the action as a "very strategic and well-planned filing" (Creno, 2000). He said the schools will remain open and operations will not be interrupted.

As of spring 2001, Spataro had kept his word. TesseracT sold two private schools—its biggest money-losers—to parents groups that had formed nonprofit corporations for that purpose (Mattern, 2001). Gan Yeladeem Learning Center, a Phoenix charter school, offered to buy a third. Court approval was pending (Ryman, 2001). The Catholic Diocese of Phoenix outbid another parents group for a fourth school, also pending court approval (Ryman, 2001).

On March 15, 2001, declaring that he had succeeded in selling some schools while keeping all schools operating, Spataro resigned (*Arizona Republic*, 2001). Chief Operating Officer Michael Lynch assumed the duties of the chief executive officer. Mr. Lynch would not discuss TesseracT's current situation or future plans, saying that he was not free to make any comments while the corporation remained in Chapter 11 (personal communication, April 4, 2001).

Needless to say, in the circumstances described above, nothing like a formal evaluation of the TesseracT schools has been forthcoming.

Edison Schools Incorporated: The Market in Theory versus the Market in Practice

No other project illustrates the attitudes toward making money in the public school sector and the cold water of reality better than the trajectory of Chris Whittle's Edison Project (so named because Edison didn't try to build a better candle, but invented a new means of producing light). No other project illustrates the differences—at times enormous—between what people theorize about market operations and what actually happens.

Whittle made a fortune early in communications, lost it, and had to sell his holdings. He then embarked on a series of adventures in other industries before announcing he planned to make his next fortune with a national system of private schools. They would be high tech, with a new, rich curriculum that Whittle would develop, a longer school day and year, and commensurate costs with public schools. Whittle scored public relations coups by hiring some highly visible people: Benno Schmidt, president of Yale University before becoming president of Edison, Chester E. Finn, Jr., former assistant secretary of education, and John Chubb of the Brookings Institution and coauthor of *Politics, Markets, and American Schools*. Finn has since left the project. At the project's inception in 1991, Whittle estimated he would have two hundred for-profit schools up and running by 1996 and one thousand by 2000.

Not everyone has been impressed. *New York Observer* business writer Christopher Byron had this take on the Whittle enterprises:

> Possessed by his own sense of visionary infallibility—and the baloney-spouting skills of a Harold Hill—Mr. Whittle soon had individuals ranging from Yale University president Benno Schmidt to President Jimmy Carter's top White House aide, Hamilton Jordan, to *Fortune* magazine editor William Rukeyser coming to work for him.
>
> Suitably adorned with such names all around him, Mr. Whittle thereafter went on to start up one wacky venture after the next. They ranged from a scheme for publishing books with ads in them, to piping advertiser-supported medical news into doctors' offices via cable TV, to the same basic idea for ad-supported news for kids in the classroom. The latter clunker, dubbed Channel One, was eventually sold to a Henry Kravis brainstorm called KIII Communications Corporation that is now spewing losses in all directions under the name Primedia, Inc. (Byron, 2000)

Going into the 2000–01 school year, Whittle has 113 schools, at least, using the Edison technique of counting, which public school folk might consider "fuzzy math." Edison can count three schools where a public district could only count one, because it considers grades K–5, 6–8 and 9–12 as separate schools, even if all grades are housed in one building. By the more usual reckoning, Edison has ninety buildings employing eighty-eight principals (Wyatt, 2001).

So far, the best that can be said is that the loss per student has fallen from $3,927 in 1996 to $603 in 1998–99, and to $389 in 1999–2000. In 1998–99, Edison had revenues of $132.8 million and lost $51 million. Since its inception, the project has lost $1.36 for every $1.00 it has made, a total of $197 million (Wyatt, 2001).

Although the company shows no profit, Whittle personally is doing quite well. His base salary for 1998–99 was $296,636, the same as his CEO Schmidt received. This is approximately three times the salary of a superintendent of a school district with as many students at Edison (38,000 pupils in 1999–2000;

57,000 in 2000–01). Whittle has also received more than $1 million from Edison for "professional services" and a loan of $5.6 million which he could use to buy 1.45 million shares of the company at $1.50 a share, tax free (the company covers them). If Whittle cashed out right now, he would make almost $32 million. And this is just for his stock option. Whittle has other holdings in Edison. After the company's public offering, the *New York Post* declared that Whittle's share of the company was worth $205 million (Miner, 2000). For his part, Schmidt received a low-interest loan of $1.8 million. If he loses his job, he receives $2.5 million and two years' salary. Other Edison officers have stock options worth, as of late October 2000, between $2.1 million and $16.8 million dollars, based on a stock valued at $27 per share.

These cozy arrangements led *Business Week* financial writer Diane Brady to declare that "Chis Whittle's IPO deserves a D–" (Brady, 1999). That grade might have been the invention of a headline writer; in the text, Brady actually writes, "this deal deserves to flunk." Brady also observes that in addition to making lots of money while the company loses lots of money, Whittle has pledged a large segment of his holdings in Edison to Morgan Guaranty Trust Co. If Whittle doesn't deliver, bankers will control about 15 percent of the company (Edison Schools, Inc., 2000). Meanwhile, not only is the number of Edison schools far fewer than the initial projections, but the schools are not new as originally conceived. Instead, they are mostly existing schools that have contracted for management services from Edison, either as public schools or charter schools.

In 1999, the Edison Project became Edison Schools, Inc., and the company went public, trading on the NASDAQ. It had hoped to offer the stock at $25 a share, but actually came out at $18. Since then the stock has risen as high as $30 per share and, as of June 2001, is selling at $25 a share.

Whittle has secured $20 million in low-cost bank loans which can be used for Edison facilities. Acquiring money for capital outlays has been problematic— banks have been skeptical about the company's long-term solvency necessary to secure mortgages (Arizona legislators attempted to overcome this problem by writing charters for fifteen years, the minimum term for a mortgage).

Early on, Edison realized that the original plan of developing a whole curriculum could not be realized. It would take too much time and money. As a consequence, the Edison curriculum includes the University of Chicago Mathematics Project materials ("based on years of systematic research," according to Edison materials), and Success For All, both programs developed by previously demeaned establishment educators.

Only some of the people currently listed as "The Edison Team" have any experience with public schools. In addition to Whittle and Schmidt, there is Chief Operating Officer Christopher Cerf, a lawyer formerly associated with arguing cases before the U.S. Supreme Court; Chief Education Officer John Chubb, a political scientist and coauthor of *Politics, Markets and American Schools;*

Executive Vice President Laura Eshbaugh, originally an editor at Whittle Communications; Executive Vice President Michael Finnerty, a former vice president for finance at Yale; Deborah McGriff, former superintendent of the Detroit (Michigan) public school system, and spouse to Howard Fuller, former superintendent of Milwaukee (Wisconsin) Public Schools and now ardent voucher advocate with a chair at Marquette sponsored by the like-minded Lynde and Harry Bradley Foundation; Executive Vice President for Development Manual Rivera, former superintendent of Rochester (New York) Public Schools; Chief Information Officer Donald Sunderland, former managing director of Global Technology and Derivative Products for the Union Bank of Switzerland; and Chief Financial Officer James L. Starr.

Starr is a certified public accountant who came to Edison from Sierra Health Services that, among other things, operates health maintenance organizations. Obtaining a person with Starr's background highlights the similarities between HMOs and the private management of schools.

Access to Information. Free-market principles hold that consumers need good information about products for markets to work properly. We have seen that EAI/TesseracT is not forthcoming with such data, and accurate information about the Edison schools can be obtained only with great difficulty. Let us examine some specific schools, and then discuss some generalizations from what we find in specific cases.

Washington Elementary School. Washington Elementary School in Sherman, Texas, run by Edison since 1995, was the first school Edison signed up. Edison's *Second Annual Report on School Performance,* issued in March 1999, gives Washington its highest rating (five stars) for "strongly positive" achievement gains (a Third Annual Report, dated August 2000, but posted only in November 2000, contains even *less* specific information than does the Second Annual Report). A report on Edison schools from the American Federation of Teachers, however, rates Washington's performance among the worst of Edison's efforts. At the end of the 1999–2000 school year, Washington's contract with Edison expired and the school chose not to renew it.

How could one school generate such disparate rankings and perceptions? Take the Edison report first. Edison provides six charts on test scores. Two show the percentage of students attaining minimum expectations on the TAAS for three years in grades 3 and 4. These charts show mixed results, with percentages both rising and falling.

The next two charts show the percentage of students meeting minimum expectations for the same cohort—the same students in grades 3 and 4 for 1995 to 1997, and for 1996 to 1998. These charts are organized differently than the previous charts, and many people would find them quite confusing and misleading. The first charts are shown with the each curriculum subject grouped together for the three years. The same-cohort charts, those which follow the same groups of children, are organized by grade and subject, not by year. The reader has to jump from one set of bars to another to see what is happening over time. When one does that, one finds that the percentage of students meeting minimum standards declined for both time periods.

Finally, two charts show changes in the Texas Learning Index from 1997 to 1998. The Texas Learning Index (TLI) is another means of tracking test scores for the same students over time. The Edison report makes no attempt to explain how the TLI is computed. It says only things like, "In 1998 Washington [Elementary School] had nearly the highest gains among the forty schools most similar to it statewide."

In the TLI, third-graders are used as a baseline and the index is calculated for the fourth grade; there is no fifth grade TLI for Washington, because it is a K–4 school. Once a school's TLI has been calculated, the Texas Education Agency compares it to those of demographically similar schools around the state. Very high-scoring students are removed from the TLI because they have no room to improve. The Edison report claiming a great TLI for Washington is accurate, but only for the year reported. In all three other years—1996, 1997, and 1999—Washington was in the bottom quartile of comparable schools.

Washington is chosen here as a concrete example because, although Edison brags about its performance, the company no longer has a contract with the school. When Washington terminated its relationship with Edison, Dallas was in the midst of initiating one. *Dallas Observer* reporter Jonathan Fox looked for reasons why Sherman Independent School District (SISD), which contains Washington, brought its contract with Edison to an end and what implications such reasons might have for Dallas (Fox, 2000).

Fox found some Edison supporters as well as detractors, and some of the dispute is a he-said-she-said affair. For instance, Sherman contends that the Edison experience cost them $4 million while Edison claims that their involvement in Sherman cost *Edison* $6 million. Other facts seem objective: Sherman administrators said that there had been some growth in test scores at Washington, but that scores had "soared" in the rest of the district.

Edison officials also seemed somewhat insensitive to the Washington neighborhood. Fox wrote that Washington Elementary School was 28 percent Hispanic and 24 percent black, and was located "in a part of the city where nearly every house needs a paint job, roofs sag, and the occasional worn sofa rests on a porch." On one trip, Edison officials arrived from the Dallas–Fort Worth airport in chauffeured Lincoln town cars (a similar gaffe occurred in Minneapolis where parents rejected Edison, in part because Edison officers were perceived as "behind this shield of Armani suits and gold jewelry" (Carter, 1999).

Edison's claims of reduced costs are also challenged both in Sherman and Dallas. One Dallas school trustee who opposed the contract wants to reduce the per-pupil stipend paid to Edison because the DISD (Dallas Independent School District) must still pay for transportation, food service, security, and other costs.

DISD superintendent Bill Rojas, an Edison advocate, said, "I know it's going to cost more money" (Rojas is a believer in Edison's pedagogy, not its business sense. He is quoted as saying "that stock is not going to be in my portfolio." The Dallas School Board terminated Rojas in May 2000, for reasons that appear to be unrelated to his Edison advocacy; he is now employed by an Edison competitor, Advantage Schools). In Sherman, the district surrendered the Edison schools' share of administrative costs, but didn't cut central office staff accordingly, thus retaining duplicate managers.

According to Sherman officials, Edison tried to save money by cutting corners on maintenance and by challenging bills. Sherman administrators ordered district staff to do maintenance work at Washington that Edison had failed to do although contractually obligated, simply because "This building belongs to SISD taxpayers. We can't afford for it to go downhill." One might have thought that Edison would have learned something from EAI, which bought a fair amount of community goodwill by making the schools it managed attractive places.

On the other hand, Edison appeared to have community support for things it did do outside of the academic arena. Mary Doclar, a reporter for the *Fort Worth Star-Telegram*, observed that even first-graders showed discipline as they moved from their classroom to a computer lab. When the teacher said "Would you please show everybody what Edison Excellence is?," a straggly line became "ruler-straight" and children folded their hands behind their backs. Edison also pleased parents by teaching what one parent called "core values: respect and honesty." This apparently had caused a substantial reduction in discipline problems (Doclar, 2000).

By selecting data and using internal testing data, the Edison annual report can claim that the seventeen schools opened between 1995 and 1997 have generated "a total of 143 trends of one, two or three years duration" (p. 10). Edison then weights these "trends" by their duration. "After weighting, for example, a positive trend that is three years long counts three times as much as a positive trend that is one year long" (p. 13). With this statistical sleight of hand, totally without any scientific merit, Edison then claims that the 143 total trends yield 176 weighted trends and that 136, or 77 percent, of these are positive. It further claims that the average annual percentile point gain on norm-referenced tests is 5 and that Edison students gain on average 6 percentage points on criterion-referenced tests (the prospectus issued to potential investors in 1999 puts the NRT gains at 4 "percentage points," whatever that might mean).

The Annual Report then contrasts these gains to "Achievement Gains in U.S. Public Schools. These are much smaller, –1 percent for reading for 9- and 13-year-olds in reading and zero for 9- and 13-year-olds in math" (p. 13).

On close examination, however, the metrics used for national trends are not the same as those used to measure Edison students. In fact, it is not at all clear what these numbers are. The legend on the chart says that they are the "Average Percentage Point Gain, National Assessment of Educational Progress, U.S. 9- and 13-year-olds, 1994–1996." The fine print, though, states that "Gains are for percentages of 9-year-olds reaching level 200 and 13-year-olds reaching level 250—minimum levels expected."

Thus the one chart implies first that they describe the percentage change in scores and second that they are changes in percentage of students reaching certain proficiency levels, proficiency levels that have been universally discredited by psychometricians. Beyond the vague specification of what the numbers refer to, there are certain fundamental problems with these data: They don't exist. There was no NAEP reading assessment in 1996 and no NAEP mathematics assessment in 1994. These statistics, whatever they might be, refer to data that have never been collected.

If the proper operation of a market requires that consumers have access to accurate information, consumers cannot make informed decisions about Edison schools. As noted, the information about Washington school is quite misleading. The NAEP information presented is not merely inaccurate; it is nonexistent.[14]

Even if one granted Edison the "5 percentile rank" gains, one could question this as a measure of efficacy. After all, the Edison day is one–third longer than the typical school day (8 versus 6 hours) and the Edison school year, even after being trimmed, is still 11 percent longer than the usual year (200 versus 180 days). Taken together, this means that students are in Edison schools fully 50 percent more hours per year than they are in regular schools (1600 [200 × 8] versus 1080 [180 × 6]). By the time students who start with Edison as first-graders finish sixth grade, they have spent as much time in school as rising sophomores in a regular public school. In addition to time in school, students in Edison schools are tested every month. Under these circumstances, one would certainly *expect* these schools to show some test score advantage.

The Thomas Edison School.   The longer day and longer year aspects of Edison have apparently taken their toll in the incidentally-named Thomas Edison School in San Francisco. An article by Tali Woodward in the July 19, 2000, *San Francisco Bay Guardian* stated that over half of Thomas Edison's teachers were quitting (Woodward, 2000a). "Frustrated by long hours, a rigid curriculum that emphasizes testing, and what they describe as a Big Brother atmosphere, teachers at [Thomas] Edison are abandoning what they initially saw as a welcome experiment. Even those who accepted the concept of a corporate schoolhouse now say ESI's cookie-cutter, bottom-line mentality harms everything from teacher morale to student development and diversity."

The scripted curriculum also turned off a number of teachers who felt they had lost all semblance of professionalism. "They literally give you a script with what you're supposed to say," said one teacher. "Every few months somebody from Edison would come in with a clipboard to make sure you had specific

---

14. During a debate with Whittle in September 2000, I mentioned these nonexistent numbers. Whittle gave no indication that they might have been merely a typographical error.

things hanging up in your classroom." According to Woodward, teachers who raised issues and proposed changes received a standard response: "Maybe our design is not for you." Teachers wondered about a company that invited them to leave rather than participate in the process of change.

Comments such as "maybe our design is not for you" evoke memories of the post-Sputnik days when curriculum development projects attempted to develop materials that would "speak directly to the child" without the intervention of the teacher. The materials were referred to as "teacher-proof." They were a disaster.

The administrators at the Thomas Edison school, all brought in by Edison, were accused of manipulating the process, instilling fear in teachers by telling them that if the teachers did not cooperate and get test scores up, the school would cease to exist. This was not true. Under those circumstances, the school simply would have reverted to the local school board's control.

There were also questions about the legality of Thomas Edison's charter and the validity of the teachers' signatures that led to Edison being brought in. School board rules forbid it to deal with a for-profit company so apparently some "fake" nonprofit entity was established as a go-between. There were allegations that teachers' signatures had been coerced in some instances and forged in others.

Discussions of vouchers, charters, privatization, and similar initiatives tend to be cast in words that carry the ring of idealism: doing right for the children, improving the system, giving poor children a chance, and so on. The above accounts from Texas and California might well be more what happens in the trenches.

Returning to the issue of costs and profitability, one way Edison cuts costs is by hiring younger, less-educated teachers. This would mitigate against high achievement because many studies have found teacher experience to be a powerful factor in student achievement. Only 12 percent of the Edison teachers in Wichita had a master's degree, compared with 47 percent nationally. Edison teachers had 5.6 years of experience compared to 10.2 years in the whole district. Although it cut its school year from 210 to 200 days as a cost-savings measure, it still runs a longer year than American public schools, with fewer holidays and more pressure to perform.

Average Edison classes contain twenty-eight students, compared to a national average of about twenty-four for elementary schools and thirty-one for high schools (National Center for Education Statistics, 1998, table 70). This again argues against high achievement as does teacher turnover which is higher in Edison schools than the national average. Edison officials in Texas balked when told that they could only put twenty-two students in a class and gave in only when shown that it was Texas *law* that caps class size at twenty-two. Edison is able to operate in similarly mandated California only because the founder of retail clothing giant Gap, Don Fisher, supplied $25 million to cover the additional costs of the smaller classes. Such resistance to small classes in the one instance and the need for additional subsidy in the other calls into question Edison's claim that their schools will not cost more than the typical public school.

In addition, the Gap deal has raised a number of eyebrows, including those of the California attorney general, Bill Lockyer (Woodward, 2000c). The Edison Schools received a gift from the D2F2[15] Foundation run by Gap's founders, the Fisher family. In return for this donation, D2F2 can purchase 1,696,750 shares of class-A stock at $7.96 a share. D2F2 unloaded 600,000 shares at $22 a share in August 2000, meaning that it has already recovered over half of its "gift." As this is written in June 2001, Edison stock is hovering around $25 a share. Should D2F2 cash in its remaining stock, it would realize some $28 million. D2F2 also has an option to pick up 188,750 heavily discounted class-B shares (Woodward, 2000b).

The California District Attorney will not say if it is looking into the matter to determine if such an arrangement compromises D2F2's status as a nonprofit, indicating that such a determination lies in the realm of the Internal Revenue Service. It certainly is a sweet arrangement: Foundation A gives company B X million dollars and gets Y million company shares at huge discount. Foundation then sells shares at market price and recoups outlay from those investing in company. This means that "D2F2 is making money off a company that it supports with tax-deductible dollars" (Woodward, 2000c).

The degree to which Edison is skimming high-achieving students from competing public and private schools is not clear. Some students in Edison schools come from outside the normal boundaries of the district that contains the Edison school. No analysis exists of these students' prior achievement, but the possibility for a selection bias is present. In addition, Edison schools accept students with special needs only if they can be instructed in regular classrooms. The costs of self-contained special education instruction is much higher than regular instruction, with multipliers running from 1.6 for mild learning disabilities to 16 for severe. Overall, the average multiple for all special education conditions is about 2.8. At a conference operated by Salomon Smith Barney for potential investors in the education industry, Edison CEO Schmidt told an audience that Edison would operate special education instruction within regular classrooms and without specialists.

The schools appeared to be carrying out Schmidt's promise. Nationally, 12 percent of students are classified as requiring special education. In Edison schools the figure was 7 percent. In Boston, the city with the highest percentage, it was 11 percent, substantially lower than the citywide average of 20 percent. Sherman officials stated that Edison's special education offerings in that district were "poor" (they also faulted Edison for not offering gifted and talented programs and for lax recruiting of bilingual teachers).

In the June 1998 issue of *The Education Industry Report*, John Fullerton, managing director of JP Morgan Capital, was quoted as saying this about Edison: "It is all about demand pull. Once it becomes objectively apparent that

---

15. D2F2 was formerly known as the Donald and Doris Fisher Family Foundation.

Edison's schools can show positive outcomes in schools, there are enough schools in the country that need improvement that it [Edison] will become an increasingly attractive alternative for districts looking to stimulate improvements through choice and competition." With JP Morgan betting on positive results, it would seem that Edison would have indeed relied on its results that are "objectively apparent," but Edison has chosen a riskier path. In July 2000, it commissioned the RAND corporation to conduct an "academic audit." Over a three-year period, RAND will examine test score changes in all Edison schools and will conduct a number of intensive case studies at particular schools.

Can Edison make money? Possibly. To date it has not. Edison staffers keep saying that the company will become profitable when it is large enough to realize "economies of scale." It is not clear where these economies reside. Whittle has missed projections of profit in the past. In 1998, Whittle told the *Education Industry Report*, "we get very close to making it in the year that starts July 1, 1998. We don't think we are going to quite make it, but . . . we will be pretty close. The '00 year, which is the year that will start July '99, we will make it easily . . ." (McLaughlin, 1998a). At a conference in September 2000, Whittle was looking more to 2004 for finally showing a profit.

It is true that the loss-per-pupil figure has fallen as Edison has grown, but, on the surface, this appears similar to the man who acknowledged he lost money on every sale, but made it up in volume. However, according to chief financial officer Starr, the individual schools are already profitable. What remains is to add sufficient numbers of these profit centers so that the general administration costs are spread across a large number of them (personal communication, August 27, 1998).

Edison's prospectus's statements about profitability are quite modest. Early on it apprises the readers of the financial losses to date and continues: "We have not demonstrated that public schools can be profitably managed by private companies and we are not certain when we will become profitable, if at all" (p. 9). The prospectus continues:

> Currently, there is a well-publicized nationwide shortage of teachers and other educators in the United States. In addition, we may find it difficult to attract and retain principals and teachers for a variety of reasons including the following:
>
> - we generally required our teachers to work a longer day and a longer year than most public schools;
> - we tend to have a larger proportion of our schools in challenging locations, such as low-income urban areas, which may make attracting principals and teachers more difficult; and
> - we believe we generally impose more accountability on principals and teachers than do public schools as a whole. (p. 10)

The prospectus probably should have also stated that Edison pays less for those longer days and years than do public schools. These factors might be the major causes behind Edison's recent announcement that it would get into the teacher-training business. One wag suggested that it would train teachers in skills that would be useful only in Edison schools, thereby binding the trainees to the corporation.

The prospectus also describes an Edison liability not commented on elsewhere: loans to charter schools that might not be repaid and loans for charter schools from financial organizations. In the latter case, Edison could be responsible for the loans even if the relationship with the school is terminated.

In what Edison calls a "research and development" and others might call a diversification plan, Edison is looking into the possibility of taking over whole districts. Unlike the EAI/TesseracT venture which collapsed in Baltimore and Hartford, Edison will be looking at some of the 13,000 districts that have 5,000 students or fewer. It refers to such arrangements as "total partnerships," shying away from the harsher-sounding "takeovers."

Edison is also moving on other fronts. It has launched a venture with Vantage Learning to put its Benchmark Assessment System online. Little is known about the Benchmark tests except that they are Edison-developed tests used as classroom exams. Tung Le, director of assessment for Edison, said that items are developed by teachers and others familiar with the curriculum. Formal studies on item characteristics, reliability, and so on, are being conducted, but no report will be forthcoming until the end of 2001. In the meantime, the tests are in use, although Le advised that teachers are told not to use the test to grade children: They are to be used to inform the teachers "where the children are" (Le, 2001).

The 2000–01 school year was not kind to Edison. In October 2000, a report from the America Federation of Teachers concluded that "Five years into the Edison experiment, ample data now exist for the public to use in making more informed judgments about progress in Edison schools. At this point, Edison schools mostly do as well as or worse than comparable (public) schools; occasionally, they do better. This mediocre record has not been evident to many observers of Edison schools for several reasons" (Nelson, 2000, p. 6). Edison presented the most favorable data, and presented it in a most favorable light, and not all data were compiled in one place.

In December 2000, an evaluation from Western Michigan University reached similar conclusions (Miron and Applegate, 2000). This report stated, "Our findings suggest that Edison students do not perform as well as Edison claims in its annual reports on student performance" (p. 21). Taking a sample of ten schools, Miron and Applegate found that Edison rated the trends as "strongly positive" in five schools, "positive" in three, and "mixed" in two. Miron and Applegate, on the other hand, found *no* "strongly positive" trends, positive trends in three schools, mixed trends in four, negative trends in two, and strongly negative trends in one.

The AFT report pointed out that much of Edison's curriculum has been well researched and is highly regarded in many quarters. Why, then, doesn't Edison do better? the report asked. It had no definitive answer because it analyzed only achievement data, not the causes, but the AFT did speculate: "Certain characteristics of current Edison schools may help explain the lower-than-expected achievement. Edison relies heavily on inexperienced teachers, and teacher turnover rates in Edison schools are higher than in most public schools" (Nelson, 2000, p. 6). The report also suggested that some segments of the curriculum were not fully implemented, a critical factor in their effectiveness.

In San Francisco, changes in the makeup of the board of education were not in Edison's favor. The board conducted an investigation and charged Edison with "discriminating against black students, urging special education kids to apply elsewhere, and threatening teachers" (Guthrie, 2001). Edison Vice President Gaynor McCown called the charges, "an outright lie" (Guthrie 2001a) and the investigation "a sham" (Wyatt, 2001a), pointing out that 80 percent of the parents at the school had signed a petition in support of Edison (Guthrie, 2001a).

The board's 6–1 vote gave Edison 90 days to correct the problems or the contract would be revoked and the school would revert to its previous status as a public school. Edison officials said they would work with the board and the district during the 90-day period, but if that fails, Edison plans to appeal the decision to the State Board of Education, which under California's charter school law has the power to overturn the decision and grant Edison a new contract.

In New York, school chancellor Harold Levy sought to convert five of the city's lowest-scoring schools to charter status, a move strongly favored by Mayor Rudy Giuliani (Wyatt, 2000; Goodnough, 2000). Several companies bid for the contract, but many community groups were eliminated from the bidding process by constraints such as prior management of schools with at least 450 students and a cash reserve of $1 million. Edison was selected, but it was not clear by what process or what criteria.

New York Times reporter Edward Wyatt thought Edison's gambit was risky and called it "Edison's biggest test" (Wyatt, 2001d). Wyatt portrayed the scheme as an if-you-can-make-it-there-you-can-make-anywhere ploy. Whittle seemed to agree, saying, "If we do a great job in these schools, we believe there will be more schools headed our way." Acquiring more schools is critical to Edison's survival because its putative strategy requires an economy-of-scale to turn a profit. According to Edison, more schools mean small "administrative costs" for each, eventually resulting in a black ledger entry. Edison also needs more funds from foundations and venture capitalists, revenue more likely to become available if the foundations and capitalists see that Edison is growing.

Levy declared that the parents of the selected schools had to approve the change. For Edison to manage them, 50 percent of the parents had to vote in Edison's favor. Initially, Edison was put in a fox-in-the-henhouse position and allowed to conduct the vote itself. Community groups, particular ACORN (Association for Community Organization for Reform Now), protested vehemently and were permitted to send out literature opposing Edison. Levy also agreed to distribute five ACORN flyers to parents, but there were allegations that ACORN had also illegally obtained confidential parent lists from the schools themselves (Campanile, 2001b).

The voting lasted more than two weeks, but well before it was over, people were talking about what went wrong for Edison:

- Parents felt blindsided about their schools being put on the management auction block.
- Only the for-profit Edison was awarded the contract. Smaller, community-based groups were shut out.
- Levy did not vigorously campaign for his own plan.
- Edison was to be reimbursed $500,000 for campaign expenses (a provision decided before the vote). (Campanile, 2001a)

Whatever the reason, the vote failed by margins that surprised everyone. Edison officials predicted victory in at least two of the five schools. Even if a majority of voters had voted for Edison, the company would have suffered defeat because fewer than 50 percent of parents voted at any given school. As it was, 80 percent of the voting parents turned Edison down. Even at the school considered most likely to accept Edison, only 34 percent of the parents voted for the contract. "Given the energy and effort and sacrifice our team put into this, I certainly thought we would have more votes," said Rev. Floyd Flake, a minister in Queens who is also the head of Edison's charter school division (Goodnough, 2001).

Mayor Giuliani announced a plan to privatize twenty schools by contract and then give parents a choice to stay or leave. Levy, backed by lawyers at the Board of Education, said that handing schools over to a private company without a vote would be illegal. Edison put on a brave face, noting that it had recently signed agreements in Chester, Pennsylvania, Clarke County (Las Vegas), Nevada, and Miami-Dade County, Florida. Edison's financial division said that Edison's revenues would rise to $370 million in the year that would end June 30, 2001, and to $560 million the following year (Goodnough, 2001).

On the other hand, shortly before the vote, Edison offered 6.7 million shares, raising $81 million. Half of the shares were sold by the company. The other half were sold to officers and other shareholders. Whittle pocketed $16 million from the sale (Wyatt, 2001c).

Sylvan Learning Systems

Twenty-year-old Baltimore-based Sylvan Learning Systems does not present itself as a competitor to public schools. Indeed, an article about a potential Sylvan contract with Kansas City, Missouri, schools observed, "Sylvan touts recommendations from public school clients that would make almost any principal or superintendent envious" (O'Connor, 1999). How has Sylvan accomplished this remarkable public relations coup, and can the good will last?

Before answering these questions, we need to track the history of this idiosyncratic organization, which got its start when Douglas Becker decided to skip college and make money. With a partner, Christopher Hoehn-Saric, Becker launched Sylvan Learning Centers, designed to provide remedial instruction in an intense setting—the pupil–teacher ratio for the centers is usually 3–1.

Sylvan's strategy over the years has been to find an area of high need and then to fill that need. When Becker sensed a lack of accessible testing, he started Sylvan Prometric in 1993, becoming the world's largest provider of computer-administered tests, administering over 300 different tests, including several from ETS. In 1999, Becker felt that Prometric, although profitable and growing rapidly, was taking up too much of the organization's time and efforts. He sold the company to Thomson Corporation, a Canadian publishing house, for $775 million.

When Becker gleaned that English was becoming the lingua franca, he set up the Wall Street Institute, now one of the largest providers of English language instruction in the world. Then, convinced that globe-trotting executives could benefit from a distance-learning setting that updated their "global marketplace skills," Becker established Caliber to provide instruction, including Wharton Direct, an attempt to provide a Wharton business education without attending the famed Wharton School of Business at the University of Pennsylvania. When he decided that European nations could not meet a growing middle class's burgeoning demand for tertiary education, he spent $50 million for a Spanish university and has plans to buy more in about ten countries.

These ventures have not always succeeded. Caliber has yet to turn a profit. When Becker took the company public, it opened at $14 a share, but by June 2001 was down to 31 cents. Sylvan's own stock opened at $5 when the company went public in 1993. Lately it has seen its stock fall from a high of $33 per share to $18 in June 2001. The reason? "Because it consisted of a number of unrelated businesses, it has been tougher for investors to understand the company's prospects and to be confident that the company was well run. That's why Sylvan Learning has been selling or spinning off its extraneous businesses. . . ." (Patalon, 2000).

Reacting to this perception, and armed with the income from the sale of Prometric, Sylvan made a strategic shift in emphasis. "After an appraisal that started last year while investors pounded Sylvan stock, three options occurred to Douglas Becker, the company's chairman and chief executive officer. Sylvan could commit to being a conventional large company, putting its management under endless pressure to increase earnings every year; go private, removing it from Wall Street's demands; or, make a more radical shift by selling some assets and becoming an investor itself. Sylvan chose the latter" (Somerville, 2000).

The "radical shift" commits Sylvan to a $500 million "incubator" project in which it will try to grow Internet-oriented companies. It expects to house a large number of these businesses on a single "campus" that would require 400,000 square feet of space and 1,000 to 3,000 high-tech workers (Ambrose, 2000).

Now, about that goodwill. Partly it comes from doing good deeds. Becker is chairman of the Children's Museum in Baltimore. He also established Book Adventure with partners Barnes and Noble, Houghton Mifflin, Lycos, and R. R. Bowker (www.bookadventure.org, or www.bookadventure.com; the latter tells you about the former). Book Adventure encourages students to read. It provides quizzes about the three thousand books on its list and children can win prizes, such as a trip to Orlando, if they take a lot of quizzes in a short time and get perfect scores on them. Of Book Adventure, Maggi Gaines, executive director of Baltimore Reads, a nonprofit literacy group, had this to say: "Education is big business, and we're naïve if we don't understand that. When I look at Sylvan, I see a corporation that's bottom-line-driven and philanthropy-driven. Those two things are compatible when executed properly" (Murray, 1999).

Perhaps more important than the altruism, however, is the fact that, from one perspective, Sylvan is free. Although Sylvan charges $1,500 per pupil, virtually all of the contracts are for services paid for with Title 1 money. It is therefore easy to consider it as "off budget." The teacher-pupil ratio does get results. Although no board would spend its own money for a program with only three pupils per tutor, it's all right if federal dollars are involved. It therefore does not appear at this time that Sylvan presents much of a threat to public schools. But if Douglas Becker ever thinks he sees an unmet demand as with his other projects. . . .

Beacon Education Management (Formerly Alternative Public Schools)

Beacon Education Management was begun in 1992 by business school graduates John Eason and William DeLoache. According to Eason, both had at one time been involved in programs to aid inner-city kids, and their interests began to focus on education as their own children entered school. They first bid on a contract in Tennessee and lost. This appears, however, to have given them connections with former Tennessee governor and former secretary of education Lamar Alexander.

Currently, Beacon provides a range of services from consulting to total school management. It has schools in Massachusetts, North Carolina, South Carolina, Illinois, Michigan, and Arizona. It recently bought a 50 percent interest in Pontiac-based JCR Inc., a charter school management firm (charter schools in Michigan are public entities, but can contract with private firms for various management services; in 2000, some 70 percent of Michigan charter schools contracted for such services). It also acquired ABS, Inc., which provides a variety of services to seventy-five charter schools in Arizona.

As Alternative Public Schools (APS), Beacon acquired a great deal of publicity with one of its first management contracts, that for Turner Elementary School in Wilkinsburg, Pennsylvania. Wilkinsburg is a town of 20,000 outside of Pittsburgh whose fortunes sank with the steel industry. At Turner, 78 percent of the students are eligible for free or reduced-price lunches.

In casting about for ways to raise achievement at Turner, a newly elected school board found APS in 1993 and awarded the company a contract in 1994 to manage their school. From the beginning, controversy swirled, as some people found it perplexing that the board would turn over Turner's management to a group that, at the time, had not managed a single school. Actually, there was already considerable hostility in the air, created by a vicious combination of teacher strikes, extraordinary teacher protection laws, tax increases, low test scores, and charges of teacher complacency and incompetence.

That incendiary mix flared when APS replaced all twenty-four teachers at Turner before starting the 1995–96 school year. A judge declared that the contract was illegal under Pennsylvania law and issued a temporary injunction. The conservative Landmark Legal Foundation showed up to represent the school board. It hired the law firm of Strassburger, McKenna, Gutnick, and Potter to argue the case. This firm also represents Richard Mellon Scaife, who provides a great deal of money to right-wing organizations, including Landmark and the Heritage Foundation.

The Pennsylvania Supreme Court permitted the contract to continue, but did not rule on specific evidence in the case, instead sending it back to the lower courts. Pennsylvania governor Tom Ridge and National Education Association (NEA) president Keith Geiger both showed up to applaud and denounce the contract, respectively. After a suit was filed by the NEA and its state affiliate, the Pennsylvania State Education Association, the case went to arbitration to reinstate the dismissed teachers. The arbitrator rule against APS, citing, among other things, the fact that there had been no decline in student enrollments, a prerequisite to any layoffs.

On August 6, 1997, Judge R. Stanton Wettich in the Allegheny Court of Common Pleas ruled that it was not legal to turn over schools to private, for-profit companies. He noted that new charter legislation permitted contracting with nonprofits, but did not authorize contracts with for-profits. At the time of the ruling, Wilkinsburg was not in a position to make itself eligible for a charter in the 1997–98 school year and the judge left the contract in place. APS–Beacon terminated its relationship with Wilkinsburg at the end of the 1997–98 school year and is awaiting further developments in charter legislation. The test scores at Turner, already low, not surprisingly fell considerably during the strife. At least two APS supporters have lost their seats on the school board.

Beacon currently operates about thirty schools around the nation and remains unprofitable. In the past, Beacon has claimed to be profitable at the school level, but not at the organizational level. All services at this point are rendered in fixed-fee contracts.

One news item presented on Beacon's website states that "George Bush Visits Newest Beacon School." The first impression was that then-presidential candidate George W. Bush had singled out the school for praise. However, it turned out to be George Prescott Bush, teen-heartthrob nephew of George W. Ironically, the St. Louis school that Bush visited was named the Thurgood Marshall School.

Nobel Learning Communities, Inc.

Founded in 1984, Nobel Learning Communities, (formerly known as Nobel Educational Dynamics and Rocking Horse Child Care Centers of America) has been called McSchool since most of its buildings are built to similar specifications. Bennigan's or TGIFriday would be a more appropriate moniker for Nobel schools. Nobel aims only for rapidly growing, upwardly mobile suburbs. It is, for the time being anyway, a niche operator. It pitches its schools at those who are interested in private schools but who are looking for a more reasonably priced alternative, with a tuition of around $6,000 a year. The average tuition range for NAIS member schools is from $8,015 for preschool to $12,834 for secondary school (McGovern, 2000). Thus, until a voucher plan comes along to provide some tuition money to lower-income families, Nobel largely appeals to yuppies.

Indeed, Nobel's CEO, A. J. "Jack" Clegg, says his company is for the two-working-parent family that needs a place to drop the kids off on the way to work and pick them up on the way home (Nobel schools mostly stay open until six or seven o'clock). In 1998, Clegg also said that once there is more standardization of charter school legislation across states, he will probably enter that market. Thus, charter schools open doors for private firms if the legislation is not restrictive. In Michigan, the number of charters soliciting management services has grown to 70 percent in 1998–99. Nobel has since moved into the charter market, acquiring two Arizona charters in 2000 from the troubled TesseracT Group.

Nobel intends to either take over or develop about seven charters per year. Nobel's income from its own schools comes from tuition. In the charter realm, it charges a percentage of income to the school. In developing a charter school, Nobel works with the group proposing the charter, then acts as the agency that manages the school's business affairs. If the charter application is rejected, Nobel realizes no income.

Nobel currently operates about 160 schools in 13 states, with most of them concentrated in California, followed by Pennsylvania, New Jersey, Virginia, and North Carolina. About two-thirds are preschools and the rest are elementary and middle schools—Nobel does not operate in high schools. Its annual report identifies it as the "largest, nonsectarian, private school system in the United States. . . ."

In articles about Nobel (named for the inventor of TNT, not the computer company; it is supposed to convey the notion of being the best), one senses an aura of mystery about how Nobel can operate with an average class size of seventeen and turn a profit, which it has done in most years, 1997 being the lone exception. One way is with low salaries. While Clegg pays himself $421,000 a year, the average teacher makes about one-tenth of that, around $26,000, with a range from $20,000 to $33,000. The average for public school teachers is around $39,000. According to Clegg, Nobel teachers will work for these smaller sums because, thanks to locations in relatively affluent areas, they are not required to be policemen, counselors, and social workers, roles often forced upon public school teachers. Nobel hires only certified teachers, and the organization was considered for admission to the National Association of Independent Schools. After deliberations, the NAIS decided to stick with its policy of admitting only nonprofits.

Official Nobel literature claims that its teachers work for low salaries because they are dedicated to teaching. However, the company experienced some difficulty when California mandated small class sizes and some Nobel teachers defected to the newly available positions. (As a small digression, we can note that so did a number of teachers in poor urban areas. Teachers in poor areas come from less rigorous universities and have less training in the subjects they teach than do those in suburban districts. The impact of the small-class mandate was in part to drain off some of the good teachers poor districts had, leaving poor urban students with even less well-trained teachers than they had before the law was passed. Even so, first and second-year evaluations find overall gains in test scores.)

Nobel also economizes by "clustering." It will establish a cluster of preschools in an area, then add an elementary school, with the preschools serving as feeders. The schools generally have only a principal and an assistant. Other support is "regionalized" to serve the whole cluster. Personnel growth in public schools has been largely in support staff—the proportion of teachers has declined from 70 percent in 1950 to 52 percent in 1995, while the proportion of administrators to teachers dropped from 2.6 percent to 1.7 percent in the same period (NCES, 1997).

As with its central offices, the Nobel libraries are "regionalized" with one library serving a number of schools, saving on both capital outlay and book acquisitions. One interviewee called the library she had seen "pathetic," about the size of a typical white-collar worker's office. The one that I visited in Loudoun County, Virginia, was about twice that size with eight computers, but books on a single wall.

Nobel also saves money by minimizing capital outlays. Most of its schools are leased. In some instances it has bought schools, but typically, when it builds something new it sells the building to a Real Estate Investment Trust, then leases the building back for fifteen to twenty years. Thus, if Nobel's market changes in a particular locale, it can move out of that locale without having to dispose of the building. It will often build in areas where rapid increases in population are occurring or are predicted to occur, such as Loudon County, Virginia, and Las Vegas, Nevada.

According to vice-president Barbara Presseisen (now retired), the schools are constructed so that they need not remain single-function buildings. Mentioning a new facility in Loudon County, she noted that when the building was started, there was nothing around it; now there are shopping centers into which the building could be integrated if it lost its value as a school.

On July 13, 1998, Nobel announced that it had received $10 million in capital from Allied Capital. This doesn't seem to have done much for its stock price. Over a fifty-two week period from May 1997 to May 1998, its stock ranged from $4.50 to $10.37, and the week of an *Education Week* story about the company, it was at $8.25. In June 2001, it was hovering around $9.

From the beginning Nobel boasted a fairly prestigious advisory board of educators: Arthur Costa, Emeritus of California State University; Drew Gitomer of ETS; Zalman Usiskin, University of Chicago; Cathy Collins Black, Texas Christian; John N. Mangieri, past president of Arkansas State University; and Barbara Presseisen, former vice president and chief education officer at Nobel, who came over from Research for Better Schools.

Presseisen advised that Nobel adopt a curriculum adapted from the company's Merryhill schools in California, which are fifty years old. In addition, the standards of various professional groups have been used to determine if the Nobel curriculum accomplishes what the organizations recommend. In the preschools, the standards for kindergartens have been "back-mapped" to determine what would be necessary at ages three and four to get students ready for the standards that first appear in kindergarten. The preschools also seek to have a "developmentally appropriate" curriculum as recommended by the National Association for the Education of Young Children.

In addition to appealing to middle-class families, the small class size also appears to be appealing to families with very bright children. Presseisen claimed that some kindergarten children at Nobel can read at fourth- and fifth-grade levels in kindergarten.

It is unlikely that a proper study of test scores will be conducted. As we have noted several times, such a study would involve collecting test information on the children *before* they received any instruction at the Nobel schools. This could be accomplished either by administering the standardized test that Nobel uses, the Stanford 9, at the time of enrollment, or by collecting information on children from their previous school. The latter procedure would be more difficult as, in all likelihood, the children would have taken a number of tests, not just the Stanford 9. The numbers of students are likely not large enough to provide reliable estimates of averages for the five most commonly used tests.

As might be expected in a press release from a for-profit corporation, the presentation of the test data is designed to put the company in the best possible light. The data are presented in grade equivalents. Grade equivalents that are better than average are more impressive because they appear to constitute whole years of time. In addition, most people draw the wrong conclusion about what a grade equivalent means (discussed below). For Nobel, we find that in 1998 their Merryhill eighth-grades scored at the grade equivalent of 11.5. This looks like they are almost four years ahead of the average student. Many parents would find this impressive. However, when converted to percentile ranks, it comes out as only the 65th percentile.

Even more misleading are grade equivalent scores from 1997, which put the reading score for the Merryhill eighth-graders at 8.6. To someone not familiar with grade equivalents, this score probably looks a little bit above average. However, it would only be average if the test were given in the sixth month of the eighth grade. There the average score *should* be 8.6. In fact, the 8.6 converts only to the 48th percentile, indicating that the norms were likely set in March and April (norms always cover about a six-week period).

Unfortunately, things get more confusing. A grade equivalent of, say, 11.5 for an eighth-grader does not mean that these eighth-graders can read material usually not seen until the middle of the junior year of high school. It refers to the score that the average eleventh-grader would make *on eighth grade material.* Moreover, the 11.5 grade equivalent is a pure statistical abstraction: No eleventh- or twelfth-graders actually took the eighth-grade test. To test children three or four years higher (or lower) than the stated grade level of the test would be prohibitively expensive for the test publishers. The 11.5 grade-level figure in an eighth-grade test is an extrapolation, likely from students taking the test in only three grades—7, 8, and 9.

Given their target audience, Nobel can make no provision for special education services. In addition, should Nobel's operation expand, it will be skimming bright students from public schools. ETS's Gitomer finds the operation "interesting"—it will be interesting, he said, to see what a school with a mostly bright population can do free of the bureaucratic constraints that afflict many public schools. It is unlikely that a research and assessment program will ever be adequately structured to permit us to know. If Nobel expands, some project might examine the impact on the affected district(s).

In late September 2000, Nobel signed a partnership agreement with South Ocean Development Corporation, thus linking the largest providers of private education in the United States with their counterparts in the People's Republic of China. According to a press release, they plan to establish a model "international school" in Beijing, which they will then market elsewhere in China, and to develop "education-based" preschools.

Advantage Schools, Inc.

Advantage Schools, Inc., is a relatively new and small operation. The 1997–98 school year was its first running schools, in Rocky Mount, North Carolina, and Phoenix. In 1998–99, it opened six new schools in Jersey City, New Jersey, Malden and Worcester, Massachusetts, San Antonio, Texas, Chicago, Illinois, and Kalamazoo, Michigan. Advantage is currently seeking partners in Philadelphia, true to its pattern of establishing schools in troubled urban areas where existing schools might be crowded or display low test scores, or where people are dissatisfied with the quality of education for any number of reasons. Here, Advantage approaches people who might be interested in serving on the board of one of their schools.

The corporation was started by William Edgerly (chairman of the board), Steven Wilson (president), and Theodor Rebarber (vice president). Edgerly was chairman of the State Street Bank in Boston and had a long-standing interest in education reform. He created "CEOs for Fundamental Change," a group of 300 Massachusetts CEOs who lobbied for education reform. Wilson had worked at the right-wing Pioneer Institute in Boston and wrote a book on reforming Boston's schools. He later became a special assistant to Massachusetts governor William Weld and helped write Massachusetts's charter legislation. Rebarber worked for the Edison Project for a time and later, with Congress, he helped write the Washington, D.C., charter law (according to the September 7, 1998, *New Yorker*, Weld now manages an equity fund focused on for-profit education).

Advantage is supported by Fidelity Ventures, part of Fidelity Investments; Bessemer Ventures; U.S. Trust out of New York; and Kliner, Perkins, Coffield, and Byers, a Menlo Park, California, venture capital firm. The company is not yet profitable but hopes to be within a year. The company extracts a flat fee, based on a fixed percentage of the school's budget. If a school operates in a deficit, Advantage must come up with the cash to cover it.

Currently, Advantage operates K–5, retrofitting buildings that were not initially designed as schools. The schools typically enroll 500 to 550 pupils. Advantage plans to add one grade each year to its existing schools. It currently utilizes the Bereiter–Engelmann DISTAR curriculum (Direct Instruction Strategies for Teaching Arithmetic and Reading). This curriculum, developed in the late 1960s, has been expanded to include natural sciences, spelling, and cursive writing. In addition to the material quoted in its introduction, Advantage has this to say about the DISTAR approach and how it contrasts with more traditional classroom techniques:

> In a typical reading program, the teacher is given guidelines on how to present the material. For example, when teaching reading comprehension the teacher might be told, "discuss the concept of main idea." Guidelines such as this leave tremendous latitude concerning what the teacher actually says and does. It is very easy for teachers to knowingly change the wording used to teach essential skills or concepts, making it especially difficult for students to learn . . . In a DI [direct instruction] lesson, what the teacher says is actually printed out on the page. The students' responses are also printed out on the page. Teacher wording is thereby controlled, making it easier for students to learn.
>
> Q: Doesn't Just Reading What Is On a Page Get Boring For The Students— Or, How About For The Teacher?
>
> . . . In fact, one of the things teachers must learn how to do is to present material in a lively manner. In order to achieve this delivery goal, lessons that are about to be delivered must be studied, especially when they contain unfamiliar formats . . . DI lessons are designed to limit the amount of teacher talk and to give students many opportunities to respond, and, in order to achieve relatively high rates of pacing, teachers must be fluent in the script.

As noted in the introduction, students might make as many as 360 responses in a half-hour lesson. The intellectual depth of such responses is necessarily low. In addition, such lessons teach that there is only one right answer.

New York Times reporter Michael Winerip visited an Advantage School and came away less than thrilled with their approach. His host, a corporate spokesman who had flown down with him to North Carolina, told Winerip, "All the kindergarten kids read, you know." Winerip became suspicious about the instruction when he found the receptionist teaching a top fifth-grade math group. She told him, "All you have to remember is you can't go off the script."

Winerip, however, did go off the script. He brought in his own books. Confronted with a story that began, "I am a ghostie," a kindergartner was unable to cope with "I." Another child fared no better trying to read a story that began, "Drip, drip, drop." Given repeated hints about the story from pictures showing raindrops, the boy finally said, "Raindrops . . . no, I don't know." A girl managed to sound out a few of these words "in agonizingly slow fashion."

The curriculum for Advantage middle and high schools is currently under construction. According to vice president for business Josh Solomon, some of it is coming "off the shelf" while other pieces are being developed. Advantage plans two tracks in high school: one leading to an International Baccalaureate, and the other to a diploma representing highly developed technical skills. This workforce-skills curriculum "will be designed and implemented in partnership with local and national business, ensuring that students will be trained to the highest skill standards and will gain a credential that is valued by employers."

In March 2001, Advantage's annual report concentrated on test-score changes. However, these changes come from fall-to-spring test administrations, which can be unreliable—fall-to-fall or spring-to-spring are preferable. In addition, because Advantage students are mostly low-scoring, one could expect some improvement in test scores simply from regression to the mean. Finally, Advantage has a 200-day academic year, and it appears that the fall administration was earlier than the norms for the test presume, potentially artificially depressing their scores. Alternatively, if the tests were given after the same number of school days, there would be twenty more days of instruction between fall and spring testing than the test norms presume.

Advantage has lost more contracts than any other EMO—five as of the end of the 2000–01 school year, including the school that Winerip visited. Various reasons have been given, including management problems, communication failures, and disillusionment with the Direct Instruction method. Advantage officers have claimed that the company can be profitable with thirty schools, but currently it has only about a dozen. In early 2001, Wilson was dislodged as CEO and Rebarber left, as did vice president for instruction Kathleen Madigan, apparently out of frustration that Advantage spent too much time on the bottom line and not enough on education (Greenberger, 2001).

Corporate Family Solutions/Bright Horizons

Corporate Family Solutions and Bright Horizons, which merged into one corporation in July 1998, are mostly involved in preschool child care, especially that provided at the workplace. However, they are worth exploring here because of their size, pedigree, and recent activities, which have taken them beyond the preschool years.

Corporate Family Solutions was founded by a genuinely odd couple: Lamar Alexander and Bob Keeshan (Captain Kangaroo). The official story is that Keeshan had always been interested in moving into preschool education but couldn't find an operation he thought worthy of his involvement until he saw an on-site day care center run by Dominion National Bank (now First Union) in Roanoke, Virginia.

Keeshan apparently spoke of this center and his enthusiasm for it at a talk he gave in Knoxville, Tennessee. In the audience was Brad Martin, CEO of Proffitt's Department Stores. Martin was a good friend of Lamar Alexander, who at the time—the mid-1980s—was casting about for a business to both invest in and operate. Martin put Keeshan in touch with Alexander. They started the CFS company in 1987. Both later left the company.

Bright Horizons was started in 1986 by the husband-and-wife team of Roger Brown, who is CEO, and Linda Mason, who is president, after they noticed a dearth of quality child care in the Boston area. Brown and Mason had worked in the field of international humanitarian aid, co-directing the Save the Children relief effort during the 1984 Sudan famine, also working in Thailand and Cambodia for CARE and UNICEF. Mason also founded The Horizons Initiative, an organization that serves homeless children in the Boston area.

In April 1998, the Nashville-based Corporate Family Solutions and Boston-based Bright Horizons announced a merger. At the time, Corporate Family Solutions operated 100 centers in 29 states and the District of Columbia while Bright Horizons operated 155 also in 29 states and D.C. Together, they have centers in forty states. Bright Horizons went into the merger with 4,600 employees and, in 1997, had $85 million in revenue and $1.473 million in net income. Corporate Family had 4,000 employees and $77.7 and $1.401 million, respectively. Both companies are traded on the NASDAQ.

Both companies have some impressive educator names on their boards: T. Berry Brazelton of Harvard University and Sharon Lynn Kagan and Edward Zigler (the father of Head Start) of Yale University sit on the board of directors at Bright Horizons. Bettye Caldwell, former president of the National Association for the Education of Young Children, and Jerome Murphy, dean of the Harvard Graduate School of Education, adorn Corporate Family's board. John McLaughlin, founder of *The Education Industry Report*, is also on the Corporate Family board. Both organizations like to boast of the number of their clients that are either in the Fortune 500 or who are picked by *Working Woman* and *Working Mother* magazines as "family friendly."

Schools at Work.   In November 1997, Corporate Family Solutions acquired the Orlando, Florida-based Schools At Work (SAW), thus breaking beyond the preschool years. SAW was started as a one-person operation by Mary Anne

Ward, who had previously worked for Schools On Location, a company that provides educational services for children making movies, working for MTV or Ringling Brothers, and so on.

SAW puts schools into corporate buildings. To date, all of these have been public schools, with the corporation supplying the facilities and maintenance, and the school district the teachers and administrators. SAW initially convinces a company to do a feasibility study in which Ward determines such factors as how much space is needed, how many employees might use the school, and how much worker turnover and absenteeism can be reduced. If the corporation then decides to move ahead, Ward works with it and the local school district to bring the arrangement to fruition.

Ward claims that test scores are high but that the corporate schools have more diversity than many neighborhood schools because all employees from the janitor to the CEO can use the facility. She also claims that the in-house schools do reduce employee absenteeism, tardiness, and turnover, to an extent that some companies have realized profits when pitting their school's expenses against money saved. Assuming that the school district involved needed the additional space for its students, it saves by not having to spend for capital development.

Because the workplace school is a public school, provisions for special education must be maintained. For the parents of some disabled children, having the child go to work with them makes life easier. Children at workplace schools are seldom those who need full-day special services. In some instances, the school district transports the child from the workplace to the school; in others, the specialist comes to the school.

Ward stated that, to date, none of her clients had produced sponsored materials of the kind described in the introduction. She did say that at some of the schools that have been in operation the longest, students often want to work for their parent's employer company because they have a more realistic sense of what their parents do and what the work world is like than do those children who never see it.

At the moment SAW "has" (in quotes because once the school is established the company has no further formal involvement, something that could change under the new management) thirty schools nationwide, including ones at Hewlett Packard, Target, American Bankers Insurance Group (Miami), and the Miami Airport. Ward helped draft Florida's new charter school legislation, establishing a provision that would permit a charter school to operate in a corporate locale. It is not clear yet how this provision will affect public school districts.

Relationships among some of the officers of the two parent groups appear to be cozy. The venture capital company, Massey Burch, has apparently funded a number of Alexander adventures and its president, Donald M. Johnson, has sat on the Corporate Family Board. The CEO of Corporate Family, Marguerite Sallee, is currently is on the board of directors of Proffitt's. It is not clear at the moment if Proffitt's is invested in Corporate Family, although it certainly has the wherewithal to do so. It operated 237 stores, not including Saks, which it acquired in 1998, and had 1997 sales of $3.5 billion.

The National Independent Private School Association (NIPSA)

At this point, the National Independent Private School Association (NIPSA) is not a large player on the private management scene. Founded in 1983, it has grown to about seventy schools. NIPSA schools are typically family-owned programs, many of the owners having been in public education. The words that seem most appropriate to them are "vision" and "control": They have a clear sense of what they want done and want to be able to do it without the hindrance of local, state, and federal rules and regulations.

NIPSA may be small but it has a symbolic value: Some people have found ways of making money operating schools. NIPSA has only recently come out of the "for-profit closet," operating in the early years on a "better silent than scathed" philosophy. According to chairman of the board Lois Gerber, however, the shift toward health management organizations has helped legitimize them. Once, the idea of making money off of hospitals was anathema, even though doctors individually turned nice profits. This is no longer the case. Of course, other issues in the health care field have surfaced concerning the quality, ethics, and efficiency of managed care.

NIPSA members are, however, dedicated entrepreneurs and the changing winds of privatization could alter their psychology. Nobel has joined NIPSA, bringing in some 17,000 new students, as has Challenger Schools, a family-owned business which operates six schools in California and another six in Utah, where it is headquartered. Whether Nobel's Clegg will seek to influence the organization is not known at this time. At the moment, the structure of NIPSA sounds more like reluctant necessity than enthusiasm: "Although we are fiercely independent, we realize that proprietary schools must work together, focus on common challenges, and speak out with pride about their contributions to American education." (Taken in 1998 from "What is Nipsa?" www.nipsa.org, not shown on the current website).

Lately, NIPSA has shown more signs of political activity. It sent representatives to Washington to lobby for a change in the federal government's definition of "school" which currently excludes all for-profits. If the definition of school included for-profits, NIPSA members (and others) would be eligible for the information technology discounts available through E-rate. It also teamed up with the Milton and Rose Friedman Foundation to conduct a survey on the public's attitudes towards private schools. The Friedman Foundation was founded specifically to advocate vouchers and a market-driven system.

The "Education Industry": Wall Street Takes Notice

On the cover of Michael Moe's and R. Keith Gay's *The Emerging Investment Opportunity in Education* (1996), Rodin's Thinker sits atop not the gates of Hell but what looks to be a petrified tree trunk, contemplating in his hand a laptop computer displaying one word—"knowledge." "The Dawn of the Age of Knowledge," reads a superscript at the top of the book.

This 120-page document builds the case that spending on public schools is horrifically high and the performance of the schools is horrifically low. Therefore, given that the United States spends $330 billion a year on primary and secondary education and another $300 billion at the college level, privatized education, which can do the same job for less, ought to be able to turn a terrific profit and is therefore a great investment opportunity .

As is usual in such arguments, data are spun. For example, a chart on worldwide spending has the United States ranked third in education expenditures among twelve nations in the Organization for Economic Cooperation and Development (OECD). Although all of the performance data concern grade school students, and although Moe and Gay don't mention it, the figures given include spending on higher education, an arena where the U.S. is outranked only by Switzerland (which, conveniently, is not included in the list).

Looking at the data for only elementary and secondary schools, one finds that the United States is ninth among nineteen OECD countries (as noted earlier, there are other ways of calculating how much nations spend on their schools, the United States looks like a big spender by some measures, a miser by others. *Per capita* GDP, a variant of the GDP indicators, is probably the best single measure. This eliminates differences due to differences in the size of nations' GDPs; that is, America's is huge, Lichtenstein's tiny. On this measure the U.S. rank remains unchanged at ninth).

Similarly, the report includes only international comparisons of math and science and only information that was obsolete even at the time of the report. Moe and Gay use data from the 1992 Second International Assessment of Educational Progress (IAEP-2), but not the eighth-grade data from the Third International Mathematics and Science study, a much larger and more carefully conducted study, on which American students did much better. American eighth-graders ranked thirteenth out of fifteen in science in IAEP-2 and fourteenth out of fifteen in math (the author also conveniently ignore the data from fourth-graders where American students ranked third in science, and they do not observe that although American *ranks* were low American *scores* were quite close to the international average). In TIMSS, American eighth-graders were nineteenth of forty-one in science and twenty-fifth of forty-one in math, with scores again close to the international averages.

There is also no mention of *How in the World Do Students Read?*, which appeared in July 1992, just five months after IAEP-2 was published. Moe and Gay discuss the National Assessment of Educational Progress in terms of proficiency levels, not noting that these levels have been rejected by psychometricians as well as by a U.S. General Accounting Office (GAO) study.

The authors ask, "Will More Money Help?" (p. 64) and then show state rankings on the SAT along with state spending levels. As with William Bennett's study described earlier in "The Master Myth," they do not mention that in the twenty top-ranked states, virtually no one takes the SAT—not even 10 percent of the seniors—instead, the states use the ACT college admissions battery. In the lower-ranked states, two-thirds to four-fifths of the seniors huddle in angst on Saturday mornings to "bubble in" answer sheets. One might have thought Moe and Gay would have become a bit suspicious of this data on noticing that Mississippi ranked twelfth, while Massachusetts, acknowledged as an education leader in the nation for over 150 years, ranked thirty-fifth. One study found that 83 percent of the differences among states was due to the differential participation rates (Powell and Steelman, 1996).

The schools are in crisis, and, "From an investment perspective, this crisis has created an enormous opportunity and powerful momentum for those companies with solutions to our educational problems, whether through better management of traditional resources or the innovative application of technology" (p. 3, boldfaced for emphasis in the original).

Special services providers (SSPs) for at-risk youth are especially exciting:

> The children of the baby boomers are about to become teenagers, indicating that the juvenile crime problem is going to get much worse before it gets better. Seventy percent of all juvenile delinquents come from single-family homes. Our juvenile population is exploding and more of them are home alone than at any other time in our history. SSPs that can provide the same or better programs [for at-risk youth] are positioned to ride a tidal wave of privatization that we believe will occur in this sector. We expect an explosion in this market similar to the tremendous growth that has occurred among the adult corrections companies such as Corrections Corporation and Wakenhut. (pp. 36–37)

The misery index is rising. What a time to get rich.

The Education Industry Report

Even though most of the new companies are not making any money yet, the Education Index, compiled by John McLaughlin in the monthly newsletter *The Education Industry Report* until early 2000, outperformed the Wall Street indices until the recent slump. McLaughlin was a professor of educational administration at St. Cloud State in Minnesota for a number of years, but left to work full time with his Education Industry Group, located in Sioux Falls, South Dakota.

The Education Index consists of thirty-five publicly traded companies categorized as Education Management Organizations (e.g., Nobel), Education Products (e.g., Scholastic), Educational Service Organizations (e.g., Berlitz, Sylvan), At-Risk Youth (e.g., Youth Services International), Postsecondary Schools (e.g., Apollo Group), and Training and Development (e.g., Learning Tree).

Each *Education Industry Report* contains several feature articles, including a profile of an organization and another of some personality, usually a player in the industry, but occasionally important "outsiders" such as Bob Chase, president of the NEA, or Alex Molnar, an antiprivatization author, or Paul Hill. Hill left the RAND corporation for the University of Washington, founding the Center for Reinventing Education—not to be confused with John Goodlad's Center for Educational Renewal at the same institution. Hill advocates contracting out services such that a school system becomes a contractor, not a provider of education in the community.

McLaughlin worries that the industry, chastened by such debacles as EAI and Beacon Education Management (in its earlier incarnation as APS), will take on charters as a safety move. "This is too bad," writes McLaughlin. "For the industry, which has proven its value for children, families, and investors on either side of the K–12 spectrum, is faltering in stepping up to the area of greatest need in the country" (1998c, p. 2).

Others in the investment community have taken notice of education as a place to make money. In February 1996, Lehman Brothers hosted a conference on the industry, and while it was noted that there have always been commercial companies providing textbooks and supplies, none of these were present. The conference featured the likes of Edison's Chris Whittle and Beacon APS's John Eason. Other presenters came from Nobel, the Princeton Review and Kaplan Educational Centers (two test "coaching" organizations), KinderCare Learning Centers, Inc., and TRO Learning, Inc., a provider of remedial software. According to an article in *Education Week*, attendees were especially impressed with Sylvan Learning Systems, Inc. (Walsh, 1996).

Commentary on the education industry in the press that monitors the industry is itself interestingly varied. Carl Horowitz, an education reporter for *Investor's Business Daily*, has commented that he thinks the criticisms of American public schools are misguided and dangerous. "I happen to take exception to the idea that our country is getting dumber and dumber. Given the rise in test scores since 1980, it is clear that we have a pretty smart and ready workforce. The bottom line is that our schools are doing a decent job, but at the same time, there is room for improvement."

Asked by John McLaughlin why IBD has had such an interest in education, Horowitz replied "The owner of the paper had a conversation with [former secretary of education] Bill Bennett, and Bill emphasized that he thought that our paper could be instrumental in hammering out an education agenda." Michael Moe's *The Emerging Investment Opportunity in Education* lists fourteen articles for that publication in 1995 and 1996, most of them either assailing schools or reporting positive results from private operations. McLaughlin in 1998 puts an undated list at "more than thirty-one cover stories" (1998c, p. 1).

McLaughlin also talked to *Washington Post* education writer Rene Sanchez, *Education Week*'s principal writer on charters and privatization Mark Walsh, and then–*New York Times* education reporter Peter Applebome. Sanchez was inclined to see charters as a flash in the pan; Applebome considered them a more important trend, and Walsh thought that the privatization efforts had reached a critical mass.

All agreed that more experimentation was inevitable and that the growth of Edison was critical to the industry—another pressure mitigating against any objective evaluation of Edison outcomes.

For his part, McLaughlin comes to profit-making schooling naturally: He founded and ran a school in Nashville for ten years before returning to graduate school and wrote his dissertation on the private sector's role in education reform. He then joined the faculty of St. Cloud State University in Minnesota, where he spent another decade.

McLaughlin apparently views education from only one of the two perspectives described by Henig at the outset of this paper—the education service deliverer. He noted in conversation that private and for-profit education on either side of K–12 has been both successful and accepted. He considers it hypocritical in the extreme to claim that it is not appropriate for K–12, that, in fact, "we have sacrificed the good of the children to stakeholders"—those who run the schools.

McLaughlin believes we need to establish choice as a plank in the education platform equal in importance to three other planks: equity, access, and performance. Education in the future will be more research and development-driven as the private sector investigates further what works, and under what conditions.

Although high on free-market reforms, McLaughlin also says that education should not educate with the purpose of preventing the creation of radicals, keeping kids out of the markets until they're nearly twenty-two, or turning them into cogs that fit the capitalist system (he observes that this statement causes a number of eyebrows to rise in business circles).

In early 2000, McLaughlin sold his share of *The Education Industry Report* back to EduVentures (see next section) and started a new group. He sits on the boards of Bright Horizons and a Michigan charter group, National Heritage Academies. He is also consulting with national education organizations about charter schools, outsourcing, online curriculum and purchasing, and other matters that involve "the education industry." He declined to name the organizations at this time.

EduVentures, Inc.   The Boston-based company EduVentures, Inc. provides consulting services to private companies that are engaged in education enterprises. Its founder, John Sandler, started the company in 1993. He is also cofounder, with John McLaughlin, of the *Education Investor* (now the *Education Industry Report*), which EduVentures has owned outright since early 2000. He was at one time an assistant to David Kearns, former CEO of Xerox, former deputy secretary of education and, at the time, CEO of the New American Schools Development Corporation, the George H. W. Bush–sponsored private initiative to build "break-the-mold" schools.

EduVentures recently represented Virtual Learning (VL) in negotiations, which led to VL's obtaining $2 million in capital from Sylvan Learning Systems. Other EduVenture clients have included Corporate Family Solutions and Wall Street Institute, the latter a part of Sylvan. Outside of education, clients include IBM, McGraw-Hill, and other companies with an interest in the development of the education industry. For these organizations, EduVentures provides "competitive intelligence" about education corporations.

Sandler distinguishes EduVentures from other brokers such as Lehman Brothers and Merrill Lynch. Those organizations, although capable, often represent the companies that they conduct research on and thus have a vested interested in presenting the companies in a favorable light. EduVentures, says Sandler, is the only independent source of such information and has the largest database in the nation about private education companies.

Some of this database can be viewed at EduVenture's online newsletter, *The Education Economy* (www.eduventures.com/news/education_economy). This weekly publication is free. EduVentures uses it to draw readers toward their services (The Education Industry Report, by contrast, costs $400 a year). After a couple of items on issues of specific companies, *The Education Economy* lists news items, giving hotlinks to the original sources of the information. Other news services from EduVentures include, "Latest Headlines," "Stock Quotes," "IPO Watch," and "Notable Hires." For the clients it serves, EduVentures provides strategic planning, business-plan writing, access to capital, and the identification of acquisition targets, merger partners, and joint-venture partners.

Getting the Word Out

In 1998 *Investors Business Daily* (*IBD*) carried an article by Hudson Institute Fellow and charter advocate Bruno Manno entitled "Still a Nation at Risk." Increasingly, one finds that conservative education reformers are bypassing educational periodicals in favor of publications that directly address the corporate community. Thus Manno writes for *IBD*, as do choice zealot Jeanne Allen of the Center for Educational Reform and Myron Lieberman, author of *Public Education: An Autopsy*. Voucher advocate Paul Peterson made his case for Milwaukee's voucher program in the *Wall Street Journal* (Greene and Peterson, 1996). Former assistant secretary of education Chester E. Finn, Jr. is a frequent contributor to the *Journal's* op-ed page. At the very least, the efforts of these authors are aimed at making the public, especially the stock-owning public, nervous about the quality of public schools.

Milken's Knowledge Universe (KU): Its Own Private Galaxy

> *To call Kalinske's operation low-profile is a laughable understatement, and the folks at KU [Knowledge Universe] get the joke. Kalinske's assistant, Mary Biondi, responds to a request for directions with a quip: "You'll have to wait by the side of the highway for one of our people to pick you up, blindfold you and bring you here.*
>
> —Jon Revelos, Director, Allen Academy of Multimedia
> August 31, 1998, www.epss.com

The Kalinske in this quote is Thomas Kalinske, the fifty-eight-year-old marketing whiz president of Knowledge Universe (KU) and former CEO of both Mattel, where he revived sales for Barbie dolls, and Sega of America, where he introduced Sonic the Hedgehog. Actually, Revelos had made great progress in uncovering information about KU compared to *Barron's* reporter Eric J. Savitz. Savitz's cover story in the March 2, 1998, edition of *Barron's*, "For Adults Only" about training workers via computers, contains only one paragraph about KU: "Lastly, in a category all its own, there's Knowledge Universe, the secretive two-year-old behemoth created by junk-bond king Michael Milken,[16] his brother Lowell Milken, and Larry Ellison [founder of Oracle]. The goal was to provide 'cradle-to-grave' educational services. If you haven't heard much about them, be patient. You will" (Savitz, 1998).

Maybe. Contacted in August 1998, Savitz could (or would) say only, "They're very frustrating. They don't even have a website." They don't even have a listed phone number, actually. They do have a website now, although it contains nothing particularly revelatory except to name the companies that comprise KU and to mention that their sales in 1997 exceeded $1 billion, a 67 percent increase from 1996, the year the company was founded. In the ensuing years, sales have grown to $1.5 billion. KU's phones were publicly listed in May 1999. (Some of the secrecy makes good business sense: KU's MO is takeovers, and if companies thought they were the objects of KU takeovers, they would attempt to raise their price).

The organization has recently divided into two smaller galaxies: the Knowledge Universe Business Group and the Knowledge Universe Learning Group. The first consists of thirty-two companies KU either owns or holds shares in. Its purpose is to "improve the effectiveness and productivity of businesses and their employees, and give people tools and services to make them more productive in life" (www.knowledgeu.com, September, 2000).

By contrast, the Learning Group's fourteen companies "enhance the adventure of learning from birth through graduate school. The range of products and services includes interactive education products; technology training and resources for teachers; early childhood education; and interactive learning websites for children, their parents, grandparents, and teachers." (www.knowledgeu.com, September, 2000).

KU does not think small. In the "vision" section of its website that first appeared in 1998, KU declared:

> Knowledge Universe seeks to create, build, and acquire education-related companies, public and private, regardless of size which:
>
> • Demonstrate a passion for improving the quality of education in the marketplaces they serve;
> • Are capable of achieving a leadership position in their respective segments of the education industry;

---

16. Milken is often credited with saying "Greed is good." That statement was actually made by Milken's co-conspirator, Ivan Boesky.

- Have the opportunity to grow dramatically with the availability of adequate capital; and
- Enjoy or have the potential to develop strong brand names recognition.

Knowledge Universe *has strong relationships with the world's leading entertainment, telecommunications and technology companies* (emphasis added). These relationships and its financial resources provide Knowledge Universe with a significant advantage as it pursues its objective of becoming a market leader in global education and learning."

By late 2000, this vision had been replaced by a more philosophical, less materialistic view: "Knowledge Universe (KU) believes that people and organizations have an almost unlimited power to improve themselves—to realize their own potential." KU helps people and businesses do this by providing learning aids based on three principles:

1. In an information economy, physical labor is less important than knowledge and wages depend on educational levels.
2. Most industrialized nations are aging, meaning that there will be fewer workers to support retirees. This in turn means that retirees will also need additional training.
3. "Skills that used to serve a lifetime now become obsolete in a few years."

This and other information can be found at KU's website: www.zknowledgeu. com/vision.html.

Underlying this vision is another, unstated one: Children will attend KU preschools and play with interactive toys produced by KU companies. Children might attend KU schools and even if they don't, their schools will utilize KU developed software. In college, they will supplement whatever they receive on campus with online courses from Knowledge University. Their teachers will receive professional training, especially in the use of information technology from Teacher Universe, a subsidiary of KU. Wherever they work, KU seminars and software will enhance their productivity. And after retirement, KU will be there with additional training so that retirees don't become obsolete and poor in their dotage.

KU Subsidiaries

Although there have been rumors of KU going public, their website notes that it is a private company and that this gives it flexibility. Observers do believe that the various KU companies will eventually become a parade of publicly traded corporations. As noted, KU has already purchased 1,283,000, or 16 percent of the shares in Nobel Learning Communities. Other directly educational acquisitions include Children's Discovery Centers (CDC) which operates 250 daycare centers and preschools and has revenues of $95 million. CDC is headquartered in San Rafael, California, across the San Francisco Bay from KU's headquarters.

There is also LeapFrog Toys, a maker of educational toys that has specialized in phonics approaches to the teaching of reading and has recently expanded to include mathematics. According to LeapFrog's website, the system was developed by Robert Calfee at Stanford University. It identifies Calfee as one of the best-known experts in reading. This might not be wholly true, but he is widely recognized in the fields of cognitive psychology and educational assessment (and departed Stanford for the deanship at the University of California at Riverside). The site also declares that LeapFrog is a division of Knowledge Kids Enterprises, Inc., but offers no Internet link to the parent company. Also in the fold is Bookman Testing Services, Inc., a specialized thirteen-year-old company that, under the brand name TeckChek, currently provides high-tech tests of students' knowledge about high-tech areas such as computer programming languages.

Finally, among the education companies, there are Knowledge University and Knowledge Universe Interactive Studio, Inc. The university was formed in 1997 to "deliver a variety of degree, certificate and continuing education programs to corporations, businesses, governments and individual learners located throughout the world" (www.knowledgeu.com/companies.html). The studio "designs and develops compelling learning products utilizing state-of-the-art technologies and modes of delivery." It is listed as the parent company of MindQ Publishing, Inc., headquartered in Reston, Virginia, that develops and delivers "multimedia learning systems . . . offering a dynamic interactive experience that is far more effective than text-based education systems." No supporting data on effectiveness is offered. Given KU's secrecy, this hardly surprises.

Another KU subsidiary is TEC Worldwide. TEC (for The Executive Committee) is described as an international membership group of CEOs who help other "CEOs become more effective in an environment of constant change." Nextera is a business consulting firm headquartered in Lexington, Massachusetts, and itself consists of four companies: Pyramid Consulting, SiGMA Consulting, Symmetric, and The Planning Technologies Group. It is the only publicly traded company in KU's firmament. Productivity Point International, Inc., is an international consulting firm that, according to KU information, trained over one million students in 1997. Another consulting group, Spring CRT Group, is headquartered in the United Kingdom.

In April 2000, KU launched KidsEdge.com from its Knowledge Kids Network (KKN). The new Internet address, according to the company, will focus on reading and mathematics "while also developing the whole child, including imagination, confidence and character." KKN will do this with "graphically rich, character-driven environments that provide age-appropriate, individualized learning activities for children." The "curriculum is based on key state standards from around the nation" (Business Wire, April 3, 2000). CEO Sarina Simon heads KKN. Simon is a former editor at Lowell House Publishing and executive producer for a number of films at Walt Disney Company. Most recently she was president of the Home and Family division of Phillips Electronics, which makes children's software, among other products (*Business Wire*, May 31, 2000). The distance between education and entertainment grows smaller, it would seem. ParentsEdge.com, GrandparentsEdge.com, and TeachersEdge.com complement KidsEdge.com and let various caretakers track the children's progress.

The business "vision" sends KU out to buy companies that are in trouble and therefore can be had on the cheap, with the eventual goal of making them into some kind of dominant, integrated education provider. "Knowledge Universe is on a quest for universal domination," said Stan Lepeak of META, a technology consulting firm. "It could easily become a Fortune 100 company" (Feldman, 1998, p. C4). Critics claim that KU appears to have no integrated purchasing strategy: It has no strong management team and has obtained little cross-fertilization or synergy from its various components.

New York Daily News business writer Amy Feldman described KU this way: "Owned directly through a complicated maze of partnerships by Milken, his brother Lowell and software mogul Larry Ellison of Oracle Corporation, the octopuslike group has snapped up a slew of education-related firms in an effort to gain dominance in areas such as computer training, private grade schools and educational toys." Contacted by phone, Feldman had no further information than that contained in her March 1998, article. In a September 7, 1998 article, *Los Angeles Times* business writer Debora Vrana didn't get much farther. "Ready or not, America, the curtain is rising on Milken's second act, one that could restructure another area of society, generate huge profits, and just maybe turn the convicted bond dealer into a hero" (Vrana, 1998, p. A1).

She does cite Milken as stating that KU wants to own a nationwide chain of private schools that will serve 2 percent of all children—about 1,000,000—something not seen in earlier dispatches. She also says, "Milken can make this work only if parents are willing to turn over their children to a brilliant fellow who says that he has come up with a better way to improve the educational system. That claim has yet to be proved, say skeptics." Vrana puts the worth of Milken's empire at $4 billion. She quotes several people whose opinions range from the belief that Milken wants to "save the next generation" to "He's always just making a buck."

According to John McLaughlin, KU's strategy is to talk to virtually everyone in a field where they are interested. McLaughlin describes companies as "awed" that Milken would want to talk with them. They then transact a deal in the field that no one expected, that surprises everyone, but that, in retrospect, makes perfect sense. McLaughlin contends that they have a stable of expert merger and acquisition specialists.

The Milken Families Foundation

If KU operates stealth-like out of Burlingame, just south of San Francisco, Milken Families Foundation in Santa Monica seeks publicity and is best known for its spring fling, which provides a three-day symposium on a chosen topic. In 1999, the theme was the education–job skills mismatch. Needless to say, there was no balance to the program.

The conference honors around thirty teachers who have made exemplary use of technology in their classrooms. They and most of their chief state school officers fly to foundation headquarters in Santa Monica and are put up in the Century Plaza Hotel. The adornments of the conference are, to put it mildly, lavish, and obviously designed to build goodwill among the attendees. It's working. When people speak of the conference, one senses they are having trouble restraining a drool.

And yet, this is small potatoes for Milken. Educators live in an economically deprived zone compared to the highfliers of finance. One wonders if, at some point Milken will reveal Knowledge Universe with the flair he once showed at an annual gathering of bond traders that was known as the Predators's Ball. At the time, Milken was in the full flush of his junk-bond successes. As he whipped the audience to a frenzy, Frank Sinatra walked onstage. "Hey, aren't you the junk-bond guy?" Sinatra asked. "Here, make sure I've got plenty of junk bonds." At this moment, the stage curtains parted, revealing a twenty-two-piece orchestra. Sinatra sang "Start spreadin' the news"[17] (Ashworth, 1999).

One imagines that Milken's flair will show again. According to one article, an upcoming conference "will begin and end with Milken-moderated panels of Nobel laureates; in between, Milken himself will deliver the keynote address. Fifteen hundred people are expected to attend, and through it all, Milken will stand at center stage, a smiling, benevolent visionary leading the discussion and masterminding the event. In short, even the conference's structure drives home the idea that this is Michael Milken's conference, for Michael Milken's institute, discussing Michael Milken's favorite issues" (Cohn, 2000).

Milken awes people. One senses that in articles written about him, at least two of which referred to his comeback after his jail term as "The Resurrection" (although at least a half-dozen others referred to "Milken's new empire"). Arthur Levine, president of Teachers College at Columbia University, met with Milken in 1998. "The message was, 'you guys are in trouble and we're going to eat your lunch.'" Levine characterized the message from Milken as "a predatory challenge" (Wyatt, 1999).

Some think Milken, a survivor of prostate cancer, does have some kind of aim at divinity. Said Stan Lepeak, "It's a big leap of faith for Mike and Co. to come in and think they can fix America's educational system. I think it's visions of godhood. After being vilified in the 1980s, he wants to go down in history as a savior in the next decade" (Vrana, 1998). Not one to limit his activities, Milken gives millions for research on prostate cancer, lectures on the subject, and has written a cookbook designed to prevent the disease.

17. For the record, Milken was shortly thereafter indicted on ninety-eight counts including insider trading, price manipulation, falsifying records, filing false reports, racketeering, defrauding customers, and "stock parking"—an arrangement to hide the true owners of stock. In a plea bargain, Milken pleaded guilty to six relatively minor charges, paid a $600 million fine and served twenty-two months in prison.

Others who have worked with Milken in his new venture contend that he is unchanged, a takeover junkie who is more interested in buying companies than delivering education. Journalist Russ Baker observed, "Milken seems most successful when he is not reinventing the wheel, but buying existing businesses in hot categories" (Baker, 1999). That approach cost him the services of one highly regarded businessman, Joseph Costello, who left KU after only three months. Costello objected to KU's lack of focus and its habit of buying firms such as existing language-training companies for $100 million, rather than creating a new model for such training for $10–20 million. Costello is one of those people who finds Milken unchanged from his earlier incarnation.

Milken's actions have contradicted his words on several occasions. He preaches a gospel of education as the savior of the underclass. He points to several factors that have prevented Watts-like riots in America's cities but claims we can experience similar urban unrest if we do not get education to all (Wiles, 2000). Yet, virtually all of the companies that make up KU presume access to information technology and would, indeed, only widen the alleged "digital divide" between poor people and the affluent.

Baker worried that Milken was unconcerned with building a stronger democracy. He also fretted over Milken's editorial control of content. When he inquired if Milken would permit KU students to do a critical assessment of the years when Milken was a junk-bond dealer, the answer from colleagues was "absolutely not." And, indeed, Baker notes that KU's *Business Encyclopedia* "approvingly cites Milken's role in the junk-bond business without mentioning the economic and social devastation associated with it." Baker also worries that in the field of entrepreneurial education, marketing will dominate curriculum: "Will it come down to how schools market themselves rather than how well kids learn and what they learn? Will students even be permitted, for example, to see the negative consequences of unfettered greed? In an era when even our most basic public institutions are being shaped by financial interest, defending these core principles has become an increasingly important struggle" (Baker, 1999).

One comes away from the literature about Knowledge Universe with the strong feeling that people like Milken not only want to provide educational services and dominate the market, but also want to control the content of that education to ensure a particular, business-sympathetic vision.

K12. Perhaps an indication of Milken's drive to control and to persuade is seen in one of his latest adventures, K12, an online K–12 curriculum. In *The Educated Child*, former secretary of education William J. Bennett, John T. E. Cribb, Jr., and Chester E. Fenn, Jr., wrote, "When you hear the next pitch about cyber-enriching your child's education, keep one thing in mind: So far, there is no good evidence that most uses of computers significantly improve learning." Well, the next pitch is coming from Bennett, via Milken.

Although a number of universities and organizations are working on online educational offerings, K12 is unique (Steinberg, 2000). Milken is backing the first effort to develop a complete K–12 curriculum based heavily on Bennett's book and strongly influenced as well by E. D. Hirsch, Jr.'s Core Knowledge program. John Holdren, K12's senior vice president of content and curriculum, oversaw the development of the Core Knowledge's "What your Xth-grader needs to know" series of books.

Also joining the K12 team as chief technology adviser is David Gelernter, a professor of computer science at Yale. Gelernter's name might strike some chord of recognition outside of his profession: He lost most of his right hand in 1993 when opening a package that turned out to be a bomb sent by the Unabomber, Theodore J. Kaczynski.

K12 is apparently making a serious attempt to assess outcomes, having lured David Niemi away from the Center for Research in Evaluation, Standards, and Student Testing, coheadquartered at UCLA and the University of Colorado at Boulder. It will be interesting to see how seriously this attempt is sustained once some of the officers not familiar with psychometrics realize what is involved in appropriate and valid assessment.

Given Bennett's association with the political right, some are worried that the program might be more of a vehicle for conservative ideology than for education (Irwin, 2000). At least one educator has expressed public skepticism. Sandra Feldman, president of the American Federation of Teachers, said, "We will have to wait and see if the quality of this particular product is as grandiose as Mr. Bennett's quotes" (Irwin, 2000).

8

Vouchers Public
and Private

Many defenders of public schools view the voucher as the most potentially dev-
astating weapon in the repertoire of those who oppose public schools. Wherever
a voucher—at least one that comes from public funds—sends money to some
agency of the private sector, that money is not available for use by the public
schools. Vouchers on any large scale, the defenders fear, would simply wreak
havoc. Their concerns are not without cause.

John Stuart Mill and the Concept of Vouchers

The idea of vouchers is not new to education or to other social programs. Food
stamps, Medicaid, and even some subsidized public housing can be considered
instances of vouchers. John Stuart Mill usually receives credit for the concept of
vouchers, although he did not use that word. In his 1838 essay, *On Liberty*, Mill
railed that families were not required to educate their children. Even when
schooling was provided free, families could avail themselves of it or not. It was
their choice. Mill argued that "it is one of the most sacred duties of the parents,
after summoning a human being into the world, to give that being an education
fitting him to perform his part well in life towards others and towards himself"
(p. 116). What to do? Mill outlined how a state could require an education, yet
not furnish it, something that Mill saw as odious:

> If the government were to make up its mind to *require* for every child a good
> education, it might save itself the trouble of *providing* one. It might leave to par-
> ents to obtain the education where and how they pleased, and content itself
> with helping to pay the school fees of the poorer classes of children, and defraying
> the entire school expenses of those who have no one else to pay for them. The
> objections that are urged with reason against State education, do not apply to the

enforcement of education by the State, but to the State's taking upon itself to direct that education: which is a totally different thing. That the whole or any large part of the education of the people should be in State hands, I go as far as any one in deprecating. All that has been said of the importance of individuality of character, and diversity in opinions and modes of conduct, involves, as of the same unspeakable importance, diversity of education. A general state education is a mere contrivance for moulding people to be exactly like one another: and as the mould in which it casts them is that which pleases the predominant power in the government, whether this be a monarch, a priesthood, an aristocracy, or the majority of the existing generation in proportion as it is efficient and successful, it establishes a despotism over the mind, leading by natural tendency to one over the body. An education established and controlled by the State should exist, if it exist at all, as one among many competing experiments, carried on for the purpose of example and stimulus, to keep the others up to a certain standard of excellence. (p. 117–118)

How would Mill decide if the schools were providing good education? Through tests. The state would administer them, beginning with reading and then extending to a "minimum competency test" of general knowledge (his actual words were a test "of a certain minimum of general knowledge"). He also proposed "voluntary examinations on all subjects." In order to keep the state from intruding where it had no business, these examinations could only test subjects of fact. In matters of politics and religion, the examination could only be in terms of what authors, schools of thought, or religions held to be true.

Although Thomas Jefferson never used the word *voucher*, his 1782 plan for a system of education in Virginia had a voucher component. Jefferson wanted to build schools within walking distance of anyone. The government would provide a child's education for the first three years. After that, a "Visitor" would visit schools and annually identify the "boys of best genius." These chosen few would continue with state-provided education, culminating at the College of William and Mary. Such a plan, Jefferson contended, would produce an "aristocracy of worth and genius," in contrast to the European aristocracy, which was based simply on the accident of birth. Persons of means could educate their children at these schools or whatever schools they chose, and to whatever levels they chose, but the family had to foot the bills.

In the late 1950s, economist Milton Friedman updated Mill's ideas and elaborated on them in his 1962 book, *Freedom and Capitalism*. In 1996, Friedman, now nearly ninety, and his wife Rose established the Friedman Foundation for School Choice in Indianapolis. The foundation's goal is to inform the public about what the Friedmans see as the advantages of voucher programs.

Comparing Vouchers and Charters

The arguments for vouchers made by the Friedmans are quite similar to those others claim for charter schools:

- Vouchers will increase the diversity of schools. Since there is no single best system, increasing the instructional options will give students a better chance to match a school to their preferred mode of learning.
- Unions and establishment educators protect the status quo, which inhibits innovation.
- Under a market-driven system, good schools will thrive and poor schools will go out of business as their disgruntled clients vote with their feet and pocketbooks.
- Schools in the present system are unresponsive because they constitute a virtual monopoly. Some voucher supporters even refer to the public schools in general and the National Education Association in particular as "The Berlin Wall of Education Monopoly."

In addition, there is one claim for vouchers not made necessarily for charter schools: They will empower poor people to obtain a good education for their children. Poor people cannot afford the tuition of nonsectarian private schools, which was on average $6,600 in 1994 (compared to $6,500 per-pupil expenditures for public schools) or even the much-lower tuition of Catholic schools, which was around $2,000. If the money follows the child to whatever school is chosen, this will give low-income families access to the kinds of education now enjoyed by affluent families in suburbs.

Except for the idea of providing better access to good schools for low-income families, the notion of a voucher contributes nothing directly to the improvement of education. A voucher scheme is a means of paying for schools, not for improving them. It offers nothing in the way of curricular or pedagogical innovations in itself. Its actions are secondary and, if the market metaphor does not fit education well, illusory.

We can state with confidence that none of the experiments currently in progress (or over, in the case of Milwaukee—no further data is being collected) will provide good evidence for whether or not choice would work at the system level on a large scale. The small experiments are just that, and they suffer from too many constraints to answer the hard questions about choice. In addition, the advocates of choice, whether politicians or entrepreneurs or philanthropists, have not shown any particular interest in asking the hard questions, much less answering them. As we shall see, the voucher experiments have become entangled in politics, with the result that those proposing the programs have shown no interest in research and evaluation that might render definitive answers to the many questions a move to a voucher system in this country would raise.

For instance, in Milwaukee, Wisconsin, voucher advocates have succeeded in killing all funds for further evaluations of the voucher program in that city. In Florida, children become eligible for vouchers if they attend public schools that receive an F grade from the state any two years out of four. The grades are determined largely by tests. The private schools that accept the vouchers do not have to administer the tests to their own enrollees or to those coming through the instrumentality of the voucher. Once these children leave the public system, all accountability for their progress is lost.

Terry Moe of the Hoover Institute has rendered the condition of research and evaluation efforts pertaining to vouchers with extreme clarity:

> Ideology aside, perhaps the most vexing problem [of voucher research] is that few researchers who carry out studies of school choice are sensitive to issues of institutional design or context. They proceed as though their case studies reveal something generic about choice or markets when, in fact—as the Milwaukee case graphically testifies—much of what they observe is due to the specific rules, restrictions and control mechanisms that shape how choice and markets happen to operate in a particular setting. As any economist would be quick to point out, the effects of choice and markets vary, sometimes enormously, depending on the institutional context. The empirical literature on school choice does little to shed light on these contingencies and, indeed, by portraying choice and markets as generic reforms with generic effects, often breeds more confusion than understanding. (1995, p. 20)

This is a remarkable statement from one who coauthored this passage five years earlier:

> We think reformers would do well to entertain the notion that choice is a panacea. This is our way of saying that choice is not like the other part of a reformist strategy for improving America's public schools. Choice is a self-contained reform with its own rationale and justification. It has the capacity all by itself to bring about the kind of transformation that, for years, reformers have been seeking to engineer in myriad other ways. (Chubb and Moe, 1990, p. 217)

Given the murkiness of the situation, it is not surprising to find different researchers taking contradictory positions on what the results of a voucher program mean. In a speech at the Cato Institute, Paul Peterson of Harvard University declared that the Milwaukee results found choice successful under "extreme duress." Hence if choice can work under such terrible constraints, it can work anywhere and, therefore, we should "scale up" to programs for the larger system. Jeffrey Henig of George Washington University, responding to Peterson's speech, contended that there were so many unusual, even unique, features to the Milwaukee program that it had little if anything to say to that larger system (Peterson, 1997; Henig, 1997). Generalization was not possible. Oddly, Henig's position was in fact Peterson's just the prior year:

> Often lost in the charges and responses is the simple fact that Milwaukee's choice plan gave low-income families only a pitifully small approximation of what theorists have always regarded as essential for choice programs to succeed. Far from being a good test of the workability of a school choice program, the legislators placed it under nine restrictions [sic]. Not unlike Dante's *Inferno*, which subjected

sinners to one of nine ever-narrowing circles of hell, each restriction was more wrenching than the preceding. . . . The end result was a program designed to fail. (Peterson and Noyes, 1996)

Nine Voucher Restrictions

Peterson follows through each restriction with citations from Dante and while these quickly become tiresome, the points that he makes are good ones.

1. Eligibility. The first restriction threw the program into limbo (Dante's first circle), because it stated that no child already in a private school was eligible for a voucher. According to Peterson, this requirement was imposed to save the state money. If a child in public school chose a private school, the state's costs were only the money already appropriated—it just followed the child. Allowing private school students into the program would have created immediate new outlays for the state. In some states, such as Florida, children in private schools are eligible to apply to vouchers.

2. Random Assignment. If more students applied than a school could accept, it was required to choose at random (how the schools, with staff untrained in the techniques of sampling, actually met this requirement—if they did—is not clear). "As a result, applicants could not be assured of a school, and schools could not select the children they thought most likely to benefit from their program. . . . Still, the costs of this restriction on choice were not excessive. The number of applicants were not greatly in excess of the number of seats available. And random assignment helped the choice program avoid the accusation that they selected only the more able and more self-disciplined students."

This would appear to be a small cost indeed, as random assignment would constitute the greatest achievement of any program evaluation. Peterson's position inherently conflicts with that of researchers. Schools will naturally want to try and match their programs with the children who apply or to weed out those they think will be problematic. Researchers will want to rid their experiments as much as possible of the selection bias this would produce. Peterson's desideratum could only be permitted in an experiment where *all* schools selected their students. In the current condition, public schools don't get to choose.

3. Limited Size. "At Hell's third circle, Dante met the Gluttons. The legislature helped preserve corpulence in public education by limiting the size of the choice program to one percent of the city's public school enrollment (with an increase to 1.5 percent in 1994). . . . In other words, the plan was designed explicitly to avoid the competition between public and private schools that choice theory says is critically important."

This is a curious objection, coming as it does from the political right. The right has many times criticized public educators for adopting programs—

Whole Language, "fuzzy math"—without conducting small-scale experiments to determine if the programs deliver on their promises. When the Milwaukee program was first considered, had the small body of extant choice research literature been brought to bear, choice would no doubt have been rejected for want of conclusive research.

4. *Limited Funding.* The legislature enacted a program to be "revenue neutral," meaning that choice schools received the same amount of state aid per pupil as the Milwaukee public schools. Schools that charged a tuition higher than the voucher amount had to either waive the tuition, admit small numbers, or decline to participate at all. Peterson cites one private school administrator as saying that his school "would participate further if we did not lose so much money per student accepted."

It is difficult to see how this posed much of a problem, unless so many students applied that schools had to hire new staff or add facilities. This never happened. Aside from textbooks and other instructional materials, the school would encounter few costs for their new pupils. It would appear that for the most part, students arriving with vouchers would constitute financial "gravy."

5. *No Parental Contributions.* Parents were not permitted to make up any difference between the tuition and the value of the voucher. "The ostensible purpose of the ban was to keep school choice from becoming elitist, but this goal was already assured by the rule that no money could go to families with income substantially above the poverty line. . . . [This restriction] guaranteed that most choice students would attend fiscally constrained institutions with limited facilities and poorly paid teachers."

This is a genuine issue from a theoretical market perspective. Peterson and some others hold that parents who invest in their children's education will endeavor to see that it pays off. They will be more likely to become involved with the school and to see that their children behave, complete homework, and so on. Several private voucher programs stipulate that parents must contribute their own funds, often as much as the value of the voucher itself. No data exist to test the hypothesis that paying parents are more involved. Studies of voucher programs do find parents more involved, but the involvement could derive from other factors. Voucher-using parents in Milwaukee and San Antonio, Texas, for instance, were more involved with school *prior* to the voucher program. In San Antonio, where parents paid 50 percent of the voucher cost, voucher-using parents did not become more involved in their children's education than they were prior to the program.

6. *No Religious Schools.* A challenge to this restriction ended with the Wisconsin Supreme Court ruling in favor of the church-affiliated schools. The U.S. Supreme Court declined to hear the case. The Wisconsin court ruled that since the money did not go to the school, but followed individual children, the program did not violate the separation of church and state clause.

In some areas, Peterson argued, no meaningful choice program could exist without the participation of church schools. In the Edgewood district of San Antonio, virtually the entire district is Hispanic and virtually all private schools are Catholic schools.

7. Schools must have non-choice students. Voucher students at new schools were limited to 50 percent of total enrollment; the other half had to pay tuition. This effectively prevented anyone from starting a new school.

8. Evaluation. Peterson impugned the skills and experience of the state-chosen evaluator of the Milwaukee program, University of Wisconsin political scientist John Witte. Peterson apparently thought that Witte lacked sufficient methodological expertise to handle the complex evaluation. And, since Witte had been picked by people opposed to the program, Peterson felt that Witte must be the same. "An acrid stench surrounds the manner in which the evaluator was chosen," wrote Peterson.

9. Hostile Implementation. According to Peterson, the Wisconsin state superintendent of public instruction, Bert Grover, did everything he could to avoid having the program in the first place. Once the program was brought into existence, Grover did everything in his power to kill it.

However one feels about any or all of Peterson's contentions, they do illustrate some of the complexities of evaluating choice programs of any kind. Evaluators do not operate in the neutral atmosphere of a laboratory. Friends of a given voucher program sometimes resort to devious means to keep it from being properly evaluated. Enemies of the program sometimes resort to devious means to paint it in the worst possible light.

Recent Vouchers Developments in Florida and Elsewhere

Fall 2000 produced a number of voucher developments. In October, an appeals court in Florida reversed a judge's earlier decision and declared the voucher program constitutional. This decision was immediately appealed, but as this is written in early 2001, the Florida Supreme Court has delivered no decision.

Earlier in the year, the schools themselves rendered the Florida program temporarily moot. Schoolchildren in Florida become eligible for vouchers if the state of Florida gives the schools an F grade in two years out of four. Two schools in the Pensacola area received their second F at the end of 1999. Some fifty-three children from these schools used vouchers to attend private schools during 1999–2000. Another seventy-eight schools received their first F that year. However, when the test scores arrived in the summer of 2000, all seventy-eight schools had improved their grades to D or better, rendering their students ineligible for voucher assistance.

Interestingly, Florida's law makes no provision for returning the voucher children to improved public schools. If we assume for the moment that the courts ultimately rule the voucher program constitutional, Florida public schools that lose students to voucher schools will have no way to re-enroll them other than to cajole them and their parents to return—no matter what letter grade the schools might attain in the future.

Two months after the Florida decisions, a federal appeals court ruled that Cleveland's voucher program was unconstitutional. The decision split the three-judge panel. The majority, one Clinton appointee and one Bush (senior) appointee, ruled that "This school involves the grant of state aid directly and predominantly to the coffers of private, religious schools, and it is unquestioned that these institutions incorporate religious concepts, motives and themes into all facets of their educational planning. . . . There is no neutral aid when that aid principally flows to religious institutions, nor is there truly 'private choice' when the available choices resulting from the program are predominantly religious choices." In 1999–2000, 96 percent of the nearly 4,000 voucher students attended sectarian schools (Wilgoren, 2000a). The Cleveland voucher program is discussed in greater depth later in this chapter.

The court also said, "Practically speaking, the tuition restrictions mandated by the statute limit the ability of nonsectarian schools to participate in the program, as religious schools often have lower overhead costs, supplemental income from private donations and consequently lower tuition needs" (Cooper, 2000). In other words, the vouchers were valued at well below tuition for most nonsectarian schools making it impossible for them to show an interest in the program.

November saw the election of a voucher-advocating president, the overwhelming rejections of voucher referenda in California and Michigan, and a major public relations media campaign by a relatively new voucher-favoring organization, the Black Alliance for Educational Options (BAEO).

The referenda in California and Michigan differed considerably from each other. The California referendum would have provided $4,000 in taxpayer money to anyone who wanted to attend a private school, including the 600,000 students already in private California schools. Supporters argued that the resulting program would have given consumers "total freedom of choice."

Not quite. While some 600,000 California children are enrolled in private schools, the state's public schools contain over 6,000,000. Even a rapidly expanding private school system could handle only a small fraction of students presenting vouchers. Indeed, as noted elsewhere, Roy Romer, former governor of Colorado and now superintendent of schools in Los Angeles, has supported the development of new charter schools in hopes of thinning his overpacked classrooms. National estimates find that existing private schools could accept only 4 percent of existing public school students (MacInnes, 2000). In addition, many private schools have no desire to expand. One story, unconfirmed but plausible, stated that 85 percent of the private schools in California had announced that they would not accept voucher students who scored below grade level.

Even if the specifics of this story are off a bit, it indicates that private schools are not opening their doors to students bearing vouchers. Catholic schools, which have been hemorrhaging students in the last decade, are more likely to accept voucher students, but to date, they have been asked to absorb only small numbers of poor and/or low-performing students.

Unlike the money-for-everyone referendum in California, the Michigan proposal would have provided up to $3,300 for students in "failing districts"— those which do not graduate at least two-thirds of their high school students within four years. Referendum proponents said it would affect about thirty districts throughout the state, but according to figures from the Michigan Department of Education, only seven districts would qualify" (Sandham, 2000, p. 1).

The California proposal, although amply funded by Silicon Valley venture capitalist Timothy Draper, met resistance early on. Homeschoolers opposed the measure on the grounds that it would lead to increased regulation of all schools (Duffy, 2000). Others objected to rich people whose children already attended private schools getting a $4,000 rebate. Even voucher advocate Terry Moe of the Hoover Institute opposed the measure. Said Moe, "There were plenty of voucher supporters who would have told him [Draper], if asked, not to do it this way. But he didn't ask" (Walsh, 2000b). For whatever reason(s), voters sent the measure down in flames by a 70–30 margin.

When first proposed, the Michigan referendum was given a fighting chance even though a seemingly natural ally, Governor John Engler, opposed it, apparently favoring his charter program instead. Throughout September and October, polls gave the measure about even odds to pass. Unlike most other voucher referenda, the proponents of Michigan's program outspent their opponents by 100 percent. It was thus something of a shock when it also failed by a margin of 70–30. Apparently, the principal reason for the shellacking was the discovery that the measure contained loopholes that rendered eligible a number of well-off students, not just the poor, for whom the measure was ostensibly intended. The *Milwaukee Journal Sentinel* (2000) opined that "had they focused on the truly needy, the [California and Michigan] initiatives might have sustained the support they earlier enjoyed."

A survey conducted a year before the 2000 election found that parents knew little about either vouchers or charters (Zehr, 1999). Even in Milwaukee and Cleveland, which have two highly visible voucher programs, the survey found that parents were confused and not very well-informed on these educational alternatives. If true, this too could have played a role in the voucher proposal defeats: People tend to be quite cautious about changes in the public schools when the impact of those changes is uncertain.

Mulling over the results, especially from Cleveland, editors at the *Washington Post* reasoned that the voucher proposals simply do not offer enough to attract schools other than those run by the Catholic Church. Cleveland's vouchers were worth $2,500. Schools that belong to the National Association of Independent Schools charge much more. In the Midwest, 1999–2000 median costs for an NAIS preschool was $8,200, while that for twelfth grade was $11,525 (McGovern, 2000). Thus the vouchers did not bring impoverished families close to the fees at even the elementary grades.

Immediate reactions to the referenda were predictable. Kathleen Lyons of the NEA said, "It's time to move on. It's time voucher proponents got that message. What people are saying is that they want a great public school in their neighborhood. Let's get on with the business of that" (Walsh, 2000b). But Nina Shokraii Rees, from the voucher-advocating Heritage Foundation, said, "It's disappointing but I wouldn't read too much into these defeats. A U.S. Supreme Court decision in favor of vouchers would single-handedly generate much more interest in creating voucher programs in other states" (Walsh, 2000b).

Given all of the uncertainty introduced by the courts and the ballot box returns, voucher supporters mobilized to decide what to do next. In general, advocates seemed to be scaling back their ambitions, taking a longer view and dumping the word *vouchers*. Harvard University's voucher proponent Paul Peterson, said, "Five percent of families will want vouchers, not 50 percent. Voucher proponents want to do something massive, and that concerns me. It's better if we crawl along." Peterson also reflected a growing tendency among voucher supporters in how to look at their movement. He stated that inadequate education in the inner cities "is the biggest civil rights question of our era" (Coeyman, 2000).

The word *voucher* currently carries so much heavy emotional and ideological baggage that even ardent advocates are dropping it. One of the most energetic voucher supporters, Jeanne Allen of the Center for Education Reform, said, "There are fewer and fewer people who think only school vouchers are the key. There are more and more people talking about choice" (Wilgoren, 2000b). Senate majority leader Trent Lott weighed in: "I think maybe the word is part of the problem. Maybe the word should be 'scholarship'" (Wilgoren, 2000b). Just how this might solve the problem is not clear, since a number of voucher programs, Cleveland and Florida included, already refer to the vouchers as "scholarships." In addition, while the Michigan referendum used the word *voucher*, the California referendum did not (although its opponents did).

Continuing the options theme, Secretary of Education Roderick Paige told senators at his confirmation hearings that "the word 'vouchers' has taken on a negative tone, but the concept should be part of a mix of school choice options available to parents." (Fletcher, 2001; Schemo 2001) And former assistant secretary of education Chester E. Finn, Jr. offered a "peace plan" to bridge the gap between voucher advocates and opponents. Likening the 107th Congress's education reform efforts to a train "that could be headed for a wreck" if it tried to incorporate vouchers, Finn proposed that federal dollars, which constitute only 8 percent of a typical school budget, should follow the child, not reside with the school. Although Finn could only describe his proposal briefly in the op-ed space allotted, it seems on the surface a plan complicated to the point of unworkability.

In any case, a relatively new organization states that it is for "options." The Black Alliance for Educational Options (BAEO) home page says the organization will work in a variety of ways to make the general public aware of choice programs and of "efforts to reduce or limit educational options available to parents" (http://www.baeoonline.org).

BAEO's president and source of inspiration is Howard Fuller, president of the Institute for the Transformation of Learning at Marquette University, and former superintendent of public schools in Milwaukee (and husband of Deborah McGriff, former superintendent of schools in Detroit and currently a vice president with Chris Whittle's Edison Schools, Inc.). BAEO grew out of symposia Fuller sponsored in 1999 on Options for African Americans and was formally organized in late August 2000. Aside from symposia, BAEO's principal activity to date has been a $1.3 million advertising campaign in Washington, D.C., media and black-owned newspapers (sponsored by the likes of the Walton Family Foundation, the Lynde and Harry Bradley Foundation, and the Milton and Rose Friedman Foundation). According to one article, "The alliance endorses all forms of parental choice—charter schools, education tax credits, private scholarships, home-schooling, public school innovations as well as the much-debated tax-supported vouchers" (Mathews, 2000).

President Bush signaled that education was indeed going to be his number one priority by calling a meeting in Austin, Texas, with both Democrats and Republicans. Its bipartisan nature was diminished a bit by the fact that the leading liberal Democratic voice on educational issues, Senator Edward Kennedy of Massachusetts, was not invited. According to reports, Bush "laid out educational proposals highlighting early literacy and school accountability, but heard warning that waging a legislative battle to funnel taxpayer money to private schools through vouchers could endanger his plans." Said Senator Evan Bayh (D-Indiana), "Bush would fight for vouchers because he believes in it." But an insistence on vouchers "could imperil all his other goals" (Oppel and Schemo, 2000).

Bush also built support for vouchers into his cabinet by choosing Roderick Paige, Superintendent of Houston Public Schools, the nation's seventh-largest district, to be his secretary of education. As noted, although Paige backed off the word "vouchers" in his confirmation hearings, he had earlier supported Bush's voucher proposals and had even installed a small voucher program in Houston to send kids with special needs and disruptive students to private schools. The program is little used, largely, it appears, because the vouchers do not provide enough money to appeal to the private schools.

Bipartisanship will not be easy on any of the important education issues—least of all, vouchers. Vouchers, along with testing and religion in the schools, deeply divided the 106th Congress. "The bickering was so bad that Congress, in the session that just ended, failed for the first in 35 years to enact a routine reauthorization of the main federal education law. When centrists offered a compromise between feuding Senate factions, only 13 people voted for it" (Hook, 2000).

In any case, given the consensus logic of the Federal Appeals Court in the Cleveland case and of the *Washington Post* editors, Bush's voucher proposal was a nonstarter. The judges and the editors found that vouchers valued at $2,500 were insufficient to allow parents to send their children to private, nonsectarian schools or to entice those schools to participate in the program. California-based columnist Matthew Miller estimated that it would take a voucher worth at least $6,000 to generate any interest in Los Angeles, where public schools' per-pupil expenditure currently runs around $8,500 (Miller, 2001). The Bush proposal would have created vouchers worth only $1,500. If Miller, the *Post* editors, and the Appeals Court are right, the Bush proposal would have been little more than a gift from American taxpayers to the Catholic Church.

Making Vouchers Accountable

In Milwaukee, no further funds have been appropriated for evaluation, and the archdiocese of Milwaukee has refused to release the test scores of voucher students, claiming that no state agency has the power to require the schools or the church to surrender the testing results.

The position of the Milwaukee archdiocese illustrates another inherent tension between church and state, one that will no doubt increase in intensity if state-funded voucher programs grow: For public schools, accountability is the word of the day. States and localities have created standards concerning what children should learn and assessments to determine if they have learned it (here, we do not question the quality or wisdom of such programs, although some of them seem to the author like cruel and unusual punishment). Accountability sanctions threaten students with retention in grade or nongraduation from high school. They threaten teachers and principals and other administrators with reassignment or removal—all in the name of accountability.

Yet, in Florida, the schools receiving voucher students do not have to administer the Florida tests that made the students eligible for vouchers in the first place. That is, on the basis of tests, Florida's accountability program has found some schools wanting and told these schools' children they may attend school elsewhere. Then the accountability stops: No one looks to see if the children are receiving a better education at these other schools.

In Milwaukee, some voucher schools have violated what few rules do exist. Examples include not admitting students at random, requiring participation in religious instruction, manipulating enrollments to screen students, and charging additional fees.

People grumble about the lack of accountability in voucher programs, but usually do not pursue their complaints because the programs are small. If the programs increase in scope, however, funding programs that have no accountability to the taxpayer will eventually annoy enough people to trigger calls for the regulation of these private schools. Why, they will say, should the private schools get a free ride when the public schools do not?

This is something John Stuart Mill, for all his considerable genius, did not think about. He thought the state could administer tests to see if children had learned what they were supposed to have learned. It's a benign scenario. But Mill ought to have asked if the state would be satisfied with this small incursion into education. He worried greatly that "State is a mere contrivance for molding people to be just like one another." Well, if the state is interested in molding people, will it not try to effect this outcome no matter what educational system is in place? If there is no state education, will the state simply resort to more indirect techniques? The answer is, to a certain extent, yes.

John Jennings of the Center on Education Policy has explored what might happen in the United States if large sums of taxpayer dollars were funneled away from the public education system and into the private sector. Many other nations have systems where a large proportion of the students are educated in private schools, but with state subsidies or at state expense. Jennings examined how schools are regulated in other nations where private schools do receive government funds. Jennings finds that "Often, subsidized private schools must follow the same national curriculum as public schools, although they may retain control over their teaching methods." In many countries, subsidized private schools must pass a government inspection before they can offer a diploma that is recognized in that country. The students must pass national exams before graduation or, in some cases, before moving on to the next level of schooling. Teachers in subsidized schools must have the same qualifications as those in public schools and, in some cases, be paid the same salaries. Teacher/pupil ratios are sometimes regulated to be the same as in public schools.

In America today, both state aid and regulation is quite limited. Thirty-eight states require certification of private schools but mostly these involve judgments about minimum criteria with regard to education, health, and safety. Jennings observes that

> [Currently], the U.S. provides only very limited kinds of assistance to private schools and regulates them far less than many other countries. But the basic impetus that has led other countries to link funding with government regulation also exists in the U.S. It is reasonable to assume that if American private schools began receiving substantially more funding through voucher and choice programs, the states or the federal government would increase the amount and scope of private school regulation beyond the current level. (Center for Education Policy, 1999, p. 12)

Some observers, especially Christian fundamentalists, have predicted that vouchers would bring just the kind of government control that Jennings found in Europe:

> If such a [choice via vouchers] plan were ever adopted, powerful interests would immediately begin lobbying in support of restrictive legislation that would undercut the element of free choice in the plan as it now stands. Under pressure from

special interest groups such as Shanker's United Federation of Teachers [sic], laws might be passed to require that teachers in private schools meet standardized licensing requirements and that the physical plant of private schools meet arbitrary standards established by the government. Laws could (and would) follow laws, self-proclaimed reformers would come to advocate the imposition, on private schools, of what they would term "academic standards; and, just as we now have a costly system of public education that wears the label "free," we may easily end up with a system of state education that bears the appellation "private." (Patton, undated, p. 24–25, probably 1991)

Similarly, Barrett Mosbacker, the headmaster of a Christian school in North Carolina, wrote, "Although vouchers ostensibly offer freedom of choice, they may actually eliminate that freedom by encumbering Christian schools with government regulations. If this happens, choice will be replaced by coercion. Unless sufficient "court-proof" safeguards are enacted that guarantee the freedom of Christian schools, vouchers should be opposed" (Mosbacker, 1998).

In more specific terms, home educator and author Cathy Duffy has argued against the California voucher proposal on the grounds that it will lead to increased regulation. "Regulation must address questions such as how to verify information provided by private schools, how to determine that children actually exist, how to deal with the fact that illegal aliens may qualify for vouchers, and how to fund and operate the bureaucracy necessary to answer the above questions as well as to process quarterly enrollment reports, payment, and mid-year transfers and dropouts" (Duffy, 2000).

Duffy argues that schools that wish to retain their autonomy by refusing vouchers will find it hard to compete. Most parents will prefer to use the vouchers rather than pay tuition, sending the schools that refuse vouchers out of business. Mosbacker voiced the same concern. Although there are not yet any reports of private schools going out of business in Michigan, we did note that private schools that remain private must compete against private schools that opt for charter status. The former must still charge tuition—the latter can offer their services free. According to Miron, no schools have yet closed, but parochial schools in some areas have lost large numbers of students to charters (Miron, personal communication, October 16, 2000).

Duffy does not emphasize a point about the voucher proposal that Columbia's Henry Levin has raised: Under a voucher system, the state would be dealing with *schools* not *districts*. Levin conjectured that the inherent inefficiency of the infrastructure needed to operate such a system would actually render vouchers more costly than the current public school arrangement.

Martha McCarthy of Indiana University has observed that recent Supreme Court rulings might open the door for spending tax dollars not only in nonsectarian schools but in church-affiliated schools as well. "The central rationale that voucher proponents use to defend the legality of voucher plans is the *private* nature of the decisions that ultimately result in government funds flowing to religious institutions. The parents, not the state, decide where to send their children to school, and the funds simply follow the child" (McCarthy, 2000, p. 375).

Although a decision by the Supreme Court might allow money to flow to sectarian schools without causing an infraction of the establishment clause, it is not clear that such a ruling alone would provide money to parents to send their kids to any school independent of state accreditation regulations. At this point we might expect the Friedmanites to argue that in a truly market-driven choice system, the market itself regulates quality.

Most of the data that have been brought to bear on the market theory are indirect at best. A common claim, for example, is that Catholic schools produce higher gains for less money. However, the manner in which costs-per-pupil are calculated and in which students are selected for these comparisons render them useless.

We can test the market hypothesis in two ways. First, we can compare existing private schools against public schools. Private schools presumably have to compete with public schools for their students and so should show the advantages that market theory claims. Second, we can look at systems that have used a market theory approach to see if the predicted changes have occurred. As an example, Chile has had a market-driven national voucher system for twenty years, certainly long enough to determine if the predicted outcomes have showed up. We first examine two ways of comparing public and private schools within this country and then turn to the results from Chile.

The National Assessment of Educational Progress provides separate results for public, Catholic, and Other Private schools. Table 8.1 presents the results of the most recent science assessment.

TABLE 8.1 *NAEP 1996 Science Assessment: Public and Catholic Schools Compared**

Grade	Percentile				
	10th	*25th*	*50th*	*75th*	*90th*
Fourth					
Public	103	127	151	172	188
Catholic	127	146	165	182	197
Eighth					
Public	102	126	151	172	191
Catholic	125	144	165	182	199
Twelfth					
Public	103	126	151	174	192
Catholic	116	136	155	174	190

The scales are independently constructed for each grade, and thus cannot be compared across grades.

*NAEP reports also contain two other categories, "Nonpublic schools," which are all nonpublic schools, and "Other Private Schools," which are those that are not Catholic. These scores are virtually identical to the scores for Catholic schools. Caution should be used, however, in speaking about "Other Private Schools," because the number of schools included is sufficiently small to yield a possibly unreliable estimate.

Source: U.S. Department of Education, Office of Educational Research and Improvement (Washington, DC: Department of Education, 1996).

Table 8.1 shows results for grades 4, 8, and 12, and for performances ranging from low (10th percentile) to high (90th percentile). The differences between public and Catholic school within any one grade are largest at the lowest performing level, and smallest at the higher performing levels. Thus, at the fourth grade, the 10th percentile school for public schools is 103 and 127 for Catholic schools, a difference of 24 points. At the 75th and 90th percentiles however, private schools outscore public schools by only 10 and 9 points, respectively.

At the twelfth-grade level, the difference between public and private schools at the 90th percentile is essentially zero, with public schools scoring two points *higher* than Catholic schools. It is sometimes alleged that this result derives from the greater holding power of Catholic schools. That is, at the upper grades, more students drop out of public schools, taking their low scores with them. No one has ever produced evidence to demonstrate that this is true. It is equally possible that these results quantify a qualitative claim made some years ago by, of all organizations, *Money* magazine.

Money set out to compare public and private schools and clearly expected to find a marked superiority for the privates. It did not. The editors declared quite candidly that "We were shocked!" This is what shocked them:

> The best news to come out of *Money's* survey of public and private schools across America was that, by and large, public schools are not lacking in experienced topnotch teachers, challenging courses or an environment that is conducive to learning. What many public schools are lacking is a student body brimming with kids eager to take advantage of what the school has to offer. But just because other kids disdain getting a good education doesn't mean your kid has to. Most teachers are dying for young, motivated minds to nurture. If they find an industrious student who is eager to learn, more often than not they will give him or her all of the personal attention that private tuition could buy.
>
> [If you live in a suburb and send you children to private schools] Here's the bottom line: You are probably wasting your hard-earned money. (p. 112)

A different set of comparisons between public and private schools was carried out by Richard Rothstein of the Economic Policy Institute, Martin Carnoy of Stanford University, and Luis Benveniste of the World Bank. Using case studies, they examined six generalizations about private versus public schools.

1. Private elementary school personnel tend to be more accountable to parents than are public school personnel.
2. Private school outputs and expectations for students tend to be more clearly defined than are public school outputs and expectations.
3. Private elementary schools tend to produce higher nonachievement outputs—behavior and values, for example—than do public elementary schools. Moreover, private schools allocate a higher proportion of resources to these nonacademic objectives than do public schools.

4. Teacher selection and retention practices at private schools are more efficient than those at public schools.
5. Private schools' academic success is accomplished with materials that are not significantly different (in standard subjects) from curricular materials found in public schools.
6. Private school innovations stimulate improved practices at the public schools with which they compete. (pp. 4–5)

They indeed found differences among the schools in their study, but not along the public-private lines of demarcation. Overall, they found that, "the social, cultural, and economic backgrounds of the parents and the community in which the school was located seemed to be the main determinant of variation, much more so than a school's public or private character or, within the latter group, whether it was religious or secular. Within these particular communities, the similarities between schools and the problems they confronted overwhelmed the differences" (p. 75).

Consider the findings on the generalization that private schools are more responsive to and more accountable to parents than the "monopolistic" "government schools."

> Our case studies suggest that parents of public schoolchildren can command as much or more control over educational issues as do parents of private school-children—when the parents are affluent, self-confident, and highly educated. But at schools in lower-income communities the pattern is different, with respect to both public and private school parents. Here, parents undertake little effort to make schools accountable for curricular offerings or academic practices; rather, the faculties perceive a serious problem of parental "meddling" in the application of policy to individual children. (Rothstein, Cannoly and Benveniste, 1999, p. 30)

Parents in affluent areas believe they have both a responsibility and a right to influence their children's education. Affluent private schools are more successful in convincing parents that matters of curriculum and pedagogy are the sole province of the school. If anything, these private schools are less responsive. In low-income areas, parents hold teachers or principals to account for the grading or disciplinary actions that the school has taken. They don't demand that phonics replace whole language. They want to know why their kid got an F or a suspension.

When it comes to academic matters, low-income schools find themselves trying to nudge the parents into taking responsibility for their children. These schools are, in a sense, attempting to hold the parents accountable. Private schools have an advantage here because they can make involvement with the school a condition of admission. Such involvements, however, usually do not occur in academic areas. The parents help with fund-raising, decorating the school, and so forth.

This research suffers from its small sample size, which constrains any generalizations to a larger system. Additionally, it provides only indirect evidence about any voucher system because the private schools in the study are not operated with vouchers. Research that did examine a larger system and also made a direct comparison between public schools and private schools operating with government-supplied money has been conducted by Patrick J. McEwan and Martin Carnoy of Stanford University.

McEwan and Carnoy observe that while advocates tout private school vouchers as a solution to the perceived low quality of public education, "most empirical evidence is unsuited to an evaluation of effectiveness and costs under a large-scale voucher system." Either the private schools are not funded through vouchers or the voucher programs are too small to provoke a great deal of interest from private schools or to make inferences about the larger system.

A Nation of Vouchers: Chile

McEwan and Carnoy found a suitable example of a larger voucher system in Chile. Influenced directly by Milton Friedman's writings, in 1980 Chile's government began a sweeping education reform effort. It transferred the management responsibility for public schools from the centralized Ministry of Education back to local municipalities through two institutions. Most schools are now operated by a part of municipal bureaucracy known as the *Departamento de Adminostracion de la Educational Municipal* (hereafter, DAEM). A much smaller number report to a quasi-autonomous municipal corporation. Teachers became employees of these municipalities, not civil servants of the state. By 1982, this transfer was essentially in place.

Funding regulations changed as well. Prior to 1980, the ministry developed budgets around the existing system, with little new money to reflect changes in student enrollments. Under the new system, the Ministry of Education disbursed payments each month based directly on the number of students enrolled multiplied by the value of the voucher. Vouchers had a base value plus adjustments based on location and grade. The law specified the factor by which the base was adjusted for each grade and additional compensations were made for schools with high levels of poverty or situated in remote locations.

The government initially indexed vouchers to inflation, but indexing ceased during Chile's economic crisis of the 1980s. In spite of this, new private schools opened and claimed a quickly increasing share of students. Existing private schools were eligible for vouchers if they did not add any tuition charges. By 1987, public schools' share of the enrollment had fallen to just over 60 percent. It has inched downward only slightly since 1987 to 58 percent.

By 1987, voucher schools had siphoned off just over 30 percent of the students; their enrollment has increased only slightly since 1987 to about 35 percent. All during this period, high-tuition private schools enrolled from 5 percent to 9 percent of the students, with the figure being 7 percent or 8 percent in most years.

In an analysis of fourth-grade data, McEwan and Carnoy found what they called "mixed" results. Nonreligious voucher schools had lower test scores than the public schools. However, they also cost less, and when costs are figured in these schools are slightly more cost-efficient than public schools. The Catholic voucher schools were more effective in producing achievement outcomes for students with similar backgrounds, but they cost *more*, and so their cost-efficiency is likewise similar to the public schools. Say the researchers:

> The results are probably not satisfying for either voucher advocates or opponents. They are inconsistent with advocates' claims that privately managed voucher schools produce significantly higher achievement than public schools for pupils with similar socioeconomic backgrounds. Even so, nonreligious voucher schools are more cost-efficient than publicly run schools. Another category, Catholic voucher schools, is able to achieve higher test scores for similar students but only by spending more. (McEwan and Carnoy, 2000, p. 23)

McEwan and Carnoy feel that vouchers and for-profit schools might be a good investment for poor nations strapped for resources. For the United States, they think the results show that "a broad caricature of private schools—either positive or negative—is misleading; in fact, different categories vary widely in their effectiveness and efficiency." Moe would certainly have predicted this. The for-profits, however, "successfully compete by cutting costs, rather than significantly raising achievement."

McEwan returned to the scene to analyze eighth-grade data which became available later. This data also had the advantage of reporting scores for individual students. The earlier fourth-grade data had already been aggregated to the school level. In addition, for the eighth grade, parental questionnaires provided a much richer set of background information on the students.

As in the earlier study, private schools that charge high tuition and don't take vouchers achieve the best results. Religious voucher schools score slightly higher than public schools while nonreligious voucher schools scored slightly lower. However, when background characteristics were taken into account, only the private, tuition-charging schools scored better than the public schools.

If voucher schools don't score higher than other schools except for the elite private schools, what accounts for their popularity? McEwan suggests that because the voucher schools contain a larger proportion of high SES students, these schools have a certain cachet of class that impresses parents. "The implication is that vouchers provided many middle-class Chilean families with the means to choose the 'right' peer group, rather than the 'best' school" (McEwan, 2000, p. 23).

The two studies described above are both cross-sectional, looking at students at a given point in time. One prediction of market theory, however, is that, given a mix of private and public schools, public schools will respond to the competitive pressure and improve. Such a prediction calls for longitudinal data. A third McEwan and Carnoy study provides just such data examining the achievement of Chilean students from 1982 through 1996.

The results are surprising in their lack of uniformity. In the rural regions outside of Santiago, the effects are negative—the public schools' achievement declined slightly. When McEwan and Carnoy analyzed the data taking parental background into account, the results were also consistently negative (McEwan and Carnoy, 1999).

In the capital region, which accounts for 25 percent of the population, and includes Santiago and its surroundings, the effects were mixed. Taking the capital region, as a whole, the results are slightly positive. Over the period from 1982 to 1996, achievement rose in the public schools by an effect size of about +0.2. When the capital region's results are analyzed by parental educational level, though, the highest and lowest categories show negative results, while the middle two show positive results. In three instances, the result is not large enough to claim a "real" effect, but in the second-lowest category, a category McEwan and Carnoy describe as "lower middle class," the effect is substantial— these schools got better.

The results flustered the researchers: "Given the weak theoretical base of the voucher literature and the constraints of our data, we are hard-pressed to explain the variable effects of competition" (p. 21). They offer several possibilities. One is that the response of some schools was not to concentrate on quality, but to lobby the government for additional funds. Second, constraints on the allocation of resources might have prevented improvement—some schools might have been unable to dump incompetent personnel or remove even competent people to reallocate their resources.

It is also possible that the schools that failed to improve were already operating close to maximal effectiveness prior to the vouchers' arrival. If this were true, however, how does one explain the popularity of the new voucher schools? "Given a choice between public and private schools of similar effectiveness, it is plausible that families would choose the more privileged peer group, especially if peer effects stood to improve their own children's outcomes" (p. 23).

The fact that the new private voucher schools attracted students whose parents are better educated is a Chilean instance of "creaming," which the researchers consider a negative outcome. They call for a more comprehensive analysis of the effects of competition. "A curious feature of the voucher literature is that advocates and critics have a tendency to emphasize one of these effects, and ignore or downplay others. For example, advocates have emphasized the positive effects of competition, while skeptics have focused on the negative effects of sorting and cream-skimming. To adequately evaluate the impact of vouchers, we need to consider both." (pp. 24–25).

Moe (1995) contends that while "private voucher programs have their own rules" which "have a lot to do with the kinds of outcomes that get generated," they also have more to offer than the mere accretion of additional evidence. "In comparison with the public programs, private voucher programs give us a simpler, more direct indication of how choice and markets actually operate when the most burdensome trappings of bureaucracy and political control are removed" (p. 20).

We shall return to private voucher programs after reviewing some of the better known public programs. In both the public and private voucher programs, the reader might be disconcerted by what appears to be a most unusual set of political bedfellows: rich, white, conservative Republicans and poor, minority, urban, most probably Democratic parents. In general, suburban families are either not interested in, or actively oppose, vouchers.

As any number of commentators have observed, this alliance, odd as it seems at first, makes sense. Conservative whites press market-oriented programs because they believe in markets (and, in some cases, hope to make money from the shift to market-driven schools). Urban minorities want to escape inner-city schools but are trapped by the harsh economic realities of those areas. Those living in suburbs have already acquired school choice: Because of their relative affluence, they can exert considerable school choice by their prior decisions of where to live. As Moe views it:

> The educational establishment is solidly behind the poor when it comes to mainstream educational programs—for compensatory, bilingual, and special education, for instance. But the establishment has its own reasons for opposing vouchers, even when poor kids are the only ones to receive them. Vouchers allow children and resources to leave the public system. A fully developed voucher system, moreover, would largely dismantle the establishment's own system of bureaucracy and political control in face of new arrangements that decentralize power to parents and schools. From the establishment's standpoint, then, vouchers are the ultimate survival issue, and they must be defeated wherever they are proposed. (p. 5)

In this statement, Moe operates partly from fact and partly from idealized theory. The "establishment" (it's not clear what Moe actually means with that loaded word) will oppose vouchers, but certainly in part because vouchers will leave the public system with fewer resources, which would reduce the system's capabilities to provide good service. Similarly, it is not at all clear that vouchers will decentralize power and put parents in charge.

Vouchers in U.S. Cities

We now turn to a more in-depth discussion of several of the better known public and private voucher ventures.

Milwaukee

The Milwaukee school choice program involves the transfer of public funds to private schools. Act 36, passed by the 1990 Wisconsin legislature, established a voucher program in Milwaukee permitting up to 1 percent of that city's low-income children to attend any private school that would accept the state's voucher (initially worth $2,446 and rising to $4,696 in 1997–98). The program has since been expanded to permit up to 15 percent of the students to attend. "Low-income" was defined as 175 percent or less than the official U. S. poverty rate—in 1990, about $14,000 for a family of four. The program has usually been under-subscribed. One percent of Milwaukee students would be about 600 pupils. The numbers rose from 300 to 771 under the 1 percent cap and with the further expansion of the program, to about 11,000 for the 2000–01 school year. With each voucher worth $5,326, the cost to Wisconsin taxpayers is almost $60 million a year to support private schools.

Participating schools had to meet one of four criteria for continued participation:

1. At least 70 percent of the students gain at least one grade level each year;
2. Attendance must average 90 percent;
3. At least 80 percent of the students demonstrate significant academic progress; or
4. At least 70 percent of the families meet the school's criteria for parental involvement.

The Wisconsin Supreme Court upheld the law in an initial suit and later concluded that religious schools can participate. The court found the law constitutional because the children, not the schools, are the beneficiaries—the vouchers go directly to the families, who then decide where to use them. This logic has also been seen in other U.S. Supreme Court rulings on vouchers and will likely hold true for any case brought before that court.

The Wisconsin Supreme Court's decision surprised some observers. To them, it seemed likely that this decision would be overturned because, although there is no religious intent in the voucher system itself, religious schools are often clear on their intention to inculcate their religion in their students. Thus Milwaukee's Gospel Lutheran School states that "children are taught to recognize God's Law and in it see their own sin. . . . Religion is taught formally in kindergarten and in all grades." St. Bernadette states that "Non-Catholic students are welcomes. Because of the nature of a Catholic School, religion is taught daily as a part of the curriculum. Catholic values are incorporated into all other aspects of the curriculum." Looking at these quotes, commentator Nat Hentoff declared that "to allow parents to use public money to put children into elementary and secondary schools that are completely devoted to inculcating a particular religious faith means that there will be, in these institutions, no separation at all between church and state" (Hentoff, 1999). Nevertheless, the U.S. Supreme Court declined to hear the case, allowing the program to continue.

The legislature initially established the program as a five-year experiment and commissioned an annual evaluation of the program. John Witte and colleagues at the University of Wisconsin conducted the evaluations. At the end of five years, Witte concluded that there were no differences between the students choosing private schools and a control group who remained in the Milwaukee Public Schools (MPS). As elaborated on pages 152 to 155, Paul Peterson, a political scientist at Harvard University, criticized the experiment, including Witte's methods and expertise. Voucher supporters lobbied successfully not to conduct more rigorous assessments of the program, but to end the evaluations—the legislature expanded the program but eliminated funds for evaluations.

In 1997–98, the vouchers were worth $4,696 and per pupil expenditures in public schools were $7,869. These figures somehow caused the usually reliable Brent Staples of the *New York Times* to claim that the vouchers cost taxpayers only $3,000—less than half of what the public schools spend. In fact, MPS elementary schools received only $4,234 in direct aid in 1997–98. Most choice students attend private schools in the elementary grades. Public schools also receive special education funds. The rest is used by the district for capital improvements, recreation programs, alternative education, food, maintenance, and transportation. MPS also must provide transportation for choice students who require it. Thus, even without factoring in the cost of transporting the private school pupils, the amount of the vouchers actually exceeds what most public schools receive in money for regular instruction (a lawsuit resulted in the private schools being exempted from having to provide special education services). The private schools do not have to disclose other sources of funds and do not.

Although Milwaukee has many private schools, initially just three of them enrolled more than 80 percent of all voucher applicants. Such a concentration of students precludes any generalization of the effect of "choice," although this has not prevented people from trying. Witte concluded after five years that there were no differences (Witte, Sterr, and Christopher, 1995). Peterson[18] and colleagues concluded that the data favored choice (Greene, Peterson, and Du, 1996). My own conclusion was that if the data favored choice, and I wasn't certain that it did, it was likely because the choice students had been in one school for four years, providing them with an academic stability rare among urban students (Bracey, 1996a). Rouse concluded that it depends on what assumptions that analyst makes and, thus, on the statistical procedure used (Rouse, 1998). In her favored analyses, there was an effect favoring choice for math but not for reading.

Rouse also noted that disadvantaged students attending a program with extra funding and small classes outperformed both students at magnet schools and the voucher students. Nelson (1998) observed that while Rouse's paper partially replicates Peterson's analysis, it can actually be taken as a rather stinging rebuke of Peterson's approach. Nelson discussed thirteen ways in which Rouse's analysis differed from Peterson's, including the type of significance test used,

18. Peterson is actually the second author on many of the articles, the lead author being one of his former students, Jay P. Greene of the University of Houston. It is Peterson, however, who has attracted the attention and fire as indicated by the page 1 story about him in the August 5, 1998, edition of *Education Week*.

assumptions about missing data, family background, and student learning rates, violations of regression analysis assumptions. and comparability of samples.

In the end, this is all much ado about very little, because the data themselves are so flawed it is not clear that they can yield any trustworthy conclusions. Among the problems:

- Researchers could collect data only on unsuccessful applicants who entered MPS, which amounted to fewer than half of those rejected. This is crucial to Peterson's analyses. He contends that those who were rejected, because they were rejected by lottery, constitute a group comparable to those admitted. Since most students were not admitted by lottery, this claim is questionable at the outset, but clearly those who were rejected by a voucher school and turned up in MPS could be quite different from those who were rejected and went elsewhere.
- Parents responded at low rates and different rates—only 37 percent of the voucher families and 22 percent of the MPS families—to a survey seeking critical background data.
- The response rate meant that test scores *and* surveys were available for only 28 percent of the voucher students and 21 percent of the MPS students.
- Random selection, much emphasized by Peterson, occurred only at schools that were oversubscribed. One of the two schools admitting most of the African American students admitted all who applied, while the other one had a waiting list.
- Siblings of already-admitted students could skip the lottery.
- There were no rules for maintaining waiting lists and no oversight of them.
- Voucher applicants with "disabilities" could be rejected with no oversight or supervision of the process. Given that most private schools have minimal expertise in special education, one wonders what they saw as a "disability."

Finally, results from another Milwaukee experiment in which additional funds were used to reduce class size indicates that smaller classes produce much more powerful effects than whatever might occur from "choice" (Molnar, 1999). Indeed, the effect seen in the Milwaukee choice project might well be due to small classes. In MPS, the pupil–teacher ratio is 19.3:1. In the voucher schools, it is 15.3:1.

It's important to note that pupil–teacher ratio is not the same thing as class size. In 1996, the pupil–teacher ratio in U.S. elementary schools was 18.8:1. The average class size was 25.2. Pupil–teacher ratio counts anyone in the building who has a teaching certificate and whose primary responsibility is to teach, including special education and Title 1 teachers as well as various specialists. Private schools seldom offer special education or remedial programs such as Title 1, and often do not have specialists. Thus, their pupil–teacher ratio is likely to be much closer to average class size than it is for public schools.

Rouse analyzed data for the voucher schools and the public schools with small classes (pupil–teacher ratio 17.0:1) and found that the improvements in reading were as large in the public schools as in the private schools. She also found a small gain for math in public schools and no gain at all (effect size = –0.05) in private schools. She suggests that *if* students in voucher schools show improvement—she still has her doubts—it is because they attend small schools with small classes (Rouse, 2000).

Small classes have emerged as an important explanatory variable in research on voucher and charter schools because they often have smaller classes than the public schools, and often smaller enrollments overall. Small schools have recently received much attention for their higher achievement as well (Wasley, Fine, King, Powell, Holland, Gladden, and Mosak, 2000).

The effects of small classes have been known for some time as a result of Project STAR in Tennessee (Finn and Achilles, 1990, 1999). The importance of the STAR experiment comes from the fact that the three treatments—regular class, regular class with full-time teacher's aide, and small class—were randomly assigned within each school, eliminating any source of selection bias. The study's evaluators found the effects strong and sustained. A recent analysis by Princeton University economist Alan Krueger, which controlled for factors that might have affected the randomness of assignment after the first year and for Hawthorne and John Henry effects (when people expend more effort because they have or have not been included as part of an experiment, respectively), not only left the initial conclusions unchanged but found that the effect was cumulative across grades (Krueger, 1998; see Bracey, 1998c, for a summary of Krueger's analyses).

That Peterson's Milwaukee study will continue to be used ideologically can be seen in how it was released initially. Most such works are reviewed by peers informally, then either presented at some professional gathering or sent to some learned journal, or both. The first appearance of Peterson's analysis of the Milwaukee data appeared as an Associated Press wire story (Estrin, 1996). The same day, the *Wall Street Journal* carried an op-ed essay (Greene and Peterson, 1996). The evening of that same day found presidential candidate Robert Dole addressing the Republican National Convention on education and calling for vouchers and choice. Within a couple of days, William Bennett and Lamar Alexander had managed to appear on television talk shows touting the study and Rush Limbaugh had sent it across the airwaves.

Peterson conducted a similar analysis drawing similar conclusions for the Cleveland voucher program (Peterson, Howell, and Greene, 1999) and has been hired in several other venues as well to evaluate the programs established by the Children's Educational Opportunity Foundation (usually referred to as CEO America), now in partnership with the conservative National Center for Policy Analysis.

Most educators are likely to see voucher issues in educational and economic terms (how it affects kids and public schools) and debate it on those grounds. But that is naïve and shortsighted. The issues are very much political and subject to all the depredations of the political process. Indeed, the Milwaukee situation has degenerated into what the *Wisconsin State Journal*, a conservative newspaper, has called "one of the largest political corruption cases in state history" (cited in Miner, 2000).

In a 1997 election for a seat on the Wisconsin Supreme Court, Jon Wilcox, on record as advocating the extension of the voucher program to religious schools, defeated opponent Walt Kelly. In 1998, when the voucher-extension case reached the Wisconsin Supreme Court, Wilcox voted with the majority to permit religious schools to participate in Milwaukee's voucher system. Kelly smelled a rat and encouraged an investigation into what became known as "The Case of the Mystery Postcards."

Just prior to the election, some 354,000 postcards urged citizens to vote for Wilcox. The postcards did not mention the voucher issue directly, but implied that Kelly was far too liberal for the state high court. As it turned out, the postcards were financed by wealthy supports of vouchers from all over the country. Patrick Rooney of Golden Rule Insurance, credited with the idea of private vouchers, sent $34,500. John Walton of Wal-Mart kicked in $25,000. Bare Seld, a Chicago businessman and voucher supporter, sent $25,000. Another $17,500 arrived from the PMA Foundation, a Philadelphia organization that supports vouchers. Even Pierre S. Du Pont, former governor of Delaware, who advocated vouchers in his brief stint as a Republican presidential candidate, sent $1,000 (Miner, 2000).

Wisconsin State Superintendent of Schools John T. Benson said, "It is obvious that the people who made contributions to this justice's campaign had one thing in mind, and that was to elect someone who would be an advocate for the voucher system." The Wisconsin Election Board has now sued the Wilcox campaign for accepting $200,000 in illegal campaign contributions. Given that without Wilcox's vote the extension of voucher eligibility to religious schools would still have passed 3–2, it is unlikely that the suit will result in anything more than a fine.

Interestingly, one judge did recuse herself from the voucher vote. People in Wisconsin think it was because she had received money from the teachers' union, but the judge provided no reasons for her actions. And some have argued that yet another judge who voted for the extension *should* have recused herself because her husband served on the board of a voucher school. If these recusals had occurred, the vote would have been a 2–2 tie, sending the matter back to a lower court.

In the absence of evaluation requirements, Milwaukee's voucher program is not being adequately studied. This is too bad because there are apparently some fascinating trends. Some private schools have 90 percent or more of their students receiving vouchers. At one Catholic school, two-thirds of the teachers quit rather than cope with voucher students. And, overall, private school enrollment has *declined* in the ten years of the voucher program (Leovy, 2000). Since there are 11,000 voucher students for 2000–01, this means that the private schools have been hemorrhaging students. This is not, according to market theorists, the way it is supposed to work.

Cleveland

In April 1995, the Ohio legislature approved the use of state funds for vouchers worth up to $2,250 that could be used to cover tuition to Cleveland private schools, including religious schools, for students in grades K–3. Proponents of the proposal had argued for vouchers in eight districts, but settled for Cleveland as a compromise preferable to no program at all. The $5.25 million for the program came from Cleveland public schools' share of state aid. The vouchers were available for up to 2,500 students, although only 1,900 ended up participating. Students already in private schools could claim up to 25 percent of the vouchers.

The ubiquitous Jay P. Greene and Paul Peterson, along with William Howell of Stanford University, were hired by the John M. Olin Foundation to evaluate the program. They found that from fall to spring, the students in the program had gained 5.5 percentile ranks in reading and 15 in math (Peterson, Howell, and Greene, 1998). No control group of any kind was established. The researchers admitted that their study was "just a start." Certainly this constituted an appropriate admission. Although their report was labeled an "evaluation of the Cleveland voucher program," their program evaluation had examined test scores in only two of the fifty-five participating schools. These "Hope" schools had been newly created by David Brennan, the Ohio entrepreneur and voucher advocate discussed in connection with Ohio charter schools.

It is indicative of how ideology, policy, politics, and the profit motive get intertwined in voucher programs when they involve for-profit schools. Ohio law forbids existing private schools from reconstituting themselves as charters, so Brennan shut down his private, voucher-using schools. He then established a nonprofit group, over which he claimed he had no direct governing authority, to run new charter schools. However, the schools' faculty and staff remained and the schools contracted with White Hat Management, Brennan's for-profit management corporation. Why would Brennan execute such a convoluted shift? Some think money plays a role. The state vouchers for private school tuition pay up to $2,250 per student. Charter schools receive $4,500 per student (Archer, 1999a).

The Ohio Department of Education commissioned a more comprehensive study by Indiana University. Researchers there tested 94 third-grade voucher recipients against a sample of 449 similar students who had remained in the Cleveland public schools, and found that "there are no significant differences in achievement between scholarship students and their [public school] peers" (Walsh, 1998). Study leader Kim Metcalf said it was too early to tell if choice made a difference (Metcalf, 1999).

The American Federation of Teachers (AFT) criticized the Greene et al. study because the test scores came from a fall-to-spring testing. Although fall-to-spring testing makes theoretical sense, it can be problematic. For one thing, people who know the purpose of the fall-to-spring testing can act in ways such as to depress scores in the fall and raise them in spring. In addition, students from low-income families have been found to show summer loss more than middle-class students, making fall-to-fall or spring-to-spring testing more appropriate for such students (Cooper, 2000). The AFT argued that the results of the Greene study were an artifact of the fall-to-spring testing procedure.

Greene and his colleagues, however, returned to administer another test in the fall. This time, the test was overseen by observers from John Carroll University. The test scores fell substantially, remaining statistically significantly higher in math (8.6 percentile rank gain) and reading (5.6 percentile gain), but not language (Peterson, Green, and Howell, 1998).

Needless to say, others found problems with the original Peterson–Howell–Greene study. As noted, the study evaluated only two schools—a combined enrollment of 352 students—that had been started by Akron industrialist David Brennan, who named them "Hope" schools. Ohio governor George Voinovich had earlier appointed Brennan to head his Commission on Educational Choice. Vouchers advocates conducted the evaluation, which was funded by a foundation (Olin) that favors vouchers. Under such circumstances, a voucher-unfriendly finding was most unlikely.

Besides the credibility problem of the test scores themselves, the study contained a number of other problems. During a suit, Judge John C. Young told a lawyer for the voucher opponents, "It seems to me the Cleveland public school system is about to go under." Yet, most of those choosing private schools were not fleeing sinking schools. Of the 1,994 students using the vouchers, 834 (34 percent) were kindergartners, in school for the first time. Given that the previous year the Cleveland public schools had eliminated full-day kindergarten in all nonmagnet schools, it seems likely that the overwhelming majority of these students were delivered to the private schools by parents seeking full-day kindergarten, an option available only in private schools. Another 496 (25 percent) of the students were already in private schools. Only 663 (34 percent) of those who used vouchers in 1996–97 actually left public schools to attend private ones.

The official cost estimate of the average voucher from the Ohio Office of Management and Budget was $1,763. However, this figure did not include $629 per pupil for transportation (most of which was provided in taxis), $257 per student for administration, or $543 per pupil in state aid already directed to private schools (in a 1996 report, *The Condition of Public Education in Ohio*, I noted that Ohio gives by far more money per pupil to private schools than any other state; it actually directed more total money to private schools than the more populous states of Pennsylvania, New Jersey, and New York (Bracey, 1996b).

An external audit by the accounting firm of Deloitte & Touche found many questionable expenditures. In the areas of residency verification, grade eligibility, guardianship, consulting services provided, transportation, and miscellaneous, the firm questioned $1,869,204, or 36 percent, of total expenditures. The effect of the first three categories would be to potentially award scholarships to students who were not eligible for them. For consulting services, the auditors could not establish that "the Department of Administrative Services had been involved in the procurement process or the services for which the Program was billed were actually provided."

In these categories, transportation ($1,882,454) and consulting services ($379,433) dominated. In a perfectly run program, not all of these costs could be recovered, of course—it would take some amount of money to transport the children, but $3.33 a day by bus compared to $15–18 by taxi.

The Ohio Department of Education has also found fault with the operation of the voucher program. For instance, although the program was intended to serve low-income families, the law places no income cap on eligibility. Consequently, some thirty students whose families make more than $50,000 a year have obtained vouchers. In addition, about one-third of the students did not have the same last name as the adults filing the application, but the program did not check to verify who had legal guardianship (Archer, 1999b).

An evaluation by the American Federation of Teachers observed that for the same money, Cleveland could have restored full-day kindergarten for 70 percent of the students or implemented Success For All in all elementary schools, serving approximately 40,000 students (Murphy, Nelson, and Rosenberg, 1997).

The Cleveland voucher program has since been through a topsy-turvy time. The Ohio Supreme Court struck it down in May 1999, but not because vouchers were inherently unconstitutional. The voucher legislation was attached to a general budget bill, something that the Ohio constitution proscribes. The legislature quickly moved to address that problem with separate legislation that was signed into law by Governor Bob Taft on June 29, 1999 (Sandham, 1999). However, on August 25, 1999, U.S. District Court Judge Solomon Oliver, Jr., issued an injunction against the program on the grounds that, because the participating schools were overwhelmingly religious, the program would not survive constitutional muster. The funds in the Cleveland program go to the schools, not to the parents, which, as we have noted, could mean the difference between a voucher program that violates the First Amendment and one that does not.

Judge Oliver's decision was immediately appealed amid general chaos. Oliver then ruled that the students already in the program could continue for the 1999–2000 school year, but that no new students could be admitted. The students are also attending private schools in 2000–01 (Metcalf, 1999).

Precisely one week after the judge's decision, a second Indiana University evaluation appeared, this one covering a three-year period and analyzing different variables, such as attendance, parental satisfaction, and student achievement. The achievement analyses were conducted separately for students who had left public schools for existing private schools, those who remained in private schools, and those who left public schools to attend the two Hope schools created by David Brennan.

Controlling for prior achievement and background characteristics, voucher students in private schools score higher in language and science (45 normal curve equivalents (NCEs) versus 40, and 40 versus 36, respectively). There were no differences in reading or mathematics. The students in the Hope schools scored significantly lower than both of these other groups.

Twenty-six of the third-grade students did not return to the voucher program for fourth grade. These students had lower test scores in reading, science, and social studies than those who remained—about 8 NCEs on average. Since these students could not be found in any Cleveland-area school, public or private, one implication is that mobile students are already low scorers because the lack of continuity in their schooling impedes academic progress.

Although the Indiana researchers attempted to gather objective information about student behavior and attendance, record keeping and policy differences made this impossible. Ratings on these variables showed no differences except that public school students, both those whose parents did not apply for a scholarship and those who applied but did not obtain one, were somewhat better rated.

Looking at parental involvement, the researchers found that the voucher parents were involved in terms of parent–teacher conferences, attending meetings and events, calling teachers, and serving on committees. Public school parents were more likely to visit their child's classroom. Interestingly, parents who had applied for a voucher but had not received one were more involved than public school parents who had not applied, often coming close to the level of voucher parents' involvement.

One might conjecture that voucher parents' lesser tendency to visit classrooms stems from their higher satisfaction ratings regarding teacher quality, academics, order in the school, social characteristics, and classmates. Public school parents were the least satisfied.

Voucher parents are generally more educated, involved, and satisfied. Similar results were found earlier in Milwaukee. As the evaluator of that program said, at one level this is precisely the kind of parent Milwaukee's voucher program should serve. On the other hand, this is precisely the kind of parent many would like to see stay with the public schools and push for improvement.

San Antonio

The previous sections on Milwaukee and Cleveland illustrate some of the characteristics, constraints, and foibles of choice programs operated with publicly funded vouchers that allow families to attend private schools. San Antonio is one of the more long-standing and larger programs wherein private individuals and corporations provide "scholarships" for students, typically economically deprived children. Summaries of smaller private voucher experiments in Milwaukee, Indianapolis, and New York City can be found in Terry Moe's *Private Vouchers* (the Milwaukee program is not the one discussed earlier in this section).

The Children's Educational Opportunity Fund, more commonly known as CEO America, financed the San Antonio program beginning in 1992. In its first year, the foundation provided 936 scholarships in an amount up to $750.

The average scholarship was $575. This is low by other cities standards, but according to the researchers who evaluated the program, the average tuition in San Antonio at the time was $1,500. The scholarships did not provide full funding because the foundation's believes that parents who personally invest in such a program will be more committed to it and will work harder to make it succeed.

Half of the children receiving scholarships attended public schools at the time. Of those receiving scholarships, 60 percent enrolled in Catholic schools, 20 percent in nondenominational schools, 10 percent in Baptist schools, one percent in nonreligious schools, and the remainder in religious schools of various denominations (Godwin, Kemerer, and Martinez, 1997, p. 2).

During the period of the program evaluation some 800 children, almost all of them in private schools, were on the program's waiting list. The program did not screen children for acceptability on any basis except need. Students had to be eligible for free or reduced-price lunches. Some schools, however, did exert admissions controls.

In the evaluation study, researchers identified six definable groups: those in private schools who received scholarships; those in private schools on the waiting lists; those in public schools who used scholarships to attend private schools; those who remained in public, neighborhood schools; and two groups involved in the district's "multilingual program"—those who enrolled in it and those who applied but were turned down because of space limitations.

Looking at the parents, the evaluators found that those who chose to use vouchers to leave public schools were better educated, wealthier, and more involved with their children's education both at home and at school, and had higher expectations for the children. The parents who chose private schools were more involved with their children's education *before* the program began, but participation in the program did not increase their involvement. These parents also had fewer children. Parents who chose private schools were very dissatisfied with public schools, whereas those who stayed in public school were very satisfied.

The evaluation did not directly test the hypothesis that parents who pay part of the cost to educate their child get more involved in the school (such a test would have been hard to arrange given the program's parameters). The evaluation did find that the scholarship program experienced a 50 percent dropout rate; lack of money and transportation were two of the most frequent reasons given for leaving the program. It thus appears that the cost-sharing requirement had a detrimental impact on at least some of the families.

For a variety of reasons, the researchers found that "comparisons between public and private school students regarding student achievement are exceedingly difficult." The children choosing private schools had "marginal improvements in standardized reading scores and marginal declines in math." These small differences, however, can take on a larger meaning when one examines the test scores of students in the public schools, where scores declined every year from third grade through ninth grade. This finding is similar to that in the

Milwaukee public voucher program except that the subjects are reversed: In Milwaukee, math improved but reading did not.

One intriguing finding that is mentioned but not discussed is that among the six groups, children who attended San Antonio's public school multilingual program showed gains in both test scores and satisfaction. Conversely, those who applied but were turned down were the most adversely affected.

The Children's Educational Opportunity Foundation (CEO America)

Take away their choice—take away their chance.
—Slogan on CEO American materials.

CEO America describes its mission as to

- Serve as the national clearinghouse for privately funded voucher program information;
- Offer and provide support services for each existing program;
- Provide matching grant money to help develop these programs; and
- Coordinate the development of new programs all across America.

To this end CEO America has undertaken, among other things, a partnership with the National Center for Policy Analysis (NCPA), a conservative think tank which provides a daily set of policy-related issues culled from various publications, but whose education-related website materials also champion choice, debase public schools, and take occasional slaps at the U.S. Department of Education. The project, called "Educating America," will "employ radio, television, and syndicated newspaper columns, as well as a series of publications," with the aim "to inject free-market ideas into the school choice debate." The two groups sponsored a "conference" in Washington, D.C. on September 23 and 24, 1998. Conference is in quotes because the CEO–NCPA conference was unlike most that the reader is likely to have attended. This one was more like a revival tent meeting complete with highly emotional testimonials from people identified as "voucher parents," one of whom turned out to work for Jeanne Allen and her arch-conservative Center for Educational Reform.

William Bennett delivered the opening after-dinner keynote speech. Having years earlier named Chicago public schools as the nation's worst, Bennett continued to hammer them with statistics that, at best, one would consider dubious. Bennett contended that 50 percent of Chicago pupils scored in the first percentile on standardized tests. The author of *The Book of Virtues* later declared that one Chicago school had a 100 percent dropout rate.

Oklahoma state representative J. C. Watts led off the next morning, following the testimonial of a voucher mom from San Antonio whose child was using a voucher to attend a Catholic school and who, in her way, gave the game away from her perspective. "I so, so wanted a *religious* education for my son." Playing off this theme, Watts declared that Catholic schools "will unleash the caged eagles in the inner cities. Catholic schools are taking the worst and making them the best." Watts offered no evidence in support of his contentions.

"There is a vast left-wing conspiracy to deprive poor children of a good education," intoned former secretary of education Lamar Alexander later in the morning. "Rarely has such a grand army as our own held the high moral ground for so long and advanced so little." Alexander harkened back wistfully to 1992 when then-president George Bush had proposed a "G.I. Bill for children," a proposal immediately labeled "G.I. Bull" by AFT president Albert Shanker (Shanker, 1992).

William Leininger of CEO America discussed changes that had taken place in Edgewood Independent School District, part of San Antonio, and CEO America's plans to provide $50 million in vouchers over the next five years. He touted the improved outcomes as proof that the market works. It was pointed out by someone in the audience (not me), however, that the information packet distributed to attendees contained a recent article from the *Wall Street Journal,* an institution presumably not part of Alexander's "vast left-wing conspiracy." The article stated that Edgewood had improved greatly *before* CEO America provided any dollars. "It opened magnet schools for math and technology and started its first-ever advanced placement classes. Elementary schools were rebuilt, their teaching revised. A high school for troubled youngsters was started. Edgewood still lags behind the state average, but two and a half times as many eighth-graders passed their math exams last year as in 1993. Dropout rates have been cut in half. SATs are up 134 points" (Kronholz, 1998). Leininger went on to his next point.

"The Berlin Wall of Educational Monopoly" was the phrase of the day. Senator Dan Coates, former Nixon attorney general Ed Meese, and the Institute of Justice's Clint Bolick all presented choice as a civil-rights issue, an approach that has since become quite popular.

CEO America initially played to fear. It's "CEO America History" (no longer available at http://www.ceoamerica.org/history.html) opened with statements having nothing to do with CEO America's history: "The American educational system is failing—and failing badly. Nowhere is this more apparent than the nation's inner-city schools where, along with lunch boxes and books, children bring guns and knives, and where metal detectors and armed guards are a common sight." Actually, these children often don't have textbooks or lunch boxes and are eligible for free or reduced-price lunches. It also seems unlikely that their teachers instructed them to bear arms—this is more likely a reflection of the communities in which these children have to spend 91 percent of their lives between birth and age eighteen.

Also rather laughable website selections are the "School Choice Debate," "School Choice Research," and "School Choice Testimonials." The debate offers a single point of view and, as well as playing to fear, it plays loose with the truth. For instance, at one point it claimed that "in Chicago 46 percent of public school teachers send their own children to non-public schools and the same is true in other cities, as well." The same is *not* true in other cities. Chicago consistently has the highest proportion, and many of the schools involved are parochial and factors other than educational quality are involved (e.g., the desire to provide their children with a religious education). In fact, Denis Doyle's study, published by the Center for Educational Reform, found that, overall, teachers make less use of private schools than the public at large. Only 12.1 percent of them send their children to private schools, compared to 13.1 percent for the general public.

This figure is all the more remarkable since better-educated and affluent parents are more likely to use private schools. Nationally, 31 percent of persons twenty-five or older have a bachelor's degree or better. For certified teachers, it is 100 percent with 50 percent holding at least a master's degree. Teachers do not receive princely wages, but they are not usually the sole wage earner in their family. In Doyle's 1995 study, the median family income of teachers was about $75,000 a year. Doyle also looked at where teachers in private schools educate their children. Only one-third of them chose private schools.

Of the "school choice testimonials" on the website, three things can possibly be said:

1. They are total fakes; or,
2. They have been heavily edited; or,
3. American public schools can be proud that they have taught low-income students—and their parents!— to write such remarkably clear, elegant, and articulate prose.

CEO America sprang from the Texas Public Policy Foundation, which liked Indianapolis insurance magnate Patrick Rooney's idea of establishing a trust to provide vouchers that poor children could use to attend private schools. CEO America's history used to note that the "groundwork" for the organization was laid by a "grant from a Texas businessman" and that things began to take off in 1994 when the Texas Public Policy Foundation received a "$2 million grant." The sources of these donations are not specified.

Former Wal-Mart executive Fritz Steiger is the president of CEO America and John Walton sits on the board of directors. James M. Mansour serves as CEO. He is also the president and CEO of National Telecommunications, a long-distance telephone service provider. They and most of the board of directors have backgrounds as activists in various Texas choice and voucher movements.

CEO America currently has programs in thirty-one cities with a goal of adding ten cities a year. Most of these programs are small (fewer than four hundred students) with Milwaukee and Indianapolis being notable exceptions. Another notable exception is the CEO Horizons program recently started in San Antonio's Edgewood school district. This is a predominantly low-income, and Hispanic school district. The district profile from the Texas Education Agency for 1996–97 shows 14,180 Edgewood students, 93.4 percent of whom are "economically disadvantaged" while some 63 percent are below the federal poverty level (Schnaiberg, 1997). Ninety-six percent of the students are Hispanic, two percent are white, and two percent are African American (for the state, the percentages are 36, 46, and 14, respectively). The average SAT combined score in Edgewood is 839, with ACT scores of 20.1 (993 and 20.1, statewide, respectively. Sixty-five percent of Texas seniors took a college admissions test, compared to only 44 percent in Edgewood).

Into this disadvantaged setting, CEO America deposited the CEO Horizon project—$50 million to provide vouchers for any student eligible for free or reduced-price lunch programs. The vouchers are worth up to $3,600 for grades K–8 and $4,000 for grades 9–12. Scholarships for students who attend schools outside of Edgewood's defined geographic area receive 100 percent of that school's tuition. These tuitions must be less than the within-district grants, because elsewhere in a Q&A section it is noted that the lesser amounts represent an attempt to keep the money concentrated in the Edgewood area. CEO America claims that once a student receives an award, it will be good for at least ten years or until such time as the state legislature provides an equivalent program. Tuition charges are paid to the schools. If parents choose a public school other than their neighborhood's, and if that school will enroll the child for a tuition charge, that school is eligible to receive the money from CEO Horizon. Transportation will not be provided.

In the first year, the Edgewood district was unaffected because state aid is based on the previous year's attendance factors. The next year was another matter. The district lost 600 students (1,350 applied and 800 were approved by CEO Horizons) to private schools and another 550 due to the closing of an Air Force base in the district. Combined, these two losses cost the district $6 million. Edgewood has since lost over 500 more students, bringing the total to 1,137.

There was some temporary benefit of the base closure and the vouchers in that for this year the district had generally smaller classes with no reduction in funding. According to David Ochoa, Edgewood director of community and public relations, the district reduced its staff by about one hundred through attrition and by offering an early retirement program (personal communication, October 18, 2000).

Edgewood superintendent Noe Sauceda was dismissive of the voucher program. He noted that there were many established private schools in the area that had always offered competition to the public schools. He was less than happy that CEO America had felt the need not only to offer the scholarships, but also to recruit students using flyers that stemmed the public schools (private communication, October 19, 2000).

In fact, the improvements noted earlier by the *Wall Street Journal* have continued, and Edgewood is now a "recognized" school district, the second-highest category in the Texas reward system. From 1996–97 through 1998–99, the proportion of students passing all Texas tests grew from 55.1 percent to 70.2 percent. SAT and ACT scores have dipped a bit (from 839 to 803 and 16.7 to 16.3, respectively), but the proportion of seniors taking the tests has grown from 44 percent to 60 percent. Sauceda insists that the gains are due to the emphasis on achievement in Texas generally, not to competition induced by CEO America's vouchers.

This situation is a bit different than when a charter school drains off some students. In theory, the charter school offers an alternative vision of education which, if successful, can be a catalyst for improvement in the district. Even if the district does not use the charter school's approach to instruction, the charter can be a goad to reform—in theory; so far, it hasn't worked out that way in practice. In Edgewood, however, the private schools are well established and overwhelmingly Catholic. Peter Cookson has observed that there is more by-the-book traditional teaching in such schools than in public schools (1994).

9

Commercialism in the Schools

This section was actually written in late 1998. It is included here because it illustrates further the corporatization of America in general and schools in particular. In "Dueling Visions," I discussed two different ways of viewing the world: the communal, democratic vision and the self-interested, commercial vision. The invasion of schools by companies helps promulgate the commercial vision. If kids can be "branded" while in school, so much the better for the branding companies. Readers interested in a more exhaustive look at commercialism and commercialization are recommended to the Center for the Analysis of Commercialism in Education (CACE) directed by Alex Molnar at the University of Wisconsin–Milwaukee, www.uwm.edu/Dept/CACE.

The activities described in this section do not involve the direct provision of either management or instruction, although they do involve in some instances the provision of instructional materials. They are discussed briefly here in the story of Mike Cameron and other related events. Although not directly operating schools now, that is a possibility. After all, one of the commentators asks at one point "What's next? Nike Elementary? Maybe, just maybe. In any case, the presence of corporations in these commercial activities is likely to be synergistic with future private management or other takeovers.

Mike Cameron Loses His Shirt: A Tale for Our Times

On March 20, 1998, the 1,230 students of Greenbrier High School in Evans, Georgia, stood in the school parking lot. The band director had arranged the seniors neatly in a giant "C." He had arrayed the juniors into an "O," sophomores modeled a "K," and freshmen shaped an "E." As some dozen-plus Coca-Cola executives looked on (Coke is headquartered in Atlanta, 130 miles to the west), photographers on a crane filmed the moment of the entire high school spelling out "COKE." As the cameras rolled, senior Mike Cameron disrobed to reveal a shirt bearing the logo of . . . Pepsi.

Principal Gloria Hamilton hustled Cameron to her office, gave him a dressing down and then suspended him, telling him the suspension was because of his disrespect and for perhaps costing the school a bundle (he said). At the time, Coca-Cola was offering $10,000 to the high school that came up with the best plan for marketing Coke-sponsored promotional discount cards. A local bottler had chipped in another $500. Mike got off lightly—one day's suspension. Normally, said principal Hamilton, such an offense draws a six-day punishment. A Pepsi spokesman called Cameron a "trendsetter with impeccable taste in clothes" and promised that Pepsi would keep him well supplied with shirts.

There were other opportunities for brand-name treason that day. Some Coca-Cola executives lectured on economics; others provided technical assistance to home-economics students who were baking a Coca-Cola cake; and still others helped chemistry students analyze Coke's sugar content. If other acts of insurrection occurred, though, they went unreported. This was "Coke in Education Day" at Greenbrier, which received no money from Coca-Cola for inviting them.

Like the first-grader who got suspended for giving a girl a kiss she asked for (according to the boy), Mike Cameron got his fifteen minutes of fame, as did Principal Hamilton and District Superintendent Tom Dohrmann. This might be the only upside positive of the story: Newspapers around the world indignantly panned the principal and Coke. "Has American society fallen so far that teens can be punished for not following the corporate party line?" asked the Baton Rouge, Louisiana, *Advocate*. "What exactly is a school doing sponsoring a "'Coke in Education Day' anyway?" queried the *Omaha World-Herald*, "Promoting a commercial product to its captive audience of young people?" The Raleigh, North Carolina, *News and Observer* invoked Hitleresque imagery: "Without even knowing it, der furious fuhrer was imparting to the students a civics lesson in obsequiousness and greed. It is disquieting to think that a kid could be kicked out of school for refusing to regard an impersonal multinational corporation with the same reverence that the principal does."

Carl Hiaasen, a columnist for the *Miami Herald*, also saw the civic consequences of the event, saying that the incident taught students

> . . . that money is more important than freedom of choice. It taught them that silence is more desirable than dissent, that conformity is better than being different and it taught them that there is no shame in selling out, if the price is right. . . . Forget individuality. Dismiss from your mischievous young minds any thoughts of freely expressing yourself. And God forbid you should have a sense of humor, or let it show in front of your classmates. Because it's all about money, boys and girls. For 10 grand you can darn well dress right and button those lips. . . . (Hiassen, 1998)

That is a terrible lesson, said the *Chicago Tribune*. "Schools shouldn't be in the position of selling captive students to advertisers, whatever the excuse. They are entrusted with children's minds and they have no right to sell access to them. Even a quick glance at the sales pitches made by marketing companies peddling promotion ideas to schools makes it clear the whole point is to make money for the advertisers, not to help kids."

In London, *The Independent* ran a story asking, "What's next? Some large company coughing up money and then telling the school's social studies department, 'We don't want you saying anything bad about our labor or investment practices?'" In a similar vein, Hong Kong's most respected paper, the *South China Morning Post* contended, "The reason why the saga [at Greenbrier High School] strikes such a chord among students and parents alike is because of the light it sheds on the steamroller tactics of soft drinks and other corporations to turn schools into nothing more than supermarkets where children can also take lessons."

As if crass commercialism and greed weren't enough of an indictment, Bud Kennedy in the *Fort Worth Star-Telegram* cautioned that Coca-Cola was nutritionally deficient as well: "Colas and other caffeinated soft drinks cause anxiety, irritability and loss of concentration." Hiaasen observed that they also make people fat and cause tooth decay. Only time will tell if the Baton Rouge *Advocate* headline writer was being prescient by leading the Mike Cameron story with, "So what's next, Nike Elementary?"

The stories did not say whether Coke had an exclusive "pouring rights" contract with the district. Perhaps Evans (pop. 13,713) is too small a market to haggle over. But there are others that aren't. Jefferson County, Colorado, needed a new football stadium. Lebanon (Ohio)'s outdoor track was crumbling. Keller Independent School District, a fast-growing, high-performing system outside of Fort Worth, Texas, wanted to make sure its high test scores didn't go unnoticed. Thanks to these school districts signing contracts with cola companies, you can only buy Pepsi in Jefferson County, only Coke in Lebanon and Keller.

So far, the soft drink companies—the most active in the field of devising exclusive contracts—haven't contacted East Harlem, or East St. Louis. The districts that are getting the easy money are affluent and high-scoring systems. Of course, district-level contracts are small potatoes. Don Baird, CEO of School Properties, Inc., goes for whole states. Under his guidance, Reebok signed a contract with the California Scholastic Federation, paying them $2.8 million over six years. In return, all playoffs and title games in the Golden State are called the CIF/Reebok State Championships. There are 3,800 such events each year.

The *South China Morning Post* worried that schools could become supermarkets where students could also take lessons. It did not note that some of those lessons might be tainted with commercialism themselves:

- "Educational materials" from the National Livestock and Meat Board claim that eating meat makes people taller.

- Procter and Gamble's materials claim that clear-cut logging—the stripping of entire hillsides of trees—is good for the environment.
- A Kellogg's cereal guide intended to teach children "how to choose healthful foods" recommends Rice Crispies Treats—a Kellogg snack food—as the one to choose most often.
- Materials from the Council for Wildlife Conservation and Education, which turns out to be affiliated with the National Shooting Sports Foundation—which happens to have the same address as the National Rifle Association—contend that there are no endangered species.
- Prego claims that proving its spaghetti sauce is thicker than Ragu's is a legitimate chemistry experiment.

The worry expressed by *The Independent* of London that corporations might try to direct a curriculum through direct assertions underestimates corporate America's ability to infiltrate the curriculum through more subtle means. The Consumer Union's (CU) analysis of sponsored materials found that many of them were commercial, incomplete, biased, and error-prone. CU found a number of materials that were little more than advertisements for the sponsoring company or organization. Actual advertisements on school property, of course, are becoming more and more common.

For $1,000, a company can put its name on a two-by-five sign in a Grapevine, Texas, gym. If the company can spring for $15,000, it gets recognition on the school's voice mail system and rights to a school roof seen by people flying into Dallas–Fort Worth International Airport. School buses in Colorado Springs carry a painting of the school mascot . . . and the Burger King logo. Thirty-three banners for everything from car dealers to doctors hang on the east wall of Plant High School in Hillsborough, Florida (Cristodero, 1998).

Steve Shulman and Michael Yanoff were twenty-five and hoping to earn enough money to buy car phones with their 1989 idea: Since most schools require kids to put covers on textbooks to protect them, why not sell corporations rights to those covers? By 1994, they were an eight-person organization with sales of $4 million. It's a win–win situation, Schulman told *Chicago Tribune* reporter Steve Mills. "Advertisers get ads in the schools, and kids get a book cover that's trendy and free" (Mills, 1997).

"Tooned-In," produced by School Marketing Partners of San Juan Capistrano, California, charges $10,000 to $478,000 per month for corporations wishing to have their message or coupons on school menus. "Tooned-In" menus were reaching 6 million kindergarten-through-sixth-graders by January 1998 ("School Lunch Special: Tuna Melt With a Side of Coupons." *Consumer Reports*, December 1997). We haven't yet reached the point of "Nike Elementary," but that might not be far in the future: Currently, corporations are taking over the schools to manage them; some provide a curriculum as well. The Edison Project or Advantage Schools can do it better—and for less.

Of course, there is some question about the curriculum these organizations offer. Edison started with the idea that it would produce its own. Freed from the incompetent government school bureaucrats, Edison would unleash the learning capacities heretofore imprisoned by schools. In reality, Edison currently manages existing schools and uses Success for All materials to teach reading and Chicago Math for mathematics, materials developed by educators (!).

As discussed earlier in Chapter 7, Advantage Schools, Inc., schools do construct their own curricula, at least for the early grades, but *New York Times* reporter Michael Winerip found these curricula less than enthralling on investigation.

If one examines the FAQ on Advantage's website, one gains additional insight into the script. One learns that in a thirty-minute lesson, "students will make eight to twelve responses each minute. This means that students will make between 240 and 360 responses in a half-hour lesson. If they have three DI [Direct Instruction, but Drill Instructor works just as well] lessons in a day, they will make between 720 and 1180 responses each day.... Q: Am I right in concluding that all students respond at the same time? A: Absolutely. It is critical that all students make the correct responses. If a child doesn't respond, the teacher can't know whether the child knows the right answer or not."

One can only imagine the cognitive depth plumbed by children who make nearly 1,200 oral responses a day. For those who think that "going off the script" is what education is all about, Advantage's Pavlovian pedagogy sounds like cruel and unusual punishment, not education. But it is among the trends in the privatization of American schools. So why are schools begging at the feet of companies and why are companies actively pursuing schools? Taking the second question first, companies feel they must "brand" children as early as possible. Exposure today means brand loyalty tomorrow. The schools, for their part, are needy. Legislation and referenda like California's Proposition 13 are starving many schools. In Texas, the wealthy Grapevine–Colleyville district lost $11.4 million to a poorer district under a new finance law.

More importantly, or at least more widely spread, companies are demanding tax breaks as a condition of relocating to or staying in a community. In 1991, businesses gave Florida schools $32 million. They extracted $500 million from the state treasury in tax breaks. There are a number of people around Tuscaloosa who will tell you that to get the Mercedes factory, state officers "gave away the farm" (tales of bribery and kickbacks also are heard occasionally). One researcher estimates that corporate tax breaks remove $1 billion out of the Wisconsin treasury each year; another has calculated that the total contributions of business and industry to America's schools would run them for two hours.

Senator Howard Metzenbaum saw the situation quite clearly:

> In speech after speech, it is our corporate CEOs who state that an educated, literate workforce is the key to American competitiveness. They pontificate on the importance of education. They point out their magnanimous corporate contributions to

education in one breath, and then they pull the tax base out from under local schools in the next. Businesses criticize the job our schools are doing and then proceed to nail down every tax break they can get, further eroding the school's ability to do the job. (Taylor, 1992)

Since 1991, there has been increasing activity in a new form of corporate extortion from states: wages rebates. As states have come increasingly to compete for companies, companies have become increasingly skilled at getting some of their money back. Whirlpool built a stove factory in Tulsa, Oklahoma, in 1996 and for ten years will get back 4.5 cents for every dollar it pays in wages. In some states, wage rebate is the most expensive corporate lure; in others, the fastest growing.

Most business complaints about schools and their graduates are not well-founded in the first place, but it appears that businessmen do not see the connection between taking money away from schools and school quality. The starvation of schools would not be permitted were it not for the widespread belief in what Alex Molnar of the University of Wisconsin at Milwaukee refers to as "the master myth": The myth that money doesn't matter. Common sense says money matters. A large number of studies exist to prove that money matters, but those who write in publications seen by businessmen choose to cite only the ideologically driven studies of Eric Hanushek at the University of Rochester. Not only have other studies found that money matters, other analyses of Hanushek's own data have shown that his research contradicts his rhetoric (these studies are reviewed in Chapter 3).

Sponsored materials, sponsored programs, exclusive contracts, privatization, electronic marketing, private vouchers. . . . Mike Cameron, you don't know the half of it.

Conclusion

At the September 2000 meeting of the Education Leaders Council, a group consisting of various conservative chief state school officers, politicians, and reformers, Frank Brogan, lieutenant governor of Florida, said that "Everyone wants the best for children." They just differ on what "the best" means. The descriptions of some of the experiments in education reform in the previous pages indicate that Brogan's statement is not always true.

Companies that charge parents $1.95 a mile for transportation are not concerned with "the best." Companies that want to brand children are not concerned with "the best." Companies that tell teachers "maybe our model is not for you" are not concerned with "the best." At best, concerns about the bottom line distract companies from paying full attention to curriculum and instruction.

Beyond that, there is surprisingly little innovation from the innovators. Perhaps this is not so surprising after all. Robert Holland, former op-ed editor for the *Richmond Times-Dispatch*, penned a book called *Not with My Child, You Don't* (Holland, 1995). Although Holland aimed his barbs specifically at outcomes-based education, his attitude probably reflects the general feeling about experimentation. As Rothstein and colleagues observed, the world after school is uncertain (Rothstein, Carnoy, and Benveniste, 1999). A school that deviates too much from what people think a "school" is runs the risk of having parents worry that they might injure their children's future by sending them there.

It will be recalled that this kind of anxiety was precisely what motivated the Progressive Education Association to conduct the Eight Year Study. They collected data for eight years to prove to parents and college admissions officers their "break-the-mold" schools provided their students with an education that was superior to the normal high school experience.

Public schools provide public forums for discussing the critical issues of how we prepare our children for the future. Many of the experiments now underway remove parents from that discussion. This is not a good path for a democracy to take.

References

"2 TesseracT Execs Quit Troubled Firm." (2000). *Arizona Republic*, February 3, p. D3.

Aikin, Wilfred. (1942). *The Story of the Eight-Year Study*. New York: Harper and Brothers.

Ambrose, Eileen. (2000). "Sylvan Rethinks Venture." *Baltimore Sun*, March 31.

American Educational Research Association. (1999). *Educational Evaluation and Policy Analysis*. Washington, DC: American Educational Research Association, Summer.

"Another Round on Vouchers." (2000). *Washington Post*, December 18, p. A26.

Archer, Jeff. (1999a). "Two Cleveland Voucher Schools Plan Rebirth with Charter Schools." *Education Week*, July 14, p. 20.

———. (1999b). "Policies of Cleveland Voucher Program Faulted." *Education Week*, January 20, p. 3.

Arsen, David, Plank, David, and Sykes, Gary. (1999). *School Choice Policies in Michigan: The Rules Matter*. East Lansing: Michigan State University.

Ascher, Carol, Fruchter, Norm, and Berne, Robert. (1996). *Hard Lessons: Public Schools and Privatization*. New York: Twentieth Century Fund (now Century Fund).

Ashworth, Jon. (1999). "Junk-Bond King Milken Took Over the Baton." *The Times* (London), July 24, Business Section.

Baker, Keith. (1991). "Yes, Throw Money at the Schools." *Phi Delta Kappan*, April, pp. 628–630.

Baker, Russ. (1999). "The Education of Mike Milken: From Junk-Bond King to Master of the Knowledge Universe." *The Nation*, May 3, p. 11.

Barbash, Fred. (2001). "Bears Breed Scapegoats." *Washington Post*, March 18, p. H1.

Barber, Benjamin, R. (1995). "Workshops of Our Democracy." *Education Week*, April 19, p. 34.

———. (1993). "America Skips School." *Harper's Magazine*, November, pp. 39–46.

Barry, John S., and Hederman, Rea S. (2000). *Report Card on American Education: A State-by-State Analysis, 1976–1999*. Washington, DC: American Legislative Exchange Council.

Barton, Paul E., and Coley, Richard J. (1998). *Growth in School: Achievement Gains from the Fourth to the Eighth Grade*. Princeton, NJ: Educational Testing Service.

Becker, Henry J., Nakagawa, K., and Corwin, R. G. (1996). "Parent Involvement Contracts in California's Charter Schools: Strategy for Improvement or Method of Exclusion?" *Teachers College Record*. 98(3): pp. 511–536.

Bennett William. (1993). *Report Card on American Education*. Washington, DC: American Legislative Exchange Council.

Berliner, David C., and Biddle, Bruce J. (1995). *The Manufactured Crisis*. Reading, MA: Addison Wesley Longman.

Bestor, Arthur. (1953). *Educational Wastelands: The Retreat from Learning in Public Schools*. Champaign: University of Illinois Press.

Blum, Justin. (2000). "Charter Schools Break D.C. Rules." *Washington Post*, May 3, p. A1.

Board of Education of the City of New York. (2000). Request for Proposal, Serial No. RFP #1B434.

Boutwell, Clinton. (1997). *Shell Game: Corporate America's Agenda for Schools*. Bloomington, IN: Phi Delta Kappa International.

Boyer, Ernest. (1995). *The Basic School*. San Francisco: Jossey-Bass.

Bracey, Gerald W. (2000a). *Bail Me Out: Handling Difficult Data and Tough Questions about Public Schools*. Thousand Oaks, CA: Corwin Press.

———. (2000b). "The TIMSS Final Year Study and Report: A Critique." *Educational Researcher*, May, pp. 4–10.

———. (1999). "The Numbers Game: A Review of Nicholas Lemann's *The Big Test*." *Washington Post*, October 17, Book World, p. 4.

———. (1998a). "'TIMSS'," Rhymes with 'Dims' As in Witted." *Phi Delta Kappan*, May, pp. 686–687.

———. (1998b). "Tinkering with TIMSS." *Phi Delta Kappan*, September, pp. 32–45.

———. (1998c). "The Eighth Bracey Report on the Condition of Public Education." *Phi Delta Kappan*, October, pp. 112–131.

———. (1997a). "What Happened to America's Public Schools? Not What You May Think." *American Heritage*, November, pp. 39–52.

———. (1997b). *Setting the Record Straight: Responses to Misconceptions about Public Education in the United States*. Alexandria, VA: Association for Supervision and Curriculum Development.

———. (1996a). "The Sixth Bracey Report on the Condition of Public Education." *Phi Delta Kappan*, October, pp. 127–138.

———. (1996b). *The Condition of Public Education in Ohio*. Columbus: Ohio School Funding Cooperative (Cooperative members include the Alliance for Adequate School Funding, Buckeye Association of School Administrators, Ohio Coalition for Equity and Adequacy of School Funding, and the Ohio School Boards Association).

———. (1995a). *Final Exam: A Study of the Perpetual Scrutiny of American Education*. Bloomington, IN: Technos Press.

———. (1995b). "U.S. Students: Better than Ever." *Washington Post*, December 22, p. A19.

———. (1993). "Filet of School Reform, Sauce Diable." *Education Week*, June 16.

Brady, Diane. (1999). "Chris Whittle's New IPO Deserves A D–." *Business Week*, September 6, p. 40.

Bratton, Samuel E. Jr., Horn, Sandra P. and Wright, S. Paul. (undated). "Using and Integrating Accessible Tennessee's Value-added Assessment System: A Primer for Teachers and Principals." Available at [no www] mdk12.org/practice/ensure/tvaas_toc.html.

Brennan, Deborah. (2000a). "A Lesson in Hard Knocks As Charter School Closes." *Los Angeles Times*, June 25.

———. (2000b). Personal communication, October 2000.

Brennor, Ethan. "U.S. 12th Graders Rank Poorly in Math and Science, Study Says." *New York Times*, February 21, p. A1.

Budde, Ray. (1996). *Strengthen School-Based Management by Chartering All Schools*. Andover, MA: The Regional Laboratory for Educational Improvement of the Northeast and Islands.

————. (1988). *Education by Charter within a Ten-Year Plan.* Andover, MA: The Regional Laboratory for Educational Improvement of the Northeast and Islands.

Bureau of Labor Statistics. (2000). *Occupational Outlook Handbook.* Washington, DC: Bureau of Labor Statistics.

Byron, Christopher. (2000). "Whittle and Benno Schmidt Try Another I.P.O. Fast One." *New York Observer,* October 13.

Callahan, Raymond. (1962). *Education and the Cult of Efficiency.* Chicago: University of Chicago Press.

Campanile, Carl. (2001a). "Education Board Concedes Edison Mess." *New York Post,* March 28.

————. (2001b). "Furor Over Edison Foe's List of Parents." *New York Post,* March 21.

Campbell, J. R., Voelkl, Kristin E., and Donahue, Patricia L. (1997). NAEP 1996 Trends in Academic Progress. Washington, DC: U.S. Department of Education, Office of Educational Research and Improvement Report No. NCES 97–985.

Carson, Huelskamp, R. M., and Woodall, T. D. (1993). "Perspectives on Education in America." *Journal of Educational Research,* May/June, pp. 249–310.

Carter, Andrew. (1999). "The Wrath of Cooper." *Minneapolis/St. Paul City Pages,* December 8.

Center on Education Policy. (1999). "Lessons from Other Countries about Private School Aid." Washington, DC: Center on Education Policy.

"Charting a Course to Reform: The Next Ten Years." (1993). *Education Week,* February 10.

Chea, Terence. (2000). "Providian Agrees to Restitution and Fine." *Washington Post,* June 29, p. E1.

Chomsky, Noam. (2000). Znet. Accessible at www.zmag.org/ZSustainers/Zdaily/2000–05/12chomsky.htm.

Chubb, John, and Moe, Terry. (1990). *Politics, Choice and America's Schools.* Washington, DC: The Brookings Institute.

Ciotti, Paul. (1998). *Money and School Performance.* Washington, DC: Cato Institute.

Class Size Consortium. (2000). Class Size Reduction in California: The 1998–99 Evaluation Findings. Accessible at www.classize.org.

————. (1999). Class Size Reduction in California: Early Evaluation Findings, 1996–98. Accessible at www.classize.org.

Clinton, William, and Gore, Albert. (1995). Letter to the editor, *USA Today,* October 11.

Cobb, Casey D. (2000). *Charter Schools As Schools of Choice: Ethnic and Racial Separation in Arizona.* Unpublished manuscript.

————. (1998). *Ethnic Separation in Arizona Charter Schools.* Unpublished doctoral dissertation, College of Education, Arizona State University.

Cobb, Casey D., and Glass, Gene V. (1999). "Ethnic Segregation in Arizona Charter Schools." *Education Policy Analysis Archives,* Vol. 7, No. 1. Accessible at olam.ed.asu.edu/v7n1.

Cobb, Casey D., Glass, Gene V., and Crockett, Carol. (2000). "The U.S. Charter School Movement and Ethnic Segregation." Paper presented at the annual meeting of the American Educational Research Association, New Orleans, April.

Coeyman, Marjorie. (2000). "Design Is Key When It Comes to Vouchers." *Christian Science Monitor,* December 12, p. A13.

Cohn, Edward. (2000). "The Resurrection of Michael Milken." *The American Prospect,* March 13.

Cookson, Peter. (1994). *School Choice: The Struggle for the Soul of American Education*. New Haven, CT: Yale University Press.

Cooper, Kenneth J. (2000). "Appeals Court Rejects Vouchers in Cleveland as Unconstitutional." *Washington Post*, December 12, p. A3.

Cremin, Lawrence. (1989). *Popular Education and Its Discontents*. New York: Harper and Row.

Creno, Glen. (2000). "TesseracT Group Files Chapter 11." *Arizona Republic*, October 10, p. D1.

Cristodero, Damali. (1998). "Schools Find Aid in Ads, Sponsorships." *St. Petersburg Times*, January 20, p. C1.

Cubberley, Elwood P. (1919). *Public School Administration in United States*. Boston: Houghton Mifflin.

Curti, Merle. (1961) *The Social Ideas of American Educators*. Patterson, NJ: Littlefield, Adams.

D'Amico, Ronald. (1984). Does Employment During School Impair Academic Progress?" *Sociology of Education*, 57(3), 152–164.

Deloitte and Touche, LLP. (1997). "Outside Audit of the Cleveland Voucher Program." June 30. Cleveland: Deloitte and Touche.

Doclar, Mary. (2000). "The Edison Enigma: School Management Company Praised, Panned in Sherman." *Fort Worth Star-Telegram*, May 1, p. A1.

Donlon, Thomas F., and Angoff, William H. (1971). "The Scholastic Aptitude Test." In William H. Angoff, (Ed.), *The College Board Admissions Testing Program: A Technical Report on Research and Development Activities Relating to the Scholastic Aptitude Test and Achievement Tests*. New York: The College Entrance Examination Board.

Donohue, Kim. (1998). "Beware the Charter Threat." *NEA Today*, September, p. 63.

Doyle, Denis. (1996). "Education." In *Issues 96: The Candidate's Briefing Book*. Washington, DC: The Heritage Foundation, pp. 261–295.

Duffy, Cathy. (2000). "Problems with the California Voucher Initiative, Proposition 38." Accessible at www.grovepublishing.com.

Edison Schools, Incorporated. (2000). *Annual Report 2000*. New York, New York.

"Edison Schools, Inc., Prices Public Offering." (2000). PR Newswire, August 3.

Elley, Warwick P. (1992). *How in the World Do Students Read?* Hamburg: International Association for the Evaluation of Educational Achievement. Available in the United States through the International Reading Association.

Eskenazi, Stuart. (1999). "Learning Curves." *Houston Press*, July 22–28. Accessible at www.houstonpress.com/issues/1999-07-22/feature.html.

Estrin, Robin. (1996). "Researchers: Milwaukee School Choice Program Boosting Students' Scores." Associated Press wire story, August 14.

Feldman, Amy. (1998). "Milken's New Empire." *New York Daily News*, March 23. p. C4.

Ferguson, Ronald. (1991). "Paying for Public Education: New Evidence on How and Why Money Matters." *Harvard Journal on Legislation*, Vol. 28, No. 2, pp. 465–498.

Finn, Chester E. (2000). "Accountability through Transparency." *Education Week*, April 26, p. 42.

———. (1998). *Wall Street Journal*, February 25.

Finn, Chester E. Jr., Bierlein, Louann, and Manno, Bruno V. (1996). "Charter Schools in Action: A First Look." Indianapolis, IN: Hudson Institute.

Finn, Jeremy D., and Achilles, Charles N. (1999). "Tennessee's Class Size Study: Findings, Implications, Misconceptions." *Educational Evaluation and Policy Analysis*, Summer, pp. 97–109.

———. (1990). "Answers and Questions about Class Size: A State Experiment." *American Educational Research Journal*, Winter, pp. 557–577.

Finnegan, William. (1998). "Prosperous Times: Except for the Young." *New York Times*, June 12, p. A23.

Fleishman, Sandra. (2000). "U.S. Conducting 240 Probes of Possible Mortgage Fraud." *Washington Post*, July 1, p. E1.

Fletcher, Michael A. (2001). "Education Nominee Sails through His Senate Test," *Washington Post*, January 11, p. A4.

Fox, Jonathan. (2000). "No Class." *Dallas Observer Online*, January 27. Accessible at www.dallasobserver.com/issues/2000–01-27/feature.html.

Friedman, Milton. (2001). Personal communication, January 12.

———. (1962). *Capitalism and Freedom*. Chicago: University of Chicago Press.

Friedman, Milton, and Friedman, Rose D. (2000). "Letter from Milton and Rose D. Friedman." Accessible at www.friedmanfoundation.org/about_milton_rose.htm.

Gelberg, Denise. (1997). *The "Business" of Reforming American Schools*. Albany: State University of New York Press.

Gerstner, Louis V. Jr. (1999). Keynote Address to the "Education Summit." Palisades, NY, September 30.

———. (1994). "Our Schools Are Failing: Do We Care?" *New York Times*, May 27, p. A27.

Gifford, Mary, Phillips, Karla, and Ogle, Melinda. (2000). *Five Year Charter School Study*. Phoenix, AZ: Center for Market Based Education, The Goldwater Institute. Accessible at www.goldwaterinstitute.org.

Gladden, R. (1998). "The Small School Movement, A Review of the Literature." In Michelle Fine and Janis Somerville (Eds.), *Small Schools, Big Imaginations: A Creative Look at Urban Public Schools*. Chicago: Cross City Campaign for Urban School Reform.

Glaser, Robert. (1987). A Review of the Report by a Committee of the National Academy of Education. In Lamar Alexander and H. Thomas James, (Eds.), *The Nation's Report Card: Improving the Assessment of Student Achievement*. Cambridge, MA: National Academy of Education.

Godwin, R. Kenneth, Kemerer, Frank R., and Martinez, Valerie J. (1997). *Final Report: San Antonio School Choice Research Project*. Denton: Center for the Study of School Reform, School of Education, University of North Texas.

Gonderinger, Lisa. (2000). "Parents Fret About TesseracT's Future." *Arizona Republic*, March 1, p. A10.

"Good News: Our 9-year-olds Read Well; Bad News: Our 14-year-olds Don't." (1992). *American School Boards Journal*, November.

Goodnough, Abby. (2001). "Scope of Loss for Privatizing of Schools Stuns Officials." *New York Times*, April 3.

———. (2000). "Plan to Privatize 5 Schools Brings Confusion on All Sides." *New York Times*, December 22.

Gottfredson, Denise. (1985). "Youth Employment, Crime and Schooling: A Longitudinal Study of a National Sample." *Developmental Psychology*, 21, pp. 419–432.

———. (1995). *School Size and School Disorder*. Baltimore: Center for the Social Organization of Schools, Johns Hopkins University.

Greenberger, Scott S. (1991). "For-profit School Firm Falls Short on Reforms." *Boston Globe*, May 13.

Greene, Jay P., Peterson, Paul E., and Du, Jiangtao. (1996). "The Effectiveness of School Choice: The Milwaukee Experiment." Available at www.ksg.harvard.edu/pepg.

Greene, Jay P., and Peterson, Paul E. (1996). "Choice Data Rescued from Bad Science." *Wall Street Journal*, August 14, p. A14.

"Guinea Kids." (1998). *Arizona Tribune*, August 27, p. A14.

Guthrie, Julian. (2001a). "Scathing Report Card for Edison School." *San Francisco Chronicle*, March 28.

———. (2001b). "Edison Schools Accused of Discrimination in San Francisco." *San Francisco Chronicle*, March 27.

Hanushek, Eric A. (1999). "Some Findings from an Independent Investigation of the Tennessee Class Size Experiment." *Educational Evaluation and Policy Analysis*, Summer, pp. 143–164.

———. (1997). "Assessing the Effects of School Resources on Student Performance: An Update." *Educational Evaluation and Policy Analysis*, Summer, pp. 141–164.

———. (1989). "The Differential Impact of School Expenditures on School Performance." *Educational Researcher*, April, pp. 45–51.

Henig, Jeffrey. (1997). "School Choice in Milwaukee: The Evidence for Gains. A Response to Peterson." Address at the Cato Institute, Washington, DC, February.

———. (1994). *Rethinking School Choice: Limits to the Market Metaphor.* Princeton, NJ: Princeton University Press.

Henig, Jeffrey, Moser, Michele, Holyoke, Thomas T., and Lacireno-Paquet, Natalie. (1999). *Making a Choice, Making a Difference? An Evaluation of Charter Schools in the District of Columbia.* Washington, DC: George Washington University.

Hentoff, Nat. (1999). "Church-State Tangle." *Washington Post*, December 18, p. A27.

Hiassen, Carl. (1998). "Be True To Your School . . . and Its Cola." *Miami Herald*, March 31, p. A4.

Hill, Paul. (1995). *Reinventing Public Education.* Santa Monica, CA: RAND Corporation.

Hodgkinson, Harold. (1985). *All One System.* Washington, DC: Institute for Educational Leadership.

Holland, Robert. (1995). *Not with My Child, You Don't: A Citizen's Guide to Eradicating Outcomes Based Education and Restoring Education.* Richmond, VA: Citizens Projects Publishing.

Hook, Janet. (2000). "Bush Education Agenda Must Span Partisan Splits in Congress: Rancor Lurks over Testing, Prayer, Vouchers." *Los Angeles Times*, December 25.

Horn, Jerry, and Miron, Gary. (2000). *An Evaluation of the Michigan Charter School Initiative: Performance, Accountability, and Impact.* Kalamazoo: The Evaluation Center, Western Michigan University.

———. (1999). *Evaluation of the Michigan Public School Initiative, Final Report.* Kalamazoo: The Evaluation Center, Western Michigan University.

Howell, William G., Wolf, Patrick J., Peterson, Paul E., and Campbell, David E. (2000). "Test-Score Effects of School Vouchers in Dayton, Ohio, New York City, and Washington, D.C.: Evidence from Randomized Field Trials." Accessible at data.fas.harvard.edu/pepg.

"Individualized Learning Adventure Featured in New Website from Knowledge Universe." (2000). *Business Wire*, April 3.

Irwin, Neil. (2000). "E-Schooling Firm Set to Open." *Washington Post*, December 28, p. E1.

Johnson, Eugene G. (1998). *Linking the National Assessment of Educational Progress (NAEP) and the Third International Mathematics and Science Study (TIMSS).* Washington, DC: Office of Educational Research and Improvement, U.S. Department of Education. Report No. NCES 98–500.

Judy, Stephen J., and D'Amico, Carol. (1998). *Workforce 2020.* Indianapolis, IN: The Hudson Institute.

Kantrowitz, Barbara, and Wingert, Pat. (1992). "An 'F' in World Competition." *Newsweek*, February 17, p. 57.

Khouri, Nick, Kleine, Robert, White, Richard, and Cummings, Laurie. (1999). *Michigan's Charter School Initiative: From Theory to Practice.* Lansing, MI: Public Sector Consultants Inc., and MAXIMUS, Inc.

Knight, Edgar. (1952). *Fifty Years of American Education, 1900–1950.* New York: Ronald Press.

"Knowledge Universe Names Sarina Simon President, CEO." (2000). *Business Wire*, May 31.

Kolderie, Ted. (1995). *The Charter Idea: Update and Prospects, Fall 1995, Public Services Redesign Project.* St. Paul, MN: Center for Policy Studies.

Kronholz, June. (1998). "A Poor School District in Texas Is Learning to Cope in a Test Tube." *Wall Street Journal*, September 11, p. A1.

Krueger, Alan, B. (2000). "Economic Considerations and Class Size." Working paper 447, Industrial Relations Section Princeton University. Accessible at www.irs.princeton.edu/pubs/working_papers.html.

———. (1998). "Experimental Estimates of Education Production Functions." *Quarterly Journal of Economics*, Vol. 114, No. 2, pp. 497–532.

Krueger, Alan B. and Whitmore, Diane M. (1999). "The Effect of Attending a Small Class in the Early Grades on College-Test Taking and Middle School Test Results: Evidence from Project STAR." Accessible at www.irs.princeton.edu/pubs/working_papers.html.

"L.A. School District Likes Charter Schools." (2000). *Contra Costa Times*, September 4.

Labaton, Stephen. (2000). "Generic Drug Maker Agrees to Settlement in Price Fixing Case." *New York Times*, July 13.

Lapointe, Archie. (1995). Personal communication, June.

Le, Tung. (2001). Director of Assessment, Edison Schools, Inc., personal communication, January 12.

Legislative Office of Education Oversight. (2000). *Community Schools in Ohio: First-Year Implementation Report.* Columbus, OH: Legislative Office of Education Oversight.

Leo, John. (1998). "Hey, We're #19!" *U.S. News and World Report*, March 9, p. 14.

Leovy, Jill. (2000). "School Voucher Program Teaches Hard Lessons." *Los Angeles Times*, October 9.

Life. (1958). "Crisis in Education." March 24, pp. 26–35.

Lockwood, Robert, and McLean, James. (1993). "Educational Funding and Students Achievement." Paper presented at the Mid-South Educational Research Association annual conference, November.

Lynch, Michael. (2001). Personal communication, April 4.

MacInnes, Gordon. (2000). "Kids Who Pick the Wrong Parents and Other Victims of Voucher Schemes." Washington, DC: Century Fund.

Manning, Anita. (1992). " U.S. Kids Near Top of Class in Reading." *USA Today*, September 29, p. A1.

Maraghy, Mary. (1999). "Loaded Up for Learning." *Florida Times-Union*, December 16, p. A1.

Massey, Joanna. (2000). "Exodus Threatens Catholic Schools." *SouthCoast (MA) Today*, September 17.

Mathews, Jay. (2000). "Group Pushes for Vouchers." *Washington Post*, December 9, p. A26.

Mattern, Hal. (2001). "TesseracT Selling School Assets to Parent Groups." *Arizona Republic*, January 5, p. D1.

Mattern, Hal. (2000a). "TesseracT Crisis Watched As Bellwether for Private Schools." *Arizona Republic*, February 20, p. A1.

———. (2000b). "TesseracT Nears $50 Million Deficit Mark." *Arizona Republic*, May 23, p. D1.

————. (2000c). "Schools Changing Hands, TesseracT Trying to Stop Bleeding." *Arizona Republic*, May 24, p. D1.

Maxwell, William. (1914). "On a Certain Arrogance in Educational Theorists." *Educational Review*, February, pp. 175–176.

McCarthy, Martha. (2000). "What Is the Verdict on School Vouchers?" *Phi Delta Kappan*, March, Vol. 81, No. 5, pp. 371–378.

McEwan, Patrick J. (2000). "The Effectiveness of Public, Catholic, and Nonreligious Private Schools in Chile's Voucher System." *Education Economics*, in press.

McEwan, Patrick J., and Carnoy, Martin. (2000a). "The Effectiveness and Efficiency of Private Schools in Chile's Voucher System." *Educational Evaluation and Policy Analysis*, in press. [publication date not yet known, 8/9/00]

————. (2000b). "Choice between Private and Public Schools in a Voucher System: Evidence from Chile." Unpublished paper, Stanford University, undated.

————. (1999). "The Impact of Competition on Public School Quality: Longitudinal Evidence from Chile's Voucher System." Unpublished paper, Stanford University.

McGovern, Myra. (2000). Public Information Specialist, National Association of Independent Schools, personal communication, October 4.

McKnight, Curtis C., Crosswhite, F. Joe, Dossey, John A., Kifer, Edward, Swafford, Jane O., Travers, Kenneth J., and Cooney, Thomas C. (1987). *The Underachieving Curriculum: Assessing U.S. Mathematics from an International Perspective*. Champaign, IL: Stipes Publishing.

McLaughlin, John. (1998a). "The Edison Project: Closing In on Profitability." *Education Industry Report*, June, p. 1.

————. (1998b). "Covering the Industry: Four Writers' Perspectives." *Education Industry Report*, January, p. 1.

————. (1998c). "Grow, Baby, Grow." *Education Industry Report*. January, p. 2.

McLaughlin, Milbrey. (1990). The RAND Change Agent Study: Macro Perspectives and Micro Realities." *Educational Researcher*, November, pp. 11–16.

Metcalf, Kim. (1999). *Evaluation of the Cleveland Scholarship and Tutoring Grant Program, 1996–1999*. Bloomington: Indiana Center for Evaluation, Indiana University.

Mill, John Stuart. (1838). "On Liberty." In *On Liberty and Other Essays*. New York: Oxford University Press, 1991, pp. 5–130.

Miller, Bill. (2000). "Group Home Ex-Chief Is Indicted." *Washington Post*, July 11, p. A1.

Miller, Julie A. (1991). "Report Questioning 'Crisis' in Education Triggers an Uproar." *Education Week*, October 9.

Miller, Matthew. (2001). "Bush Must Be Bold on Vouchers." *Washington Post*, January 1, p. A23.

Mills, Steve. (1997). "Marketing Idea: Be True to Your School—with VISA." *Chicago Tribune*, August 11, p. 1.

Miner, Barbara. (2000). "Voucher Backers Illegally Funnel Money: Wisconsin Supreme Court Race Tainted by Corruption Scandal." *Rethinking Schools*, Summer, p. 5.

Miron, Gary, and Applegate, Brooks. (2000). *An Evaluation of Student Achievement in Edison Schools Opened in 1995 and 1996*. Kalamazoo: The Evaluation Center, Western Michigan University. Accessible at www.wmich.edu/evalctr.

Moe, Michael T., and Bailey, Kathleen. (1999). *The Book of Knowledge*. San Francisco: Merrill Lynch.

Moe, Terry (Ed.). (1995). *Private Vouchers*. Stanford, CA: Hoover Institution Press.

Molnar, Alex, Smith, Philip, and Zahorik, John. (2000). "1998–99 Evaluation Results of the Student Achievement Guarantee in Education (SAGE) Program." Accessible at www.uwm.edu/Dept/CERAI/documents.

Molnar, Alex. (1999). *Class Size and Education Vouchers: An Update*. Harrisburg, PA: Keystone Research Center.

———. (1996). *Giving Kids the Business*. Boulder, CO: Westview Press.

Mosbacker, Barrett. (1998). "School Vouchers: Blessing or Threat to Christian Schools?" Accessible at www.charlottechristiannews.com/mosbacker/vouchers.htm.

Murphy, Dan, Nelson, F. Howard, and Rosenberg, Bella. (2000). *The Cleveland Voucher Program: Who Chooses, Who Gets Chosen, Who Pays?* Washington, DC: American Federation of Teachers.

Murray, Shanon D. (1999). "Sylvan to Launch Free Reading Site Today on Internet." *Baltimore Sun*, April 21, p. C1.

Myrdal, Gunnar. (1969). *Objectivity in Social Research*. New York: Pantheon Books.

Naisbitt, John. (1982). *Megatrends*. New York: Warner Books.

Nasar, Sylvia. (1994). "The American Economy, Back on Top." *New York Times*, February 27, Section 3, p. 1.

Nathan, Joe. (1996). *Charter Schools: Creating Hope and Opportunity for American Education*. San Francisco: Jossey-Bass.

National Center for Education Statistics. (1998). *Digest of Education Statistics*, Table 70, p. 80. Report No. 1998–036.

National Center for Education Statistics. (1997). *Digest of Education Statistics*, Table 82, p. 89.

National Commission on Excellence in Education. (1983). *A Nation at Risk*. Washington, DC: National Commission on Excellence in Education.

National Committee for Responsive Philanthropy. (1997). *Moving a Public Policy Agenda: The Strategic Philanthropy of Conservative Foundations*.

National Research Council. (1999). *Grading the Nation's Report Card: Evaluating NAEP and Transforming the Assessment of Educational Progress*. Washington, DC: National Research Council.

National School Boards Association. (1995). *Private Options for Public Schools*. Alexandria, VA: National School Boards Association.

Nelson, Howard F. (2000). "Trends in Student Achievement for Edison Schools, Inc.: The Emerging Track Record." Washington, DC: American Federation of Teachers. Accessible at www.aft.org.

———. (1998). "Thirteen Ways Rouse Disagrees with GPD's Methodological Perspective." Accessible at www.aft.org/research/Vouchers/mil/13ways.htm.

Nelson, Howard F., Muir, Edward, and Drown, Rachel. (2000). *Venturesome Capital: State Charter School Finance Systems*. Washington, DC: Office of Educational Research and Improvement, U.S. Department of Education, December.

Newman, Arthur, J. (1978). *In Defense of the American Public School*. Berkeley, CA: Schenkman Publishing.

Nowicki, Dan. (1998). "Governor Aims at Charters." *Arizona Tribune*, August 28, p. A1.

O'Connor, Phillip. (1999). "Reading Tutors Seen as Remedy: K.C. Schools Weigh Pact with Sylvan." *Kansas City Star*, February 26, p. A1.

Office of Educational Research and Improvement. (2000). *The State of Charter Schools 2000*. Washington, DC: U.S. Department of Education.

On Thin Ice. (1999). New York: Public Agenda.

Oplinger, Doug, and Willard, Dennis J. (1999a). "In Education, Money Talks." *Akron Beacon Journal*, December 13, p. A1.

———. (1999b). "Voucher System Falls Far Short of Goals." *Akron Beacon Journal*, December 14, p. A1.

———. (1999c). "Campaign Organizer Pushes Hard for Changes." *Akron Beacon Journal*, December 15, p. A1.

Oppel, Richard A., and Schemo, Diana Jean. (2000). "Bush Is Warned Vouchers Might Hurt School Plans." *New York Times*, December 22.

Organization for Economic Cooperation and Development. (2000). *Education at a Glance*. Paris: Organization for Economic Cooperation and Development.

———. (1993). *Education at a Glance*. Paris: Organization for Economic Cooperation and Development.

Oshrat, Carmiel. (2000). "Parents and Doctors Say the Load Students Are Carrying Is Too Heavy. My Aching Back. Make That Backpack." *Philadelphia Inquirer*, May 21, p. A1.

Packer, Arnold. (1999). "Bracey's Applesauce." *Phi Delta Kappan*, May, p. 696.

Patalon, William III. (2000). "Sylvan Has Deal to Sell Prometric." *Baltimore Sun*, January 27, p. D1.

Patton, Robert. (1991). "The Voucher System: Trap for the Unwary." In James R. Patrick, (Ed.), *Choice in Education! It Sounds Wonderful But. . . .* East Moline, IL: The MacArthur Institute.

Payne, Kevin, and Biddle, Bruce. (1999). "Poor School Funding, Child Poverty, and Mathematics Achievement." *Educational Researcher*, August/September, pp. 4–13.

Peterson, Paul. (1997). "School Choice in Milwaukee: Evidence for Gains." Address given at the Cato Institute, Washington DC, February.

———. (1990). "Monopoly and Competition in American Education." In William H. Clune and John F. Witte, (Eds.), *Choice and Control in American Education*. London: Falmer Press.

Peterson, Paul E., Greene, Jay P., and Howell, William. (1999). "New Findings from the Cleveland Scholarship Program: A Reanalysis from the Indiana School of Education Evaluation." Accessible at data.fas.harvard.edu/pepg.

Peterson, Paul E., Howell, William G., and Greene, Jay P. (1998). "An Evaluation of the Cleveland Voucher Program after Two Years." Available at www.ksg.harvard.edu/pepg.

Peterson, Paul E., and Noyes, Chad. (1996). "Under Extreme Duress, School Choice Success." Available at www.ksg.harvard.edu/pepg.

Powell, Brian, and Steelman, Lala Carr. (1996). "Bewitched, Bothered, and Bewildering: The Use and Misuse of State SAT Scores." *Harvard Educational Review*, Fall, pp. 29–59.

Rasell, Edith, and Mishel, Lawrence. (1988). *Shortchanging Education: How U.S. Spending on Grades K–12 Lags behind Other Industrialized Nations*. Washington, DC: Economic Policy Institute.

Raspberry, William. (1998). "The Good News about U.S. Schools." *Washington Post*, March 6, p. A25.

Raubinger, Frederick M., Rowe, Harold G., Piper, Donald L., and West, Charles K. (1969). *The Development of Secondary Education*. Toronto: Collier Macmillan.

Richards, Craig E., Shore, Rima, and Sawicky, Max B. (1996). *Risky Business: Private Management of Public Schools*. Washington, DC: Economic Policy Institute.

Rickover, Hyman. (1959). *Education and Freedom*. NY: E. P. Dutton.

Robinson, Glenn, and Brandon, David. (1992). *Perceptions about American Education: Are They Based on Facts?* Arlington, VA: Educational Research Service.

Rofes, Eric. (1998). *How Are Districts Responding to Charter Laws and Charter Schools?* Berkeley, CA: Policy Analysis for California Education (PACE).

Rothman, Robert. (1992). "U.S. Ranks High in International Study of Reading." *Education Week,* September 30, p. 1.

Rothstein, Richard, Carnoy, Martin, and Benveniste, Luis. (1999). *Can Public Schools Learn from Private Schools?* Washington, DC: Economic Policy Institute.

Rothstein, Richard, and Miles, Karen Hawley. (1997). *Where Has the Money Gone?* Washington, DC: Economic Policy Institute.

Rouse, Cecilia Elena. (2000). "School Reform in the 21st Century: A Look at the Effect of Class Size and School Vouchers on the Academic Achievement of Minority Students." Working Paper #440, Industrial Relations Section, Princeton University, June. Available at www.irs.princeton.edu/pubs/working_papers.htm.

―――. (1998). "Private School Vouchers and Student Achievement: An Evaluation of the Milwaukee Parental Choice Program." *The Quarterly Journal of Economics,* May, pp. 553–602.

Ryman, Anne. (2001). "Charter Offers to Buy TesseracT School." *Arizona Republic,* February 9, p. B7.

Safire, William. (2001). "The Sinking Sun?" *New York Times,* March 15.

Sanchez, Rene. (1998). "U.S. High School Seniors Rank Near Bottom." *Washington Post,* February 25, p. A1.

Sandham, Jessica L. (2000). "Vouchers Facing Two Major Tests." *Education Week,* September 27, p. 1.

―――. (1999). "Ohio Lawmakers Reinstate Voucher Program." *Education Week,* July 14, p. 17.

Savitz, Eric J. (1998). "For Adults Only." *Barron's,* March 2, p. 31.

Schemo, Diana Jean. (2001). "Easy Approval Seen for Education Official." *New York Times,* January 11, p. A19.

Schnaiberg, Lynn. (1997). "Firms Hoping to Turn a Profit from Charters." *Education Week,* December 10, p. 1.

Schulenberg, John, and Bachman, J. G. (1993). "Long Hours on the Job? Not So Bad for Some Adolescents in Some Types of Jobs: The Quality of Work and Substance Use, Affect, and Stress." Paper presented at the biennial meeting of the Society for Research in Child Development, New Orleans, March.

Schultz, Karen. (1999). "Millions Go to Charter School Management Companies." *Michigan Live,* August 29. Accessible eventually at www.mlive.com. As of January 2001, the archives of *Michigan Live* are under construction, but will contain all articles since its founding in 1997.

Secretary's Commission on Attaining Necessary Skills (SCANS). (1991). Washington, DC: U.S. Department of Labor.

Shanker, Albert F. (1988). Speech to the National Press Club, Washington, DC, March 31.

―――. (1998). "Convention Plots New Course—A Charter for Change." *New York Times,* July 10, Section 4, p. 7.

―――. (1992). "GI Bull." *New York Times,* July 5, Section 4, p. 7.

Shatz, Adam. (2001). "The Thernstroms in Black and White." *The American Prospect,* March, pp. 32–40.

Silberman, Charles. (1970). *Crisis in the Classroom.* New York: Random House.

Slavin, Robert. (1989). "PET and the Pendulum: Faddism in Education and How to Stop It." *Phi Delta Kappan,* June, pp. 752–758.

Solmon, Lewis, Paark, Kern, and Garcia, David. (2001). *Does Charter School Attendance Improve Test Scores? The Arizona Results.* Phoenix, AZ: The Center for Market-Based Education, The Goldwater Institute.

Somerville, Sean. (2000). "Sylvan's Choice: Bigger Isn't Better." *Baltimore Sun,* March 5, p. D1.

Steinberg, Jacques. (2000). "Skeptic Now Sees the Virtue in Teaching Children Online." *New York Times,* December 28, p. A13.

Taylor, Jay. (1992). "Desperate for Dollars." *American School Boards Journal,* p. 23.

"TesseracT Leader Says Job Is Done." (2001). *Arizona Republic,* March 6, p. D2.

"Texas Charter School Moratorium Urged." (2000). *Washington Post,* December 29, p. A6.

Texas Education Agency. (1998). *Open Enrollment Charter Schools: Second Year Evaluation.* Austin, TX: Office of Charter Schools. Accessible at www.tea.state.tx.us/charter/eval98/index.html.

Toch, Thomas. (1998). "The New Education Bazaar." *U.S. News & World Report,* April 27, p. 24.

Todd, Cece. (1998a). "Oversight Overlooked." *Arizona Tribune,* August 25, p. A1.

——. (1998b). "Nobody's Watching Charters." *Arizona Tribune,* August 24, p. A1.

Topolnicki, Denise M. (1994). "Why Private Schools Are Rarely Worth the Money." *Money,* October, pp. 98–112.

Tortora, Andrea. (2000). "Charters Will Cost CPS $21 Million." *Cincinnati Enquirer,* November 2.

Tyack, David. (1974). *The One Best System: A History of American Urban Education.* Cambridge, MA: Harvard University Press.

Tyack, David, Thomas, James Thomas, and Benavot, Aaron. (1987). *Law and the Shaping of Public Education.* Madison: University of Wisconsin Press.

U.S. Department of Education. (2000). *The State of Charter Schools Fourth-Year Report.* Accessible at www.PDFDocs/4yrrpt.pdf.

Van Der Werf, Martin. (1998). "ASU Dean: We're Losing Battle for Public Schools." *Arizona Republic,* August 26, p. B3.

Viadero, Debra. (1998). "U.S. Seniors Near Bottom in World Test." *Education Week,* March 11, p. 1.

——. (1997). "Statistics from Cleveland Add Fuel to the Voucher Debate." *Education Week,* August 6.

"Vouchers Not Free-For-All." (2000). *Milwaukee Journal Sentinel,* November 25.

Vrana, Debora. (1998). "Education's Pied Piper with a Dark Past." *Los Angeles Times,* September 7, p. A1.

Wainer, Howard. (1993). "Does Spending Money on Education Help?" *Educational Researcher,* December, pp. 22–24.

"Wake Up, Keegan!" (1998). *Arizona Tribune,* August 27, p. A14.

Walsh, Mark. (2000a). "Campaign Cash from Voucher Backers at Issue in Wisconsin." *Education Week,* May 24, p. 21.

——. (2000b). "Voucher Initiatives Defeated in California, Michigan." *Education Week,* November 13, p. 14.

——. (1998). "Audit Criticizes Cleveland Voucher Program." *Education Week,* April 14, p. 9.

————. (1996). "Brokers Pitch Education as Hot Investment." *Education Week*, February 21, p. 1.

Wasley, Patricia A., Fine, Michelle, King, Sherry P., Powell, Linda C., Holland, Nicole E., Gladden, Robert M., and Mosak, Ester. (2000). *Small Schools, Great Strides*. New York: Bank Street College of Education.

Weir, Fred. (2000). "More Charter Schools." *Christian Science Monitor*, January 31.

Wells, Amy Stuart. (1993). "The Sociology of School Choice: Why Some Win and Others Lose in the Educational Marketplace." In Edith Rasell and Richard Rothstein (Eds.), *School Choice: Examining the Evidence*. Washington, DC: Economic Policy Institute, pp. 29–48.

————. (1998). *Beyond the Rhetoric of Charter School Reform: A Study of Ten California School Districts*. Los Angeles: UCLA.

Wenglinsky, Harold. (1998). *How Educational Expenditures Improve Student Performance and How They Don't*. Princeton, NJ: Educational Testing Service.

Wiles, Russ. (2000). "Internet, Education Are Saviors of Underprivileged, Milken Says." *The Arizona Republic*, April 11, p. D1.

Wilgoren, Jodi. (2000a). "A Ruling Voids Use of Vouchers in Ohio Schools." *New York Times*, December 12, p. A1.

————. (2000b). "Vouchers' Fate May Hinge on Name." *New York Times*, December 20, p. A20.

Will, George F. (2001). "A Second Decade of Economic Trouble?" *Washington Post*, March 25, p. B7.

————. (1993). "Meaningless Money Factor." *Washington Post*, September 24, p. A22.

Willard, Dennis J., and Oplinger, Doug. (1999a). "Charter Experiment Goes Awry: Schools Fail to Deliver." *Akron Beacon Journal*, December 12, p. A1.

————. (1999b). "Voucher Plan Leaves Long List of Broken Vows." *Akron Beacon Journal*, December 14, p. A1.

————. (1999c). "School Battle Eludes Voters, Takes Its Cues from Coalitions." *Akron Beacon Journal*, December 15, p. A1.

Williams, Lois C., and Leak, Lawrence. (1995). *The UMBC Evaluation of the TesseracT Program in Baltimore City*. Baltimore: Center for Educational Research, University of Maryland, Baltimore County.

Wilson, Sloan. (1958). "It's Time to Close Our Circus." *Life*, March 24, pp. 36–37.

Winerip, Michael. (1998). "Schools for Sale." *New York Times Sunday Magazine*, June 14, p. 42.

Wingert, Pat. (1996). "The Sum of Mediocrity." *Newsweek*, December 2.

Wirtz, Willard, and Howe, Harold II. (1977). *On Further Examination: Report of the Advisory Panel on the Scholastic Aptitude Test Score Decline*. New York: The College Board.

Witte, John F., Sterr, Troy D., and Thorn, Christopher A. (2000). *Fifth-Year Report: Milwaukee Choice Program*. Madison, WI: Department of Public Instruction.

Woodward, Tali. (2000a). "Edison Exodus: Will a Teacher Revolt Spell an End to the School Privatization Experiment?" *San Francisco Bay Guardian*, July 19, p. 1.

————. (2000b). "Fisher Nonprofit Nets Millions from Edison Inc. Stock Deal." *San Francisco Bay Guardian*, August 23, p. 12.

————. (2000c). "Attorney General Investigates Fisher Charity." *San Francisco Bay Guardian*, October 4, p. 25.

Wyatt, Edward. (2001a). "Defeat Aside, Edison Plans to Expand." *New York Times*, April 1.

———. (2001b). "School Management Company Faces Ouster in San Francisco." *New York Times*, March 28.

———. (2001c). "Founder of Edison Schools Sells Some of His Stock in Company." *New York Times*, March 23.

———. (2001d). "Challenges and the Possibility of Profits for Edison." *New York Times*, January 1.

———. (2000). "5 Poor New York Performers Could Be Run by Company." *New York Times*, December 21.

———. (1999). "Investors See Room for Profit in the Demand for Education." *New York Times*, November 4, p. A1.

Zehr, Mary Ann. (1999). "Vouchers, Charters, A Mystery to Most." *Education Week*, November 24, p. 1.

Zernike, Kate. (2000). "New Doubt Is Cast on Study That Backs Voucher Efforts." *New York Times*, September 15, p. A21.

Index

207